From the Cook's Garden

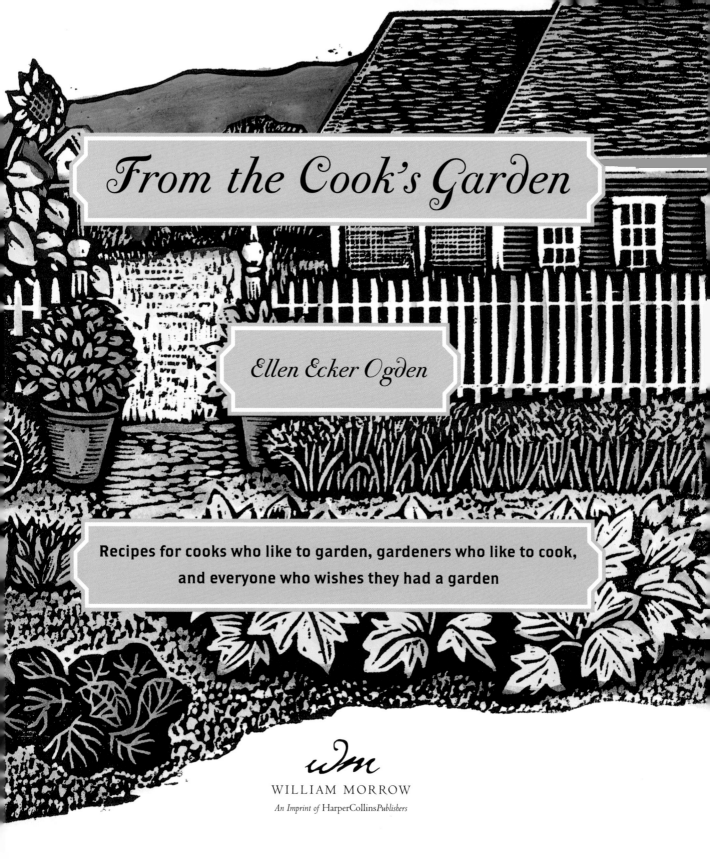

From the Cook's Garden

Ellen Ecker Ogden

Recipes for cooks who like to garden, gardeners who like to cook, and everyone who wishes they had a garden

WILLIAM MORROW

An Imprint of HarperCollinsPublishers

HarperCollins books may be purchased for educational, business, or
sales promotional use. For information please write:
Special Markets Department, HarperCollins Publishers Inc.,
10 East 53rd Street, New York, NY 10022.

The Cook's Garden is a registered trademark of Park Seed Co.

FIRST EDITION

Designed by Leah Lococo Ltd

Illustrations by Mary Azarian

Printed on acid-free paper

Library of Congress Cataloging in-Publication Data
Ogden, Ellen.
From the cook's garden : recipes for cooks who like to garden, gardeners
who like to cook, and everyone who wishes they had a garden
/ Ellen Ecker Ogden.—1st ed.
p. cm.
Includes index.
ISBN 0-06-000841-5
1. Cookery. I. Title.
TX714.O34 2003
641.5—dc21

2002027485
03 04 05 06 07 WBC/RRD 10 9 8 7 6 5 4 3 2 1

Dedication

$\mathcal{T}$his book is dedicated to Shepherd Ogden, whose creative vision

in founding The Cook's Garden made this book possible.

As gardener and cook, we make a good team.

Contents

Foreword

by Deborah Madison

With its annual arrival in my mailbox each winter, The Cook's Garden catalogue signals the distant promise of summer and the closer anticipation of spring. I don't think I've ever thrown away one of these catalogues. I keep them on the shelf, along with my cookbooks.

As a cook and, to a lesser degree, a gardener, I look upon them as telling a short history of the evolution of edible garden plants in late-twentieth-century America and beyond. Reading about the new varieties that are introduced with enthusiasm each year, seeing which ones stay on to become true perennials in The Cook's Garden catalogue, has served as a looking glass into our evolving tastes in vegetables, herbs, and flowers. You can spot a new seed variety one year, then see a particular lettuce or bean crop up on restaurant menus across the country. And, of course, these same vegetables, herbs, and flowers crop up in the backyards of home gardeners everywhere.

The Cook's Garden catalogue, begun by Ellen and Shepherd Ogden in 1983, was one of the first that strayed far from the huge red tomatoes and giant-sized pumpkins promised by other glossy seed catalogues. The offerings were not about size and primary colors, but about more exotic and subtle nuances of flavor, pattern, color, and form. I remember the wonder of seeing my first planting of Marvel of Four Seasons, a deeply bronzed red lettuce that took diners at Greens restaurant in San Francisco by surprise more than twenty years ago. "What gorgeous lettuce was that?" they asked in amazement. Today, they might be asking about another wine-hued lettuce, one that was first featured in the catalogue only a few years ago, called Merlot, or perhaps a charming speckled Romaine called Freckles. The Cook's Garden was one of the first catalogues to offer slender green beans or ones of purple hue, or the pale curvaceous Armenian cucumber or the heirloom lemon cucumber. All of these new offerings played a role in my cooking, especially in the early years at Greens restaurant. There I was fortunate to have a gardener-partner in Wendy Johnson, who eagerly planted these new, exotic seeds at Green Gulch Farm. At a time when the delights of vegetable varieties hadn't yet caught on the way they have today, it was very special to be able to feature a salad made of five different kinds of cucumber, or a dozen kinds of lettuce, or a dish of tender, skinny green beans or the sweetest carrots imaginable.

Of course, it makes little sense to go on about seeds in a seed catalogue if one can't talk about what they turn into and how they behave in the kitchen. Another reason I've kept my collection of catalogues is that they're laced with Ellen's recipes. These recipes, which are entirely guided by her garden and choice of seeds that grow in it, bridge the gap between a dream on a page promised by a seed packet and how the seeds can be used in the kitchen.

I've always considered the recipes to be an especially thoughtful gesture on Ellen's part. Here is someone who loves to cook, and who cooks from what she grows. And her new book brings many of these garden recipes together in one convenient place.

I met Ellen Ogden in person many years after knowing her through her recipes and her catalogue. It was at her home in Vermont, during the season of the late summer garden. The first thing we did was walk through the rows of beds filled with plants, which looked much like some of the illustrations in the catalogue. What a verdant place that garden was!

Compared to our New Mexico gardens, where I live with their parsimonious servings of water and inhospitable beds of gravel or clay, each one of Ellen's plants seemed amazingly profuse, green, and tender. There were innumerable lettuces, all of them pristine, rows of herbs, hedges of berries, red and golden oregano, beds of flowering cucurbits, great stands of chard and black kale, arching branches of sweet-smelling nicotiana. The flowers were enchanting varieties of simple charm and haunting color rather than loud, top-heavy types with double and triple rows of petals. Sunflowers lined the garden in russets and deep reds as well as bright yellow. Hummingbirds were everywhere.

With the cool of the day's end, we went into her house. Boxes of potatoes, platters of tomatoes, jars of herbs, melons, and squash covered every available surface as they do in any farmhouse kitchen. Volumes of produce were in various stages of kitchen production, some awaiting washing, canning, drying, or cooking. Others became our dinner a few hours later—fresh pasta with pesto and a huge salad of all kinds of lettuces and herbs—nothing startling by way of a recipe, but astonishing in terms of taste. This was real food, not a shadow or a memory of it, but the real, vital thing itself. What surprised me was Ellen's restraint; she didn't use every vegetable available, which I might have done, since I was starved for this kind of quality and taste.

"Seasonal recipes are at the spiritual heart of any kitchen garden,'" writes Ellen. When we cook from a garden naturally, our recipes reflect what's in season at that moment. My cardinal rule, one shared by anyone who gardens, is that plants that come to fruition at the same moment always taste good together. It is something you can pretty much count on when shopping at farmers' markets—or from your own garden or other local sources. Plants that bear fruiting at the same time often end up in the pot together, as in such classic dishes as ratatouille and caponata, tomato and onion salads, or asparagus with wild mushrooms and ramps.

Classic food combinations are based on what's in season, be it the garden or the wild plants of the field and the forest. They're not based on the timeless season of the supermarket. But if you have grown your garden to such amazing potential as Ellen has, new combinations will arise effortlessly in your kitchen. So an autumn pie of leeks, Brussels sprouts, and horseradish makes perfect sense, as does a pesto composed of spinach and arugula, both plentiful and at their best at the same time. Ellen also

knows well about how to deal with those items that gardeners encounter, such as the bumper crops of green tomatoes at the end of the summer and the runaway zucchini. Her experience has taught her how to distinguish among all the different varieties of squashes and pumpkins, sunflowers, herbs, and lettuces and lettuce mixes so that we might know what to expect and where to start. I especially love Ellen's ability to go into the whys and wherefores of plants. In one recipe introduction, she tells us about the carrot that she's found to be the best of them all, Touchon. It has to be pulled by hand because its tops are weak, which is precisely why it will never serve as a commercial machine-harvested crop appearing in a store near you. What a tease! You have to grow it yourself if you want to taste it. As you page through these garden-based recipes, you'll find some that are familiar friends and you'll make some new ones. And you might notice a growing desire to plant some of the seeds that got them started in the first place. You can always send for a catalogue.

Acknowledgments

A cookbook is never born alone but is the collective vision of many that contribute to the development of the final product. First, I must thank my editor, Harriet Bell, for her enthusiasm and vision. It was her keen interest in both gardening and cooking that fueled the passion for this book. And thanks to my agent, Colleen Mohyde, for providing me with the opportunity to write this book and for the faith that it could be done. Great credit must be given to talented artist Mary Azarian for her major contributions. We are fortunate to have her illustrations grace the pages of this book as well as our catalogue. Thanks to Deborah Madison, whom I deeply admire, and her articulate foreword to this book, and to Rick Rodgers, who helped sculpt the finished manuscript into an orderly final draft.

I also wish to thank all those who have participated in The Cook's Garden since its inception in 1984. To all the employees who have helped us in the garden, at the farmstand, or packing seeds and shipping orders. To my father, who creatively designed the initial business plan to get us started. And to those offered generous support and advice in the early years, which was instrumental to our success. And to the Park family, who have maintained the business with a high level of integrity and dedication to our original mission for the business.

Thanks also to the recipe testers who contributed in numerous ways, specifically Dorothy Rankin and Jon Gatewood for their professionalism and knowledge of food. And my deepest gratitude to all my friends and family, who have come to the table and engaged in the process of recipe tasting. I am grateful to all for your participation and inspiration.

With all my heart, I especially acknowledge my children, Molly and Sam, for all their help in our family business. I'm certain there have been many times that they would've preferred I was working on a book about desserts instead of vegetables. And last but not least, special thanks to my mother, who more than anyone else introduced me to the wonderful recipes and the pleasures of bringing good food to the table.

Introduction

We moved to our ten-acre farm near Londonderry, Vermont, in 1980, reclaiming land that had, years before, been harrowed, then abandoned, leaving behind ridges and pockets of scrub, stones, and poor soil. At the top of the south-facing hillside, we built a post-and-beam house designed to be a passive solar system with a woodstove as our only source of heat. We planted a market garden and sold lettuce and salad greens to the local restaurants.

Down the hill from the house we reconstructed an old barn to raise livestock, sheep, pigs, waterfowl, and poultry, including a turkey for Thanksgiving. It took us four years to finish the house and we camped during the first summer in a perch above the animals in the barn. Our first major purchase was a chest freezer, which we filled with homegrown vegetables and meats to tide us through the winter.

Unlike those who garden for pleasure, we gardened to supply our farm stand. We chose varieties with an eye to sell and included only a few unfamiliar vegetables and herbs that we wanted to try. Seeds were planted in plastic plug trays that held 162 seedlings each and we grew them in four full-sized, plastic-domed greenhouses. To keep the plants warm on cooler days, a heater was fired up with a loud blast that shook the plastic walls; on sunny days, fans hummed to circulate and vent the heat away from the seedlings.

Living off the land was a dream my husband, Shepherd, and I both shared, but our farm quickly became less about the garden and more about running a business. Growing our own food was important, but figuring out a way we could work the land to provide us with an income became the challenge. Customers stopped by our farm stand to purchase our Romanesco broccoli, Freckles lettuce, Triomphe de Farcy filet beans, and Selvatica arugula. We sold organically grown sweet corn and berries from other local farmers and we grew acres of cut flowers that filled our farm stand shelves.

After a few years, we began importing organic seeds in bulk from Europe. Because there were more seeds than we could use, we repacked the extra seeds in small packets to sell at the farm stand. The living room bookshelves held crates of seed packets; the dining table was the weighing station; the kitchen counter the packing area.

We printed our first seed catalogue in 1984, a two-page listing of mostly lettuce and salad greens. Unlike in many seed catalogues, there were no glossy photos promising 200-pound pumpkins and fast-growing, huge tomatoes. Mary Azarian created black-and-white woodcuts to illustrate and convey our way of life—a cozy farm kitchen with a woodstove, big baskets overflowing with harvested vegetables, canning jars waiting to be filled. We wanted to share our way of life with our customers.

As the catalogue business and our family grew, we built a barn exclusively for the seed business. We designed elaborate gardens that served as trial plots for our seeds and grew seeds from other catalogues to compare the results. We eventually decided to ask for customer feedback. This led to the highlight of our gardening year, which is our open house held each summer at the end of August. Customers drive from all over New England to join us in tasting the crops grown in our garden. As customers crunch their way through six types of carrots, twelve varieties of beans, fourteen kinds of cucumber, and hundreds of tomatoes, they fill out evaluation charts rating flavor characteristics along with comments on color and appearance. By doing this, we are able to evaluate "new and improved" varieties to add to our growing catalogue.

The Cook's Garden evolved into a 112-page catalogue with color woodcuts by Mary. Our original goal was simply to find unusual varieties that we could grow for our farm stand, but our interest in food and cooking began to play a big part in the business. We learned how to cook the food that we grew. The recipes in our catalogue started off as a lure to encourage customers to try something new in their gardens, and as the cook of The Cook's Garden, it was my job to create the recipes.

My cooking often starts with the same routine. I heat a little olive oil in a pan, chop an onion and some garlic, and start to sauté them. While the kitchen fills with a luscious aroma, I run to the garden to see what I can harvest and cook. Cooking from the garden should be simple, inspired by the ingredients rather than by a recipe.

The sight of a countertop full of bright fresh vegetables that have just been brought in from the garden or bought at a farmers' market has inspired some of our most memorable meals. Capturing that inspiration is what this book is all about.

Soups

$\mathcal{M}$aking soup is like arranging flowers. A flower arrangement often begins with a few spiky twigs to act as the display's backbone; a soup uses onions and garlic as the foundation. The large focal flowers are added to provide substance and, for the soup pot, we are talking about the carrots, squash, or other primary flavor. The flower arrangement is brought together by the fillers that act as support; the cook will use broth and herbs to achieve the same effect.

I often take a flower vase into the garden to obtain a natural design that mimics the flowers' growth in their natural environment. Think of soups in the same light, of cooking ingredients from the same growing season. Tomatoes, eggplant, and basil in the summer; lettuce and chervil in the spring; potatoes and leeks in cool weather—these are natural, classic combinations that are hard to improve upon.

Floral designers warn against overfilling the vase, suggesting that we leave enough space to "allow butterflies to fly in between the stems." The same goes for the soup pot. Keep it simple.

Tips for Soups

- Use a large (at least 6-quart), heavy-bottomed pot for making soup. The thick bottom will discourage scorching and promote even simmering. The pot should have a tight-fitting lid.

- Nothing beats the flavor of homemade broth, and making it is an easy habit that a good cook should acquire. When making homemade broths and stocks, don't add salt. Unsalted stock gives you more control over seasoning the finished dish, which can be important in recipes where the stock is reduced. (The terms *broth* and *stock* are considered interchangeable; a stock is, however, made with bones, but they are not required in a broth.)

- To purée soups, you can use a blender, a food processor, or a hand-held blender. Each one has its advantages. A blender makes the smoothest purée, but you may have to process the soup in batches. A few short pulses of the blender avoids a geyser of hot liquid, but replace the lid with a towel just in case. Cooling the soup prior to blending is also helpful. With a hand-held blender you can purée the soup right in the pot. A food processor works fairly well, especially for large quantities, but the soup could leak out of the central stem area. To avoid this, drain the soup, reserving the liquid. Process the solids and gradually add the liquid through the feed tube. Puréeing will cool the soup a little, so return it to the pot and reheat before serving.

- Chilled soups may thicken too much for your taste during refrigeration, so thin them, if desired, with additional broth, milk, or even a little water.

Purée of Vegetable Soup

Makes 4 servings

Vegetable purée is my favorite soup. It is easy and the vegetables and legumes provide enough substance to thicken the soup. There are many ways to personalize your creation. Use the chart on page 11 for ideas for vegetable and herb combinations. A small quantity of dry sherry or cream can be added to the soup to vary the flavor. For a fresh green color, add a handful of fresh leafy greens (such as spinach or even arugula for a peppery taste) when blending the soup. Serve hot or chilled, with a sprinkle of fresh herbs or a spoonful of sour cream or yogurt.

2 tablespoons olive oil
1 medium onion or 2 medium leeks,
    white and pale green parts only,
    coarsely chopped
2 garlic cloves, chopped
2 teaspoons finely chopped fresh herbs
    or ½ teaspoon dried herbs
3 cups chopped mixed vegetables
1 medium potato, such as Yukon Gold,
    peeled and cut into 1-inch cubes
4 cups Vegetable Broth (page 27)
    or Chicken Stock (page 29)
Salt and freshly ground pepper, to taste

Heat the oil in a large pot over medium-low heat. Add the onions and garlic and cook, stirring often, until softened, about 5 minutes. Stir in the herbs, then the vegetables and potato, and cook gently, stirring often, for 5 minutes to blend the flavors.

Add the broth and bring to a simmer over medium heat. Simmer, partially covered, until the vegetables are tender, about 30 minutes. For a smooth soup, purée the soup in batches in a blender or food processor. For a chunkier soup, purée only half of the soup, and return it to the pot.

To serve hot, season with the salt and pepper and reheat the puréed soup until piping hot. To serve cold, transfer the soup to a large bowl and cool. Cover tightly and refrigerate until chilled, at least 2 hours. Season shortly before serving.

Chilled Sorrel Soup

Makes 4 servings

Sorrel, with its distinctive lemony tartness, appears in the early spring. It's a hardy perennial and one plant will provide years of abundant spring greens. If unavailable, substitute spinach seasoned with a fine grating of nutmeg and a bit of minced rosemary. For a striking garnish, top each serving with a sprinkle of fresh chives and some colorful edible flowers, such as violas, Johnny-jump-ups, or chive blossoms, broken into tiny florets.

2 tablespoons unsalted butter
1 medium onion, chopped
2 medium Yukon Gold potatoes, scrubbed but not peeled, cut into 1-inch cubes
4 cups stemmed and coarsely chopped sorrel leaves
4 cups Chicken Stock (page 29)
1 cup half-and-half
Salt and freshly ground pepper, to taste
Edible flowers, such as violas, and chopped chives, for garnish

Melt the butter in a large pot over medium heat. Add the onion and cook, stirring occasionally, until lightly browned around the edges, about 6 minutes. Stir in the potatoes. Add 3 cups of the sorrel and stir until the sorrel wilts, about 1 minute. Add the stock and bring to a simmer. Cook over medium-low heat, partially covered, until the potatoes are tender, about 30 minutes.

In batches, purée the soup in a blender or food processor, along with the remaining 1 cup sorrel (the fresh leaves will heighten the color and flavor) and half-and-half. Transfer to a large bowl and cool completely. Cover and refrigerate until well chilled, at least 4 hours or overnight.

Season with the salt and pepper and serve chilled, topping each serving with a sprinkle of flowers and chives.

Herbed Gazpacho with Garlic Croutons

Makes 8 servings

A blender makes a smooth gazpacho with a quick push of the button, but the hand-chopped version makes a more substantial texture that I find much nicer. If you want to make the smooth gazpacho, work in batches, and add two cups iced water to the blender to help liquefy the ingredients. Depending on the size of the blender, soup may need to be processed in two batches. For a colorful variation, use yellow tomatoes and bell peppers—you can call it "golden gazpacho."

HERBED GAZPACHO
4 large tomatoes, seeded and finely chopped
1 large cucumber, peeled and finely chopped
1 medium onion, finely chopped
1 medium red bell pepper, seeded and finely chopped
1 cup chopped arugula
½ cup chopped fresh basil
½ cup chopped fresh parsley
2 garlic cloves, minced

⅓ cup rice vinegar
3 tablespoons olive oil
Salt and freshly ground pepper, to taste
Thinly sliced basil leaves, for garnish

GARLIC CROUTONS
4 slices French or Italian bread, cut into ½-inch cubes
3 tablespoons olive oil
2 garlic cloves, minced
Salt, to taste

To make the gazpacho, mix all of the ingredients, except the salt and pepper and the basil, in a large bowl or purée in a blender. Cover and refrigerate until well chilled, at least 4 hours, preferably overnight.

Meanwhile, make the garlic croutons. Preheat the oven to 400°F. Toss the bread cubes, oil, and garlic with your hands in a large bowl until well mixed. Spread in a single layer on a large baking sheet. Bake for 5 minutes. Stir to turn the croutons, and bake until golden brown, about 5 more minutes. Cool completely. (The croutons are best used within a few hours, but they can be stored in an airtight container at room temperature for up to 3 days.)

Serve the soup chilled, seasoned with the salt and pepper and garnished with the croutons and the sliced basil.

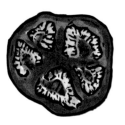

Vegetable and Herb Combinations

𝒽ere are some suggestions for Purée of Vegetable Soup. Keep these combinations in mind, too, when cooking vegetable side dishes.

Beans, green or shell	Sweet basil, sweet marjoram, summer savory
Beets	Dill
Broccoli	Sweet marjoram
Brussels sprouts	Caraway, sweet marjoram, parsley
Cabbage	Fennel fronds and seeds, sweet marjoram, tarragon, thyme
Carrots	Chervil, cilantro, dill fronds and seeds, tarragon
Cauliflower	Sweet marjoram, tarragon
Celeriac	Chervil, chives, parsley
Corn	Basil, cilantro, parsley, sweet marjoram
Cucumber	Dill, fennel fronds and seeds
Eggplant	Scented and sweet basil, fennel fronds and seeds, oregano
Peas	Chervil, mint
Potatoes	Cilantro, chives, parsley
Spinach	Chives, rosemary, sorrel
Summer squash	Sweet basil, oregano, sweet marjoram, summer savory
Tomato	Sweet basil, lovage, fennel
Winter squash	Cilantro, sage

Zesty Lemon Cucumber Soup

Makes 6 servings

Round, bright yellow lemon cucumbers are a real treat to eat right off the vine. In a bumper crop year, the plants are so abundant that a good soup recipe is needed to make a dent in the harvest. This refreshing chilled soup is uncooked and ideal for hot days. If you wish, substitute sunflower seeds, cooked in a dry skillet over high heat until lightly toasted, for the pecans.

6 lemon cucumbers or 2 large unwaxed
    cucumbers, cut into large chunks
3 cups yogurt
1 small fennel bulb, trimmed, fronds
    removed
2 scallions, trimmed, or 1 small onion,
    coarsely chopped
2 large eggs, hard boiled
¼ cup pecans, toasted (see Note)
1 tablespoon chopped fresh dill
1 tablespoon chopped fresh mint
1 tablespoon chopped fresh parsley
1 tablespoon olive oil
Salt and freshly ground pepper, to taste

In batches, purée the cucumbers, yogurt, fennel, scallions, eggs, pecans, dill, mint, parsley, and oil in a blender or food processor. Transfer to a bowl, cover and refrigerate until well chilled, at least 2 hours.

Season with the salt and pepper. Serve chilled.

NOTE: To toast nuts such as almonds, walnuts, and pecans, spread them on a baking sheet. Bake in a preheated 400°F oven, stirring occasionally, until fragrant and toasted, about 10 minutes. Cool completely.

Ginger Carrot Soup

Makes 6 servings

≈

Carrots are always fun to compare because their flavor differences are so pronounced. The sweetest by far is the Touchon, a French heirloom we grow all year round. Plant a fall crop to overwinter in a cold frame and sweet carrots will be ready to harvest in the early spring. This soup, which certainly can be made with any carrot variety, has a rich color and a fragrant bouquet of spices. Vanilla yogurt enhances the carrots' sweetness. Serve it hot or cold.

2 tablespoons olive oil

2 tablespoons unsalted butter

2 shallots, minced

1 garlic clove, minced

1 tablespoon minced crystallized ginger

¼ teaspoon ground turmeric

¼ teaspoon ground cumin

¼ teaspoon ground cinnamon

¼ teaspoon crumbled saffron threads

8 medium carrots, scrubbed, sliced into ¼-inch-thick rounds

2 cups peeled and seeded butternut squash, cut into 1-inch cubes (about ⅓ medium squash)

5 cups Vegetable Broth (page 27) or water

½ cup apple cider

1 cup vanilla-flavored yogurt

Salt and freshly ground pepper, to taste

Heat the oil and butter in a large pot over medium heat. Add the shallots and garlic and cook, stirring often, until golden, about 2 minutes. Add the ginger, turmeric, cumin, cinnamon, and saffron and stir until very fragrant, about 1 minute. Stir in the carrots and squash and cover. Cook, stirring often, until the carrots begin to soften, about 5 minutes.

Add the broth and cider and bring to a simmer. Reduce the heat to low and cover. Simmer, stirring occasionally, until the vegetables are very tender, about 45 minutes.

In batches, purée the soup with the yogurt in a blender or food processor until smooth. If serving hot, return to the pot, season with the salt and pepper, and gently reheat, being sure not to boil the soup or the yogurt will curdle. If serving cold, transfer to a bowl and cool. Cover and refrigerate until chilled, at least 2 hours. Season with the salt and pepper shortly before serving.

Chilled Lettuce and Chervil Soup

Makes 4 to 6 servings

Often our trial gardens are filled with hundreds of heads of lettuce that are all ready at the same time. We make lots of salads, give plenty of heads away, but more often than not, a good amount ends up on the compost pile. Luckily, lettuce can also make a delicate and refreshing chilled soup. In place of chervil, substitute tarragon or lovage in reduced proportions to taste.

4 tablespoons (½ stick) unsalted butter
2 medium leeks, white and pale green parts
    only, well rinsed and coarsely chopped
1 garlic clove, minced
4 cups Vegetable Broth (page 27) or Chicken
    Stock (page 29)
1 medium head Romaine lettuce, rinsed,
    cut into 1-inch strips
⅓ cup finely chopped fresh chervil
Salt and freshly ground pepper, to taste
Crème fraîche, thinned with milk or heavy
    cream, for garnish

Melt the butter in a large pot over medium heat. Add the leeks and garlic and cook, stirring often, until the leeks are softened, about 5 minutes. Pour in the broth and bring to a simmer. Cover and reduce the heat to low. Simmer until the leeks are tender, about 15 minutes.

Stir in the lettuce, increase the heat to high, and bring to a boil. Cook, uncovered, until the lettuce is completely wilted, about 5 minutes.

In batches, purée the soup in a blender or food processor, along with the chervil. Season with the salt and pepper. Return the soup to the pot and gently reheat until hot. Serve hot, with a dollop of the thinned crème fraîche in each bowl.

Creamy Red Beet Soup with Pistachio Mousse

Makes 8 servings

〜

We grow white beets, which are great for salads, and Chioggia or candy-striped beets for dazzling side dishes, but red beets are my favorite for this colorful soup with its light fruity flavor. The pistachio mousse topping adds an exciting visual contrast.

2 tablespoons olive oil

6 medium beets, peeled and cubed

1 small onion, chopped

2 garlic cloves, minced

1½ cups semidry white wine, such as Riesling

2 cups apple juice or cider

Dash of ground allspice

1 cinnamon stick

1 bay leaf

1 pint sour cream or yogurt

Salt and freshly ground pepper, to taste

PISTACHIO MOUSSE

1 cup ricotta cheese

½ cup chopped pistachio nuts

8 sprigs fresh chervil or 4 sprigs fresh
   tarragon

4 fresh mint leaves

Pinch of salt

Pinch of cayenne pepper

Heat the oil in a large pot over medium heat. Add the beets and onions and cook, stirring often, until the onions soften, about 5 minutes. Add the garlic and cook, stirring often, until fragrant, about 2 minutes. Add the wine and bring to a boil over high heat. Cook until the wine is reduced by half, about 5 minutes. Add the apple juice, allspice, cinnamon, and bay leaf, and return to the boil. Reduce the heat to medium-low and cover. Cook until the beets are tender, about 45 minutes. Remove the cinnamon stick and bay leaf. Stir in the sour cream or yogurt.

Transfer to a bowl and cool. Cover and refrigerate until chilled, at least 2 hours.

Meanwhile, make the pistachio mousse. Process all of the ingredients in a blender or food processor until smooth. Transfer to a bowl, cover, and refrigerate until ready to serve.

Serve the soup chilled, seasoning with the salt and pepper and garnishing each bowl with a spoonful of the mousse.

Curried Summer Squash Soup

Makes 6 servings

Gardeners can't resist growing summer squash, and with good reason—they are as versatile as can be. From soups to entrées, from side dishes to cakes, you always can find a way to use up that surplus of zucchini or yellow squash. This cold soup has a pastel hue and subtle squash flavor that changes with the specific variety.

2 tablespoons unsalted butter

1 large onion, chopped

2 garlic cloves, minced

1 tablespoon curry powder

1 teaspoon ground ginger

½ teaspoon ground turmeric

3 medium summer squash or zucchini, trimmed and coarsely chopped (about 4 cups)

4 small red-skinned potatoes, peeled and coarsely chopped (about 2 cups)

½ cup canned unsweetened coconut milk, as needed

Salt and freshly ground pepper, to taste

Heat the butter in a large pot over medium heat. Add the onion and garlic and cook, stirring occasionally, until the onion is softened, about 5 minutes. Add the curry powder, ginger, and turmeric and stir until very fragrant, about 30 seconds. Add the squash and potatoes and cover. Cook, stirring often, until they begin to soften, about 5 minutes.

Add 6 cups of water and bring to a boil. Reduce the heat to medium low and cover. Simmer until the vegetables are tender, about 30 minutes.

In batches, purée the soup in a blender or food processor, along with the coconut milk, adjusting the quality of coconut milk to reach the desired consistency and flavor. Transfer to a bowl and cool. Cover and refrigerate until chilled, at least 2 hours. Season with the salt and pepper and serve chilled.

Leek, Celeriac, and Potato Soup

Makes 6 to 8 servings

Leeks are easy to grow, but they do require a long growing season. If you grow your own, harvest them in the fall, and store in a cool, dry place for a few weeks. You can also chop them into ¼-inch slices and freeze for a few months. Most leek and potato soups look bland, but my version gets a colorful lift with the addition of spinach leaves.

4 tablespoons (½ stick) unsalted butter

3 medium leeks, white and pale green parts
    only, coarsely chopped

2 garlic cloves, minced

4 medium red-skinned potatoes, peeled and
    cut into 1-inch cubes

1 small celeriac (celery root),
    pared and cut into 1-inch cubes

6 cups Vegetable Broth (page 27)
    or Chicken Stock (page 29)

½ teaspoon freshly grated nutmeg

1 bay leaf

1 cup coarsely chopped and
    packed fresh spinach leaves

Salt and freshly ground pepper,
    to taste

Heat the butter in a large pot over medium-low heat. Add the leeks and garlic and cook, stirring often, until the leeks are tender, about 15 minutes. Add the potatoes and celeriac and cook, stirring often, to blend the flavors, about 5 minutes. Add the broth, nutmeg, and bay leaf and bring to a simmer over high heat. Return the heat to medium low and cover. Simmer until the potatoes are tender, about 30 minutes. Remove the bay leaf.

In batches, purée the soup in a blender or food processor until smooth. Add the spinach leaves and pulse to blend. If serving hot, return to the pot, season with salt and pepper, and gently reheat. If serving cold, transfer to a bowl and cool. Cover and refrigerate until chilled, at least 2 hours. Season with salt and pepper shortly before serving.

Tomato and Celeriac Soup with Basil Sorbet

Makes 6 to 8 servings

≈

Celeriac, a knobby root vegetable, provides a subtle hint of celery flavor to soups and stews. A scoop of basil sorbet makes this an especially inviting dish for a summer meal.

2 tablespoons olive oil

¼ cup finely chopped shallots

1 garlic clove, minced

2 medium Yukon Gold potatoes, peeled and cut into ¾-inch cubes

1 medium celeriac (celery root), pared and cut into ¾-inch cubes

2 teaspoons chopped fresh rosemary

8 large ripe tomatoes, seeded and coarsely chopped

1 red bell pepper, roasted (see page 40), skinned, and cut into thin strips

1 cup Vegetable Broth (page 27)

Salt and freshly ground pepper, to taste

BASIL SORBET

½ cup sugar

1½ cups finely chopped fresh basil

½ cup finely chopped fresh parsley

Zest and juice of 2 lemons

Heat the oil in a large pot over medium-low heat. Add the shallots and garlic and cook, stirring often, until the shallots are golden around the edges, about 3 minutes. Stir in the potatoes, celeriac, and rosemary. Cook, stirring often, to blend the flavors, about 10 minutes. Add the tomatoes, red pepper, and broth and bring to a simmer over high heat. Return the heat to medium low and cover. Simmer until the potatoes are tender, about 25 minutes.

Transfer to a bowl and cool. Cover and refrigerate until chilled, at least 4 hours or overnight.

Meanwhile, make the sorbet. Pour 1½ cups of water into a medium saucepan and stir in the sugar. Bring to a full boil over high heat, stirring constantly just until the sugar dissolves. Remove from the heat and stir in the basil, parsley, and lemon zest and juice. Let stand for 30 minutes. Strain, discarding the solids, and cool the basil syrup completely.

Transfer the syrup to a sorbet maker and process according to the manufacturer's instructions. Cover and freeze for up to 1 day.

Lacking a sorbet maker, freeze a 9- × 13-inch metal baking dish until cold. Pour in the syrup. Freeze until the mixture is beginning to freeze around the edges, about 2 hours. Stir well with a sturdy metal spoon, breaking up the ice crystals. Freeze again, stirring every hour or so as the edges freeze, until the mixture forms an icy slush. (The sorbet can be prepared to this point up to 1 day ahead.) Just before serving, freeze the bowl of a food processor until well chilled. Break up the slush with a sturdy metal spoon, and whirl in the food processor to give the sorbet a smoother texture. Use immediately.

Serve the soup chilled, seasoned with the salt and pepper and garnished with a spoonful of the sorbet on top.

Smoked Salmon and Asparagus Bisque

Makes 4 servings

⌒

Smoked salmon slices are often wrapped around asparagus spears and served as an appetizer, and the combination inspired me to use the same flavors in a soup. This can be left as a chunky chowder or puréed to make a creamier version. In the spring, Johnny-jump-up flowers make a nice garnish.

2 tablespoons unsalted butter

1 medium onion, finely chopped

3 medium red-skinned potatoes,
    peeled and cut into ½-inch dice

4 cups Vegetable Broth (page 27)
    or Chicken Stock (page 29)

8 asparagus spears, trimmed, and cut into
    ½-inch lengths

4 ounces sliced smoked salmon,
    chopped

½ cup half-and-half

Zest of 1 lemon

Salt and freshly ground pepper, to taste

Melt the butter in a large pot over medium heat. Add the onion and cook, stirring often, until golden, about 6 minutes. Add the potatoes and cook, stirring occasionally, to blend the flavors, about 5 minutes. Add the broth and asparagus and bring to a simmer over high heat. Reduce the heat to medium low and cover partially. Simmer until the potatoes are tender, about 20 minutes.

Stir in the smoked salmon, half-and-half, and lemon zest. Season with the salt and pepper. Continue to cook over low heat for 10 minutes before serving. For a smoother version, process about half of the soup in a food processor or blender until puréed, and stir back into the pot; reheat. Serve hot.

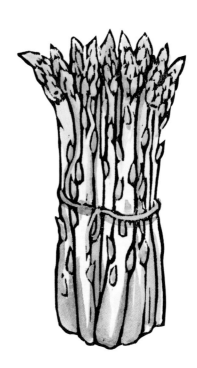

Fiesta Black Bean and Tomato Soup

Makes 6 to 8 servings

This hearty soup makes a perfect lunch or après-ski snack. On many a winter night, I've served it with open-faced grilled Vermont Cheddar sandwiches for a light dinner. Nothing beats my own home-canned tomatoes, but a can of store-bought stewed tomatoes will work just fine.

2 tablespoons olive oil

2 tablespoons unsalted butter

I medium onion, chopped

2 garlic cloves, minced

2 medium carrots, chopped

½ teaspoon ground cumin

½ teaspoon dried summer savory

I bay leaf

½ cup dry sherry

2 cups stewed tomatoes, homemade or canned

I cup dried black beans, soaked overnight in water and drained, or two 15- to 19-ounce cans black beans, drained and rinsed

I tablespoon brown sugar

Salt and freshly ground pepper, to taste

Heat the oil and butter in a large pot over medium heat. Add the onion and garlic and cook until the onion is golden, about 6 minutes. Add the carrots, cumin, savory, and bay leaf and stir to coat. Add the sherry and cook until it evaporates slightly, about 3 minutes. Stir in I quart of water, the tomatoes, soaked beans (add the canned beans later), and brown sugar. Bring to a simmer over high heat. Reduce the heat to low and cover partially. Simmer until the beans are tender, about 2 hours. If using canned beans, add them during the last 10 minutes of cooking.

Purée about half of the soup in a blender or food processor until smooth, and stir back into the pot. Season with the salt and pepper. Gently reheat and serve hot.

Italian Borlotti Bean Soup

Makes 6 to 8 servings

For this recipe, we've used all kinds of fresh shelling beans. Any type will do, but we prefer the Borlotti variety from the Veneto. These are the famous Lamon beans that make Italian soups so hearty and are the foundation of the classic *pasta e fagioli*. Speckled with red and white streaks, they are much like a cranberry bean, which can be substituted. If you wish, used dried beans, soaked overnight in lots of water.

2 tablespoons extra virgin olive oil,
   plus more for serving
1 medium onion, finely chopped
1 cup fresh shelling beans, preferably
   Borlotti or cranberry
1 medium carrot, finely chopped
1 head roasted garlic (see page 38),
   squeezed to remove the soft pulp
2 sprigs fresh thyme
1 sprig fresh rosemary
2 bay leaves
6 cups Vegetable Broth (page 27) or water
Salt and freshly ground pepper, to taste
Finely chopped fresh rosemary, for serving

Heat the oil in a large pot over medium heat. Add the onion and cook, stirring often, until the onion is golden, about 6 minutes. Stir in the beans, carrots, roasted garlic pulp, thyme, rosemary, and bay leaves. Stir in the broth and bring to a simmer over high heat. Reduce the heat to low and partially cover the pot. Simmer until the beans are completely tender, about 30 minutes (45 minutes or longer for dried beans).

Remove the herb stems and bay leaves. Season with the salt and pepper. For a chunky soup, leave as is. For a smoother soup, process about half of the soup in a food processor or blender until smooth, and stir back into the pot. Serve hot, with a swirl of olive oil and a sprinkle of rosemary.

Vermont Gouda and Broccoli Soup

Makes 6 to 8 servings

Just down the road from our place is Taylor Farm, a dairy farm whose owners have recently begun to make cheese. At their very first competition, they won a blue ribbon from the American Cheese Council for their excellent smoked Gouda cheese. Its well-deserved success inspired this recipe.

2 tablespoons unsalted butter

I medium leek, white and pale green parts
    only, coarsely chopped

2 medium Yukon Gold potatoes,
    peeled and cut into I-inch cubes

2 garlic cloves, minced

6 cups Vegetable Broth (page 27)
    or Chicken Stock (page 29)

I bay leaf

I head broccoli, trimmed into bite-sized
    florets, stems peeled and chopped into
    ½-inch dice

2 tablespoons fresh lemon juice

A few gratings of fresh nutmeg

I cup yogurt or sour cream

2 large egg yolks

½ cup shredded smoked Gouda cheese,
    preferably Vermont Gouda

Salt and freshly ground pepper, to taste

Melt the butter in a large pot over medium heat. Add the leek and cook, stirring often, until tender, about 5 minutes. Add the potatoes and garlic and cook, stirring often, until the garlic is fragrant, about 2 minutes. Add the broth and bay leaf and bring to a simmer over high heat. Reduce the heat to medium low and partially cover the pot. Simmer until the potatoes are just tender, about 20 minutes. Add the broccoli and cook until the vegetables are very tender, about 10 minutes. Remove the bay leaf.

In batches, purée the soup in a food processor or blender. Return to the pot. Stir in the lemon juice and nutmeg. In a medium bowl, whisk the yogurt and egg yolks to combine, then add the cheese. Whisk a large ladle of soup into the cheese mixture, then gradually whisk this mixture into the soup. Cook over low heat, stirring constantly, just until the soup is hot and slightly thickened. Do not let the soup boil or the yolks will curdle. Season with the salt and pepper. Serve hot.

Brilliant Butternut Bisque

Makes 8 servings

Of the many varieties of winter squash, the butternut is my favorite for soups because of its smooth texture, bright color, and mellow flavor. This recipe makes a pretty big batch, so it is a fine first course for a holiday meal.

4 tablespoons (½ stick) unsalted butter

4 cups pared and seeded butternut squash,
    cut into 1-inch cubes

2 medium carrots, chopped

1 medium leek, white and pale green parts
    only, coarsely chopped

2 garlic cloves, minced

1 bay leaf

1 cup dry white wine, such as Chardonnay

2 cups half-and-half

½ cup pure maple syrup

A few gratings of fresh nutmeg

Salt and freshly ground pepper, to taste

Heat the butter in a large pot over medium heat. Add the squash, carrots, and leek, and cook, stirring often, until the leek is wilted, about 5 minutes. Add the garlic and bay leaf and cook, stirring often, until the garlic is fragrant, about 1 minute. Stir in the wine and bring to a boil over high heat. Cook, uncovered, until the wine is almost completely evaporated, about 10 minutes. Stir in 4 cups of water and return to the boil. Reduce the heat to medium low and simmer until the squash is very tender, about 30 minutes.

In batches, purée the soup in a food processor or blender. Return to the pot. Stir in the half-and half, maple syrup, and nutmeg. Cook over low heat, stirring constantly, just until the soup is piping hot. Season with the salt and pepper. Serve hot.

Kale and Sausage Soup

Makes 6 servings

The kale in our garden grows late into the fall. We now grow an Italian variety called Lancianto or Black Tuscan kale. Its long, narrow leaves are smoother and more tender than American kale. Look for it in farmers' markets or specialty food stores that stock local produce.

⅓ cup olive oil

½ pound cooked sausage, such as kielbasa, cut into bite-sized pieces

1 medium onion, chopped

1 medium red bell pepper, ribbed, seeded, and thinly sliced

1 jalapeño chile, seeded and finely chopped

2 garlic cloves, minced

1 teaspoon ground cumin

1 large bunch kale, preferably Black Tuscan, stemmed, well washed, and coarsely chopped (8 cups packed)

6 cups Chicken Stock (page 29)

2 cups chopped tomatoes, fresh or drained canned

½ cup brown rice

Salt and freshly ground pepper, to taste

Heat the oil in a large pot over medium heat. Add the sausage and cook, stirring occasionally, until browned, about 5 minutes. Add the onion, red pepper, chile, and garlic, and cook them until they soften, about 5 minutes. Stir in the cumin and cook for 1 minute.

A handful at a time, add the kale, stirring each addition and letting it wilt before adding another handful. Add the stock and tomatoes and bring to a boil over high heat. Reduce the heat to medium low and partially cover the pot. Simmer for 30 minutes.

Add the rice and cook until it is tender, about 45 minutes. Season with the salt and pepper, but use a light hand, because the sausage may have provided enough seasoning. Serve hot.

Moroccan Eggplant Soup

Makes 4 to 6 servings

Of the many ways to serve eggplant, soup is often overlooked. But this one, nicely flavored with cumin and fennel, serves as an excellent first course to pique the appetite. To toast the spices, a step that really brings out their flavor, heat a small, empty skillet over medium heat. One spice at a time, add to the skillet and toast, stirring often, until very fragrant (you may see a wisp of smoke), about 2 minutes or so. Transfer to a plate and cool. Grind the spices in a mortar and pestle or spice grinder.

2 tablespoons olive oil

1 medium onion, chopped

6 garlic cloves, minced

One 1½-pound eggplant, peeled and cut into
    1-inch cubes

1 red bell pepper, roasted (see page 40) and
    thinly sliced, plus additional strips of red
    pepper for garnish (optional)

2 teaspoons cumin seeds, toasted and ground

2 teaspoons fennel seeds, toasted and ground

6 cups Chicken Stock (page 29)
    or Vegetable Broth (page 27)

1 cup basmati rice

Salt and freshly ground pepper, to taste

Yogurt, for garnish

Chopped fresh cilantro, for garnish

Heat the oil in a large pot over medium heat. Add the onion and garlic and cook, stirring often, until the onion softens, about 5 minutes. Add the eggplant and red pepper and cook, stirring often, to blend the flavors, about 3 minutes. Stir in the cumin and fennel. Add the stock and rice and bring to a boil over high heat. Reduce the heat to medium low and partially cover the pot. Simmer until the eggplant is very tender, about 20 minutes. Season with the salt and pepper.

For a chunky soup, leave as it is. For a smoother soup, purée about half of the soup in a blender or food processor, return to the pot, and reheat gently until piping hot. Serve hot, garnishing each serving with a dollop of yogurt and a sprinkle of the cilantro.

Chicken and Barley Soup

Makes 8 servings

My recipe for curing the wintertime blues is a big pot of chicken and vegetable soup. It's a good way to sample everything from the root cellar or vegetable bin and provides a rib-sticking family meal.

> 2 tablespoons olive oil
>
> 3 medium leeks, white and pale green parts only, chopped into ½-inch dice
>
> 2 garlic cloves, minced
>
> 1 hot chile pepper, preferably cayenne, seeded and minced
>
> 6 medium carrots, cut into ½-inch dice
>
> 4 medium red-skinned or Yukon Gold potatoes, peeled and cut into ½-inch dice
>
> 4 ounces portobello or stemmed shiitake mushrooms, chopped
>
> ½ cup pearl barley
>
> 8 cups freshly made Chicken Stock (page 29)
>
> 1 teaspoon finely chopped fresh thyme
>
> 2 cups bite-sized chunks of cooked chicken (reserved from Chicken Stock)
>
> 1 cup packed chopped fresh spinach leaves
>
> Salt and freshly ground pepper, to taste

Heat the oil in a large pot over medium heat. Add the leeks, garlic, and chile and cook, stirring, until the leeks soften, 5 minutes. Add the carrots, potatoes, mushrooms, and barley, and cook to blend the flavors, 3 minutes. Add the stock and thyme and bring to a boil over high heat. Reduce the heat to medium low and cover. Simmer until the barley is tender, 45 minutes. Add the chicken and spinach and heat through. Season with salt and pepper. Serve hot.

Thai Lemon and Arugula Soup

Makes 4 servings

Quick and light, this soup is simple to make and simply delicious. The recipe is for four servings, but you will easily see how it could be turned into a fast lunch for one. The lemon and garlic add a zing that can be intensified with a splash of hot sauce or a grating of fresh ginger.

> 2 cups cooked jasmine rice
>
> Grated zest of ½ lemon
>
> 1 teaspoon fresh lemon juice
>
> ½ pound medium shrimp, cooked, peeled, deveined, and halved lengthwise
>
> 2 cups chopped arugula
>
> 2 medium carrots, finely shredded
>
> 2 garlic cloves, minced
>
> 4 cups Chicken Stock (page 29), heated to a simmer
>
> 8 lemon balm or mint leaves

Fill 4 soup bowls with boiling water and set aside to heat the bowls. Toss the rice with the lemon zest and juice in a medium bowl.

When ready to serve, pour out the water from the bowls. Place a mound of the rice in each bowl and add equal quantities of the shrimp, arugula, carrots, and garlic. Ladle the stock into each bowl, and add the herb leaves. Serve immediately.

Vegetable Broth

Makes about 2 quarts

A good vegetable broth is a must in my kitchen. I use it to provide depth and flavor to soups and sauces, as well as to make risotto. The trick is creating a broth that is well balanced without the flavor of one vegetable dominating the broth. If you have the time, try the roasted vegetable broth variation, as roasting coaxes extra sweetness from the vegetables.

1 medium leek, white and pale green parts only, coarsely chopped

1 medium carrot, cut into thin rounds

1 medium celeriac (celery root), pared and quartered

1 medium turnip, pared and quartered

1 wedge (¼ head) green cabbage, coarsely chopped

1 small fennel bulb, fronds trimmed, cut in half lengthwise

½ cup chopped mushrooms

2 garlic cloves, smashed under a heavy knife

A handful of fresh parsley sprigs

2 sprigs fresh thyme

2 bay leaves

Salt and freshly ground pepper, to taste

Place all of the ingredients in a stockpot and add 4 quarts of cold water. Bring to a boil over medium heat. Reduce the heat to low and cover. Simmer for 1 hour. Season with the salt and pepper. Strain into a large bowl, pressing hard on the solids to extract as much liquid as possible. Cool, cover, and refrigerate for up to 1 week or freeze for up to 1 year.

ROASTED VEGETABLE BROTH. Place all of the vegetables (except the parsley and bay leaves) in two large, lightly oiled roasting pans. Drizzle the vegetables in each pan with 2 tablespoons olive oil and toss to coat. Roast in a preheated 400°F oven, stirring occasionally, until the vegetables are softened and tinged with brown, about 45 minutes. Transfer to a stockpot, add the remaining ingredients, and proceed as directed.

SUMMER GARDENS BLOOM
GLORIOUS IN WINTER DREAMS.

Chicken Stock

Makes about 2 quarts

Canned broth is convenient, but so is making and freezing home-made stock—and there is no comparison in flavor and quality. As for the vegetable broth, I give a roasted variation for the times when you want a more intense flavor and darker color.

One 3- to 4-pound organic chicken, giblets included (no liver), cut into quarters

3 carrots, coarsely chopped

2 medium onions, each studded with 5 cloves

2 garlic cloves, smashed under a heavy knife

3 bay leaves

8 sprigs fresh thyme, or $^1\!/_2$ teaspoon dried thyme

5 sprigs fresh sage, or $^1\!/_2$ teaspoon dried sage

2 sprigs fresh tarragon, or $^1\!/_4$ teaspoon dried tarragon

Salt and freshly ground pepper, to taste

Place all of the ingredients in a stockpot and add enough cold water to cover by 1 inch. Bring to a boil over high heat, skimming off any foam that rises to the surface. Reduce the heat to low and partially cover the pot. Simmer until the chicken is tender, about 1 hour. Remove the chicken from the pot and reserve for another use. Season the stock with the salt and pepper.

Strain the stock into a bowl. Cool, cover, and refrigerate for up to 3 days, or freeze for up to 6 months.

BROWN CHICKEN STOCK. Spread the chicken, giblets, carrots, onions, and garlic in a large lightly oiled roasting pan. Roast in a pre-heated 400°F oven until the chicken is golden brown, about 1 hour. Remove the chicken meat from the bones, reserving the skin and bones. Save the chicken meat for another use. Place the chicken skin and bones, giblets, and vegetables in a stock pot. Place the roasting pan on the stove over high heat. Pour 2 cups cold water into the pan and use a wooden spoon to scrape up the browned bits. Transfer to the pot. Add the remaining ingredients, and add enough cold water to cover them by 1 inch. Proceed as directed above, simmering for 1 hour.

Salads and Dressings

*L*ettuce is the queen of the salad bowl. Quick-growing, adaptable to different seasons, and tolerant of most conditions, it is an ideal crop, equally at home in a simple kitchen plot and an intensive, full-blown vegetable garden. We complement our lettuce patch with other greens that can be added to salads to vary the flavor, color, and texture. Many of these greens are cultivated versions of wild plants; others are new, improved varieties, such as a milder purslane that grows upright instead of hugging the ground and a more compact arugula.

Let the greens dictate the dressing you choose. Tender and subtle-flavored greens such as mâche are best with a light vinaigrette of mild oil and a gentle vinegar. More assertive greens such as arugula or dandelion can handle a dressing with dominant flavors, such as garlic and shallots. In this chapter, I've collected recipes for every season and every taste, gathered from many years of growing and harvesting mountains of greens.

We began growing gourmet salad greens in the early 1980s, mostly because they were the only fast-growing crop that would be ready when we opened our farm stand in May. But we were also curious to try some of the new greens that were beginning to appear in specialty food markets and high-end restaurants. Mesclun, now ubiquitous at the supermarket, was familiar only to traveling gourmets. We began growing a range of different greens and created mesclun mixes that reflected our own preference as well as the classic combinations that have been grown for centuries in France and Italy.

At first, most of our esoteric seeds came from friends who brought them back from their European travels, usually accompanied by a story about a unique salad they enjoyed at an elegant restaurant or family-run bistro or trattoria. We did a trial planting, usually with no more information than the picture on the seed packet and a verbal description from the traveling friend. After a few seasons, our farm stand customers and local chefs were so enthusiastic that we soon found ourselves importing seeds by the kilo!

Tips for Salads and Dressings

■ Every kitchen should have a large wooden salad bowl. They are so beautiful, and salad made in one just seems to taste better, especially if the bowl is seasoned with salt and garlic before the greens are added. Cut a clove of garlic in half and rub all over the inside. Transfer the crushed garlic to a cutting board and chop it finely. Return it to the bowl. Sprinkle the inside of the bowl with a pinch of sea salt. Consider the garlic and salt to be the beginning of your dressing. A wooden salad bowl should never be washed with hot water and soap—it will remove the natural oil protection and repeated washings and drying could cause warping and cracking. To clean a wooden bowl, wipe it out with a moist paper towel or a clean kitchen cloth. Sprinkle with salt, and scour the inside of the bowl with the towel to pick up any residual moisture and kill bacteria. Wipe the salt out of the bowl.

■ Salad greens, especially wild or bitter greens that may have been grown in sandy soil, should be washed well in lots of cold water to remove any grit. Fill a sink with cold water, add the greens, and agitate them. Let the greens stand in the water for a few minutes so the grit can settle to the bottom. Lift the greens out of the water, and transfer to a colander, leaving any dirt behind. If necessary, wash the greens again in a fresh sink of water.

■ All salad greens should be dried thoroughly before dressing in order for the oil to coat the leaves. A salad spinner does the best job here. To keep the greens well chilled, spread a single layer on a paper towel, loosely roll, and place in a plastic bag. Seal and refrigerate.

Basic Vinaigrette

Makes about ⅓ cup

The quality of the ingredients will directly affect the outcome of anything you cook, but it is especially important to use top-notch olive oil and vinegar to make the best vinaigrette. I prefer making a vinaigrette directly in a garlic-and-salt-rubbed wooden salad bowl, but you can whisk the ingredients in a separate small bowl, if you wish. This makes enough salad for four, with a week's worth of vinaigrette as a variation.

I garlic clove, cut in half lengthwise

⅛ teaspoon fine sea salt

¼ cup extra virgin olive oil

2 tablespoons herb-infused or sherry vinegar

I teaspoon Dijon mustard or ½ teaspoon dry mustard

I teaspoon pure maple syrup or honey

I teaspoon finely chopped fresh parsley, chervil, chives, or basil

Freshly ground pepper, to taste

To make the dressing in a wooden salad bowl, rub the inside of the bowl with the garlic, then with the salt. Mince the garlic and add to the bowl. Add the oil, vinegar, mustard, maple syrup, parsley, and pepper. Whisk until the dressing is combined and thickened. (Or, mince the garlic and place in a small bowl. Add the remaining ingredients and whisk until combined and thickened.)

LARGE BATCH VINAIGRETTE. Makes 1⅔ cups. If you want to store a large batch of vinaigrette in the refrigerator, use these proportions. With the machine running, drop 2 garlic cloves into a food processor or blender and process until minced. Add I cup extra virgin olive oil, ¼ cup herb-infused or sherry vinegar, I tablespoon Dijon mustard or I teaspoon dry mustard, 2 teaspoons pure maple syrup or honey, 4 teaspoons finely chopped fresh herbs, and ½ teaspoon freshly ground pepper, and process until smooth. Transfer to a covered jar. Store in the refrigerator for up to I month. Shake well before using.

Garlic-Honey Vinaigrette

Makes about ⅔ cup

⌒

For spring salad greens with tender textures and gentle flavors, use a simple, tart dressing such as this tarragon-scented vinaigrette. It's made with garlic-infused honey, an easy-to-make ingredient with plenty of uses for a creative cook.

    6 garlic cloves

    ¼ teaspoon fine sea salt, plus more to taste

    ½ cup extra virgin olive oil

    2 tablespoons tarragon vinegar

    ½ cup Garlic Honey or plain honey

    1 teaspoon Dijon mustard

    1 teaspoon finely chopped fresh chives

    1 teaspoon finely chopped fresh chervil

    1 teaspoon finely chopped fresh parsley

    Freshly ground pepper, to taste

Chop the garlic and place in a mortar. Sprinkle with the salt and mash to a paste with the pestle. (Or chop the garlic on a work surface, sprinkle with salt, and chop and smear the garlic until it makes a paste.) Transfer to a jar. Add the oil, vinegar, garlic honey, mustard, chives, chervil, and parsley, and season with the pepper. Cover and shake well to combine. Store, covered and refrigerated, for up to 1 week. Shake well before using.

GARLIC HONEY. Process 12 peeled garlic cloves and 1 cup of honey in a blender until smooth. Transfer to a covered jar. Store, refrigerated, for up to 1 month.

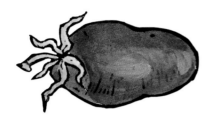

Lemon-Tahini Dressing

Makes ¾ cup

≈

This light-bodied dressing is a refreshing spring tonic, and a fine partner on soft, sweet butterhead lettuce.

> 1 garlic clove
> ⅛ teaspoon salt, plus more to taste
> ¼ cup fresh lemon juice
> 1 tablespoon tahini (sesame seed paste)
> ½ teaspoon sugar
> ½ cup olive oil
> Freshly ground pepper, to taste

Chop the garlic and place in a mortar. Sprinkle with the salt and mash to a paste with the pestle. (Or chop the garlic on a work surface, sprinkle with ⅛ teaspoon salt, and chop and smear the garlic until it makes a paste.) Transfer to a covered jar. Add the lemon juice, tahini, sugar, and oil. Shake well until combined. Season with the salt and pepper. Store, refrigerated, for up to 1 week. Shake well before using.

Goat Cheese and Tomato Dressing

Makes about 1½ cups dressing

≈

A creamy dressing will often tame the bite of bitter greens. This recipe, with a whole ripe tomato as its base, makes a lovely light pink dressing that offsets the deep greens in a flamboyant way. It yields a big batch, so plan on using it in other ways with sliced tomatoes, or as a mayonnaise substitute.

> 2 ounces rindless goat cheese (chèvre)
> 2 tablespoons tarragon vinegar
> 1 tablespoon finely chopped fresh basil leaves
> 1 garlic clove, smashed under a heavy knife
> 1 or 2 ripe medium tomatoes, coarsely
>   chopped (1 cup)
> ½ cup olive oil
> Salt and freshly ground pepper, to taste

Pulse the goat cheese, vinegar, basil, and garlic in a blender to combine. Add the tomato and purée. With the machine running, gradually add the oil until the mixture is smooth. Season with the salt and pepper. Store in a covered jar in the refrigerator for up to 2 weeks. Shake well before using.

Roasted Garlic, Dill, and Ginger Dressing

Makes 1½ cups dressing

Roasted garlic is mild, and its sweet flavor pairs well with any member of the cabbage family, including kale, bok choy, or kohlrabi. Here, the sturdy texture of roasted garlic purée is used to create a thick and versatile dressing that not only works for a cabbage slaw, but could also be served as a sauce over baked potatoes, steamed vegetables, or grilled fish.

3 heads roasted garlic (see Note)
¾ cup olive oil
¼ cup chopped fresh dill
¼ cup rice vinegar or sherry vinegar
2 tablespoons fresh lime juice
1 tablespoon peeled and
    grated fresh ginger
2 tablespoons sesame seeds
2 tablespoons dark Asian sesame oil
Salt and freshly ground pepper, to taste

Process the garlic pulp, olive oil, dill, vinegar, lime juice, ginger, sesame seeds, and sesame oil in a blender or food processor until smooth. Season with the salt and pepper. Store in a covered jar, refrigerated, for up to 1 week. Shake well before using.

NOTE: To roast garlic, wrap a whole large and firm head of garlic in aluminum foil. If you wish, add a sprig or two of fresh rosemary, thyme, or sage before wrapping. Place on a baking sheet. Bake in a preheated 400°F oven until the head feels tender when squeezed through the foil, about 1 hour. Unwrap and cool. Using kitchen scissors or a sharp knife, snip off the top ½ inch or so from the head. Squeeze the soft garlic pulp out of the hull; discard the hull. Or use kitchen scissors to snip through the skin of each clove, and remove the whole cloves from the hull.

Each season has cultivated and wild greens and edible flowers that are at their best during that time of year. Here is a list of salad possibilities that can be gathered in season, depending on your locale.

Winter

GREENS Arugula, cress, chickweed, mâche, *shungiku* chrysanthemum, kale, dandelion leaves, wild sorrel, shepherd's purse, salad burnet, radicchio and other chicories, claytonia (miner's lettuce)

FLOWERS Viola, mustard blossoms, arugula blossoms, pansy

Spring

GREENS Arugula, salad burnet, chicory, chervil, cress, chickweed, comfrey, dandelion leaves, fiddlehead ferns, kale, *shungiku* chrysanthemum, good king henry, mâche, mustard greens, French and wild sorrels, radish tops, shepherd's purse, salad orach, parsley

FLOWERS Arugula blossoms, chive blossoms, forget-me-nots, pansy and viola, plum blossoms, primrose, mustard blossoms, wood violets

Summer

GREENS Amaranth, basil, beet greens, celery leaves, cilantro, lemon balm, lovage, watercress, comfrey, cress, chickweed, fennel, kale, lamb's quarters, mâche, mint, mustard, nasturtium, perilla, purslane, sorrel, *shungiku* chrysanthemum, salad burnet, spinach, shepherd's purse, wild or cultivated sorrel, chicory, chervil, salad orach, parsley

FLOWERS Anise hyssop, arugula blossoms, borage, calendula, nasturtium, marigold, red clove, rose, sage, sugar peas, purple vetch

Fall

GREENS Bok choy, cabbage, chickweed, spinach, kale, lamb's quarters, mustard, nasturtium, salad orach, purslane, mâche, mint, mustard, wild sorrel

FLOWERS Calendula, pansy and viola, chrysanthemum, thyme, rosemary

Roasted Red Pepper Dressing

Makes 1½ cups

Roasted red peppers turn this dressing an amazingly brilliant red. There are many ways to roast peppers, but I find the broiler method, with the peppers flattened, to be the best. Note that with this method, the seeds and ribs are removed before roasting. The dressing can be used on assertive salad greens such as mustard or arugula, or use as a sauce on steamed kale or Swiss chard.

2 medium red bell peppers, roasted (see Note)

¼ cup fresh lemon juice

2 tablespoons sherry vinegar

2 tablespoons minced shallots

½ teaspoon cumin seeds, roasted
   (see page 25)

½ cup olive oil

Salt and freshly ground pepper, to taste

Purée the roasted peppers, lemon juice, vinegar, shallots, and cumin in a blender or food processor. Gradually add the olive oil and process until smooth. Season with the salt and pepper. Store in a covered jar, refrigerated, for up to 5 days. Shake well before using.

NOTE: To roast bell peppers, position a broiler rack 6 inches from the source of heat, and preheat the broiler. Trim the stem end from each pepper and discard (or poke out and discard the stem, and save the trimmed pepper top). Cut the peppers lengthwise, spread open, and press down on the peppers with your hand to flatten them. Trim out the ribs and seeds and discard. Place the flattened peppers (with the stemless tops, if you wish), skin side up, on the broiler rack. Broil until the skin is charred and blistered, about 5 minutes. Transfer the peppers to a bowl and cover tightly with plastic wrap or place in a paper bag and close the bag. Let stand until the peppers are cool enough to handle, about 10 minutes. Scrape off the blackened skin. Try not to rinse the peppers under cold water unless absolutely necessary.

Spring Greens Salad with Sour Cream Dressing

Makes 4 servings

The first salads of early spring are made with pleasantly piquant leaves, be they perennial chicories from our garden or foraged greens from the wild. Our spring salad usually features Ceriola, a beautiful spoon-shaped chicory, and the wild Selvatica arugula, but any combination of similar greens will be equally delicious, especially with this soothing dressing.

DRESSING

3 tablespoons olive oil

2 tablespoons sour cream

2 teaspoons sherry vinegar

1 teaspoon balsamic vinegar

Salt and freshly ground pepper, to taste

1 garlic clove, cut in half lengthwise

Salt, as needed

5 cups loosely packed perky salad greens (such as dandelion, curly chicory, frisée, radicchio, and other mildly bitter greens), rinsed, dried, and torn into bite-sized pieces

½ cup coarsely chopped sun-dried tomatoes

¼ cup freshly grated Parmesan cheese

To make the dressing, whisk together all of the ingredients until smooth in a medium bowl.

If you have a wooden salad bowl, rub the bowl with the garlic, and a sprinkling of salt. Mince the garlic and add to the bowl. (Or, mince the garlic and toss it into a large bowl.) Add the greens, then the dressing, and toss. Sprinkle in the tomatoes, add the cheese, and toss again. Serve immediately.

Balsamic-Thyme Dressing

Makes 1½ cups

When our own bed of cultivated greens is not quite ready to be cut, we're happy to use wild greens. In the Northeast, we've got plenty of volunteers, from purslane, dandelion, and chickweed to edible flowers such as Johnny-jump-ups, calendula, and nasturtiums. Here is a robust dressing that allows the individual flavors of the greens to shine through. To keep the greens crisp, it's best to pass this dressing, which also allows the guests to use the amount they prefer.

¼ cup balsamic vinegar
2 tablespoons tamari or soy sauce
1 tablespoon finely chopped fresh thyme
    or 1 teaspoon dried thyme
1 tablespoon Dijon mustard
1 tablespoon honey
2 garlic cloves, smashed under a heavy knife
    and peeled
1 cup olive oil
Salt and freshly ground pepper,
    to taste

Pulse the vinegar, tamari, thyme, mustard, honey, and garlic in a blender or food processor to combine. With the machine running, gradually add the oil and process until smooth. Season with the salt and pepper. Store in a covered jar, refrigerated, for up to 1 month. Shake well before using.

Belgian Endive Salad with Raspberry-Walnut Dressing

Makes 4 servings

To achieve the characteristic ivory color of Belgian endive *chicons*, the gardener must be intrepid. The seed is sown outdoors to sprout the fat cigar-shaped shoots that grow from a thick root. The roots are then transplanted inside to grow out in a dark place (to deprive the shoots of the sunlight that would develop their chlorophyll and turn them green). The pale endive is enhanced by an exuberant burst of color from the red raspberry dressing. Serve this vibrant salad on plates with a dramatic, stylized design.

DRESSING
½ cup fresh raspberries
3 tablespoons raspberry vinegar
1 tablespoon honey
1 tablespoon sour cream
1 tablespoon Dijon mustard
⅓ cup extra virgin olive oil
Salt and freshly ground pepper, to taste

2 Belgian endive, separated into leaves
1 clementine, peeled and separated into
    sections
½ cup toasted (see page 12) and coarsely
    chopped walnuts

Purée the raspberries, vinegar, honey, sour cream, and mustard in a blender or food processor. With the machine running, gradually add the oil and process until smooth. Season with the salt and pepper. If desired, strain the dressing through a fine wire sieve to remove the seeds.

Arrange equal quantities of the endive leaves in a spoke pattern on four salad plates. Scatter with the clementine and sprinkle with the walnuts. Drizzle with the dressing.

Serve chilled.

Herbed Sea Salt

Makes about 2 cups

Keep a small container of this secret ingredient next to your stove and use it in savory recipes to replace plain salt. This is a clever way to use up the dregs in those aging jars of dried herbs in the cupboard and add a tasty seasoning to your food at the same time.

2 cups coarse sea salt
I teaspoon dried basil
I teaspoon dried rosemary
I teaspoon dried sage
I teaspoon dried summer savory
I teaspoon dried tarragon
I teaspoon dried thyme
½ teaspoon dried lavender

Pulse the salt, basil, rosemary, sage, savory, tarragon, thyme, and lavender in a food processor until the herbs are crushed. Transfer to an airtight container. May be stored indefinitely at room temperature.

Marinated Green Beans

Makes 4 servings

Most of the green beans we grow are the narrow, tender varieties, such as *haricots verts* or French filets. You can use these beauties in this salad, but it is also wonderful with thicker, meatier beans such as stringless Kentucky Wonders or old-fashioned snap beans. For the best results, dress the beans while they are hot, then chill, but serve them at room temperature.

I pound green beans, trimmed
¼ cup extra virgin olive oil
I tablespoon sherry or herb-flavored vinegar
I teaspoon finely chopped fresh thyme or summer savory
Salt and freshly ground pepper, to taste

Bring a large pot of lightly salted water to a boil over high heat. Stir in the beans, being sure they are submerged. Cover and cook the beans until they are crisp-tender, about 5 minutes. They will make a snapping sound when cooked. Drain and rinse under cold water to stop the cooking.

In a large bowl, preferably a wooden salad bowl, whisk the oil and vinegar until combined. Season with fresh thyme or savory and the salt and pepper. Add the warm green beans and toss well. Cover and refrigerate until chilled, at least I hour. Let stand at room temperature for 30 minutes before serving.

Sweet Corn, Tomato, and Cucumber Salad

Makes 6 to 8 servings

This cool and refreshing salad has the consistency of a chunky salsa, but without the heat. Top-notch summer corn will supply plenty of sweetness without sugar. For a decorative touch, spoon the salad into a cup of tender lettuce, such as butterhead.

6 large ears fresh corn
2 large ripe tomatoes, seeded and
    chopped into ½-inch cubes
1 medium cucumber, chopped
    into ½-inch cubes
1 small onion, finely
    chopped
⅓ cup finely chopped
    fresh parsley
⅓ cup finely chopped
    fresh cilantro
2 tablespoons fresh lemon
    or lime juice
2 tablespoons Basic
    Vinaigrette
    (page 35), or as
    needed
Salt and freshly ground
    pepper, to taste

Place the corn in a large pot and add enough cold water to cover by 2 inches. Cover and bring to a boil over high heat. Cook until the corn is tender, about 10 minutes. Drain and cool the corn. Cut each ear in half. Stand each half ear on end, and cut the kernels. You should have about 3 cups.

Combine the corn, tomatoes, cucumber, onion, parsley, and cilantro in a large bowl. Add the lemon juice and toss. Toss with the vinaigrette, using more if you like.

Season with the salt and pepper. Cover and refrigerate until chilled, at least 2 hours or up to overnight. Serve chilled.

*W*hile chicories have been cultivated for centuries, all are cool weather crops, but each type has slightly different needs. The endives and escaroles are grown much like lettuce as an annual crop. There are three types of perennial chicory; root and forcing chicory, spring cutting and rosette chicory, plus red and green leaf heading types, otherwise known as radicchio.

ENDIVE AND ESCAROLE. The only physical difference between endive and escarole is the shape of the leaves. Endive is also known by the name frisée and has deeply cut, feathery foliage while escarole has broad leaves like lettuce. Both are slightly bitter in flavor. Endive is usually blanched before harvest to lessen its natural bitterness.

ROOT AND FORCING CHICORY. These chicories are grown for their large roots, eaten as a cooked vegetable, or dried and ground as a coffee substitute. The misnamed Belgian endive, or witloof (Dutch for white leaf) chicory also forms a large root. The small elongated heads are a delicate and expensive salad fixing.

SPRING CUTTING AND ROSETTE CHICORY. The cutting and rosette chicory are perennials, and so deserve a place in such a permanent salad bed along with sorrel and dandelion. We grow Catalogna chicory (or Radichetta), Spadona (also good as an annual), and Grumulo, also known as Ceriolo.

These spring chicories are used in a variety of ways, depending on type. If picked when young, spring chicory can go in a salad, with a creamy dressing to tame the bitterness. Or strip the leaves from the stems and these tender stalks make a crisp addition to a salad or crudité platter. They can also be steamed lightly and served with a drizzle of good olive oil.

RED AND GREEN RADICCHIO. These chicories form small, tightly packed heads that weigh a quarter to half pound apiece. Their form ranges from tight balls to loose elongated leaves, both with striking variegated leaves. Try them painted with olive oil, grilled, and then splashed with balsamic vinegar. They'll lose their distinctive wine red color when cooked, but the flavor is unsurpassed, especially if paired with a soft chèvre.

Insalata di Misitcanza

Makes 4 servings

Romans love *insalata di misitcanza*, a piquant salad with a complex combination of fresh and wild greens and herbs. Some versions of this wildly healthy dish include up to fifteen different ingredients, but the common denominator seems to be arugula. The exact combination will depend entirely on what is available, but here is the basis for a classic recipe.

> 6 cups loosely packed mixed greens
> (such as arugula, mâche, radicchio,
> flat-leafed young spinach, purslane,
> curly endive, dandelion, mint, sorrel,
> and valerian), washed, dried, and
> torn into bite-sized pieces
> 1 small fennel bulb, trimmed, fronds
> removed, and finely chopped
> 2 spring onions, white bulb only,
> thinly sliced, or 4 scallions,
> white and green parts, chopped
> ¼ cup finely chopped fresh flat-leaf parsley
> ¼ cup finely chopped fresh mint
> 2 tablespoons finely chopped fresh chives
> ¼ cup Basic Vinaigrette (page 35)

Combine the greens, fennel, onions, parsley, mint, and chives in a large bowl. Drizzle with the dressing and toss. Serve immediately.

Dutch Mâche and Beet Salad

Makes 2 to 4 servings

Mâche, also called lamb's lettuce, is a delicate spoon-shaped green, prized for its subtle nutty flavor and its ability to grow vigorously during cool weather in the early spring and late fall. This classic recipe is improved with white or golden beets because they do not "bleed" their juices as the more common red types do.

> 4 medium white, golden, or red beets, well
> scrubbed but not peeled
> ⅓ cup olive oil
> 2 tablespoons tarragon vinegar
> Salt and freshly ground pepper, to taste
> 2 cups mâche, well washed and dried
> 2 hard-boiled eggs, chopped
> 1 small red onion, thinly sliced
> ½ cup Garlic Croutons (page 10)

Position a rack in the center of the oven and preheat to 400°F. Wrap each beet in aluminum foil and place on a baking sheet. Bake until the beets are tender, about 1 hour. Cool completely. Peel the beets and cut into ¼-inch rounds.

Whisk the oil and vinegar in a large bowl, preferably a wooden salad bowl, and season with the salt and pepper. Add the mâche, beets, eggs, onion, and croutons and toss. Serve immediately.

Greens are among the most satisfying vegetables to grow, and many grow so quickly that they are ready to harvest within a month after sowing. Spring and fall are the natural seasons for greens in Vermont because they prefer cool weather, but with some forethought, you can produce good crops right through the summer in all but the hottest climates. During early and late summer, when a little shade will suffice to shield the plants, we plant our greens in beds between north-south rows of beans and peas to provide semishade for most of the day. When the real dog days take hold, we put shade cloth–covered wire hoops over the greens. Protected in this fashion, most greens will grow throughout the summer. We have over forty types of salad greens in our catalogue but this list reflects our favorites.

ARUGULA *(Eruca sativa)*. Currently one the most popular and best-known salad greens, arugula has oak-shaped leaves with a sharp, mustardy flavor; the longer the plant stays in the ground, the spicier the taste. Selvatica arugula is a compact miniature of its better-known cousin, and remains green and harvestable throughout the year in temperate climates. Like many other greens, arugula has been around a long time, dating far back through European recorded history (it was a favorite of the Romans).

CRESS *(Lepidium sativum)*. Just about the easiest crop to grow, cress is the perfect plant for a child's first garden. Quick growing, it is also quick to pass its prime, and should be used when it is barely past the seedling stage. If you've ever seen one of those ceramic sheep covered with "woolly" green sprouts, you were probably looking at cress. Grown for sprouts, cress can be harvested in about a week to ten days, and lends a clean, peppery taste to salads. In winter up north, it can be grown indoors in pots and window boxes, or year-round outdoors in milder climates. The three common kinds of cress are plain (with mildly serrated leaves), curly (deeply serrated leaves, like curly parsley), and broadleaf (with 1-inch wide by 4-inch-long leaves).

WATERCRESS (*Nasturtium officinale*). Not actually a cress, but rather a member of the nasturtium family, watercress shares the sharp, clean taste of other so-called cresses. To grow well, it needs lots of water, an alkaline soil, and full sun. Its natural habitat is the eddies of clear-running streams or at the inlets and outlets of ponds. In fact, a planting of watercress established in such places will do much better than one sown in a garden plot. You might try to establish a bed of watercress near your garden hose bib, where the plants will get plenty of splash and spray. Start the plants in sterile potting soil in early spring.

MUSTARD (*Brassica*). Often grown as a companion to cress in gardens and used with it as a traditional British tea-sandwich filling, white mustard (*B. alba*) is the most common type grown in Britain. We prefer Japanese purple mustard (*B. juncea*) mostly because of its striking color, superior growing habits, and flavor.

MÂCHE (*Valerianella locusta*). Also known as lamb's lettuce and corn-salad (because it was often found wild in grain fields), mâche will produce nearly year-round in mild climates. Don't expect large heads— the rosettelike leaf bunches are usually served whole in a salad. To showcase its mild, nutty flavor and delicate texture, it is best served alone with just a hint of dressing.

CHERVIL (*Anthriscus cerefolium*). This is a small parsleylike plant with curly, deep green leaves and a slight anise flavor. Rarely used alone, it is a fine accent for many vegetables and greens, and is a major component of the classic French herb mixture known as *fines herbes*. Chervil may resemble parsley, but unlike that hardy biennial, it is an annual. You can tell when your chervil plant is past its prime by the lengthening of the central stems, a fact that holds true for many salad plants.

PURSLANE (*Portulaca oleracea*). Purslane has a salty and succulent flavor, best eaten straight from the garden. Originally from eastern India, it is familiar to many gardeners as a tenacious ground-hugging weed. The cultivated form is more upright, and is easier to harvest. Golden purslane, a slower growing, upright variety, is plumper than its wild cousin. Both types can be cooked, but are really at their best raw, to add crunch to salads with softer greens.

CLAYTONIA (formerly *Claytonia perfoliata*, now *Montia perfoliata*). Usually gathered from the wild (where it is called miner's lettuce), claytonia can also be cultivated. Each funnel-shaped leaf encloses a tiny white flower, and the plant is a very attractive salad ingredient, especially in a mesclun salad with other greens and herbs. It is very delicate and mild, like a mâche, and best considered as a beautiful green to put in your mouth.

ORACH (*Atriplex hortensis*). Commonly called mountain spinach, orach, if grown quickly (as it should be), will have mild, tender leaves that will add variety to a mix of salad greens. Be careful not to let it go to seed, or it will be with you forever, reseeding itself into eternity.

SORREL (*Rumex acetosa*). This is the domesticated cousin of the wild sour-grass found in many New England gardens and is easily cultivated as a long-lived perennial. The pale, arrow-shaped leaves emerge very early in spring. Young sorrel leaves are tender and sour with a hint of lemon, and because of their overpowering astringency, they are a minor, but welcome, player in most spring salads. As the summer progresses, the leaves grow larger and tougher, and are then more suitable for sauces or soups.

DANDELION (*Taraxacum officinale*). Another cultivated form of a common garden weed, dandelions, when domesticated, produce larger leaves with a milder taste. To tone down their bitterness, the plants can be covered to keep out the sun (this is called blanching). To accomplish this, gather up the leaves loosely with a rubber band and cover the plant with a nursery pot for a week or so. Keep them from spreading seeds by keeping the seed stalks picked off.

Tart Cucumber and Lemon Salad

Makes 4 servings

A tangy combination guaranteed to cleanse the palate, this salad works best as an appetizer for a rich, creamy main course. Served on chilled plates and garnished with a few leaves of lemon balm, it is especially good when the weather is hot.

1 lemon, preferably organic

½ teaspoon fine sea salt, plus more to taste

4 cucumbers, peeled and thinly sliced

1 red bell pepper, roasted (see page 40) and thinly sliced

1 red onion, thinly sliced

2 tablespoons chopped fresh parsley

2 tablespoons fresh lemon juice

¼ cup olive oil

1 cup curly endive, washed, dried, and torn into bite-sized pieces

Lemon balm or lemon basil leaves, for garnish (optional)

Slice the lemon into ¼-inch-thick rounds. Stack the slices and cut into sixths to make triangles. Pick out and discard the seeds. Place the lemon triangles in a small nonreactive (glass or stainless steel) bowl and toss with the salt. Let stand to draw out the bitterness, at least 30 minutes and up to 1 hour. Place in a sieve and rinse gently under cold water to remove the salt. Drain, and pat the lemon triangles dry with a clean kitchen towel.

Combine the lemon triangles, cucumbers, pepper, onion, parsley, and lemon juice in a medium glass or wooden salad bowl. Add the olive oil and toss. Season with the salt. Cover loosely and let stand at room temperature to marinate, at least 30 minutes and up to 2 hours.

Just before serving, arrange equal quantities of the endive on four chilled plates. Top with the lemon salad, garnish with the lemon balm, if using, and serve immediately.

Rainbow Tomatoes with Fresh Basil

Makes 2 to 4 servings

This simple dish is our favorite way to show off some of the many colored tomatoes from our garden. It's especially nice to overlap slices of red, yellow, green zebra, and purple tomatoes, scattered with the finest shreds of green basil.

6 large ripe tomatoes, preferably at least
    3 different colors
8 large fresh basil leaves, finely sliced
3 tablespoons olive oil
2 tablespoons fresh lemon juice
I teaspoon sugar
Salt and freshly ground pepper, to taste

Cut the tomatoes into $1/2$-inch-thick rounds. Arrange the slices, slightly overlapping, in a single layer on a platter. Scatter the basil over the top.

Whisk the oil, lemon juice, and sugar until combined, and season with the salt and pepper. Pour the dressing evenly over the tomatoes. Cover loosely and let stand at room temperature to marinate for at least 30 minutes and up to 2 hours.

Arugula and Roasted Pear Salad

Makes 4 servings

Salad greens and pears flourish during the cooler late-autumn weather. Put them together for a great balance of piquant and sweet. Have all of the components ready ahead of time for a fast last-minute assembly. If you wish, garnish each salad with calendula flower petals.

> 4 firm-ripe Bartlett or Bosc pears, peeled, cored, and cut lengthwise into eighths
> 2 tablespoons sugar
> 1 tablespoon unsalted butter, melted
> 3 tablespoons olive oil
> 1 tablespoon rice vinegar
> Salt and freshly ground pepper, to taste
> 6 cups arugula or mixed salad greens, torn into bite-sized pieces
> 2 tablespoons pine nuts, toasted (see Note)
> ¼ cup freshly grated Parmesan cheese

Preheat the oven to 400°F.

Toss the pears, sugar, and butter in a medium bowl. Arrange the pears in a single layer on a baking sheet. Bake, turning once, until the pears are barely tender, 10 to 15 minutes.

Whisk the oil and vinegar in a large bowl, preferably a wooden salad bowl. Season with the salt and pepper. Add the arugula and toss. Place equal quantities of the salad on 4 chilled salad plates, heaping the greens on one side of the plate. Place equal quantities of the pears next to the greens. Sprinkle with the Parmesan and pine nuts and serve immediately.

NOTE: To toast pine nuts, place the nuts in a small, dry skillet over medium heat. Cook, stirring almost constantly, until the nuts are golden brown, about 3 minutes. Transfer to a plate and cool completely.

Letter from the Garden

The weather in Vermont is uneven and unpredictable, and this can have a serious effect on our gardens and crops. The typical growing season consists of the seventy days between the first frost-free day and the first frost. If the beginning of May is warm, we transplant the seedlings outside in the hope of a long growing season. But often, June will turn cloudy and cool with a killer frost in the middle of the month. We've become accustomed to recognizing the signs of cooling weather: the wind shifts, there is a crisp smell to the air, and the clouds give way to a clear night sky. All these signal a 4 A.M. watch at the thermometer.

In the summer of 1993, we planned our first trip away from the farm since we began market gardening. That year, we had chosen to focus our trial garden on the best cutting flower varieties, and we planted over four hundred test specimens. In pursuit of the best cutting flowers available to gardeners, we traveled to the annual Fleuroselect exhibition in Noordwijk, Netherlands.

The purpose of Fleuroselect is reflected in its name. This is where Europe's top flower breeders show their new flowers, those that they hope wholesalers will choose to sell in seed catalogues and garden centers all over the world. Dutch breeders are world renowned for their vegetables and flowers, and after seeing these exhibition gardens, we know why. They were spectacular, with more than twelve thousand 10-foot-long rows of annuals. In each case, the original species was planted next to a hybrid so the buyers could evaluate the differences.

In some cases, it was evident that the improved flowers had potential. But in many cases, the heirloom species were clearly superior. It was an unfortunate reminder that most horticultural enterprises look for market appeal rather than the way each plant works in relation to the others growing nearby. The heirloom species generally had more interesting flower forms with natural growth habits. Many of the so-called superior hybrids lacked vigor, and their flowers looked out of balance with the proportions of the plant.

When we returned to the farm, our flowers had survived our absence, along with our 122 varieties of tomatoes and other vegetable crops. It is always good to get away and see other gardens, take notes on new varieties to try in the future, and taste different food. But coming home to our garden and kitchen is often the best part of the trip, especially when the garden is bursting with flowers just begging to be brought inside to fill every room in the house.

Warm Spinach and Strawberry Salad

Makes 8 servings

Just as you choose one kind of potato for baking and one for cooking, you should use tender flat-leafed spinach for salads and reserve the curly variety for cooking. Strawberries are usually ready in the garden at the same time as spinach, and it may be a surprise that they can be combined to make a harmonious salad.

2 tablespoons olive oil
2 tablespoons sesame seeds
1 tablespoon poppy seeds
¼ cup raspberry vinegar
2 tablespoons sugar
¼ teaspoon sweet paprika
Salt and freshly ground pepper, to taste
8 cups loosely packed flat-leafed spinach (about 2 large bunches), well washed and dried
2 pints strawberries, rinsed, hulled, and sliced
⅓ cup thinly sliced scallions, white and green parts

Heat the oil in a small skillet over medium heat. Add the sesame and poppy seeds and roast, stirring often, until the sesame seeds are golden, about 5 minutes. Transfer to a plate to cool.

Whisk the vinegar, sugar, paprika, and the salt and pepper to combine.

In a large bowl, preferably a wooden salad bowl, gently toss the spinach with the seeds and oil, strawberries, scallions and vinegar mixture. Serve immediately.

Leaf Peeper's Carrot and Red Cabbage Salad

Makes 6 servings

The colors of red cabbage and carrots are reminiscent of fall leaves, so I can't resist the temptation to call this leaf peeper salad. (A leaf peeper is a tourist who comes to New England in the autumn just to see the leaves change color.) It is a vibrant alternative to the typical cole slaw, and also makes a great vegetarian filling in a tortilla wrap. Carrots left in the ground until the ground freezes sweeten up, and our Kuroda carrot is especially hardy. But the trick is to harvest them before the deer do.

½ cup raisins
½ medium head red cabbage, grated (4 cups)
8 medium carrots, shredded
½ cup pine nuts, toasted (see page 55) and coarsely chopped
¼ cup Roasted Garlic, Dill, and Ginger Dressing (page 38)

Place the raisins in a small bowl and cover with cold water. Let stand until plumped, about 30 minutes. Drain and pat dry.

Mix the cabbage, carrots, raisins, pine nuts, and dressing in a large salad bowl until combined. Let stand at room temperature to marinate for at least 30 minutes and up to 2 hours. Serve at room temperature.

Beet, Apple, and Goat Cheese Salad

Makes 4 to 6 servings

〜

Chioggia, or candy-striped beets, are not only the sweetest beets around, they look terrific in salads. If possible, use them in this chunky dish to show them off. Beets of any color will also be delicious, but keep in mind that red beets will bleed. A tart apple is in order here—in Vermont, we would choose Macoun, McIntosh, or Empire. In clementine season, add a few segments to the salad.

6 medium beets, preferably Chioggia or
    candy-striped, scrubbed and trimmed
    (leave about 1 inch of stem attached)
2 tart apples, preferably locally grown, peeled,
    cored, and cut into $\frac{1}{2}$-inch cubes
$\frac{1}{2}$ cup walnuts, toasted (see page 12)
$\frac{1}{2}$ cup crumbled feta cheese (4 ounces)
$\frac{1}{2}$ cup chopped fresh parsley
1 small red onion, thinly sliced
$\frac{1}{2}$ cup walnut oil or olive oil
$\frac{1}{4}$ cup balsamic vinegar
2 tablespoons finely chopped shallots
$\frac{1}{2}$ teaspoon Dijon mustard
Salt and freshly ground pepper, to taste

Position a rack in the center of the oven and preheat to 400°F. Wrap each beet in aluminum foil and place on a baking sheet. Bake until the beets are tender, about 1 hour. Cool completely. Peel the beets and cut into $\frac{1}{2}$-inch cubes.

Mix the beets, apples, walnuts, cheese, parsley, and onion in a salad bowl, preferably wooden. In a small saucepan, heat the oil, vinegar, shallots, and mustard, whisking often, until simmering, about 5 minutes. Mix as much dressing as you prefer into the salad, reserving any remaining dressing for another use. Season the salad with the salt and pepper. The salad can be made up to 2 hours ahead, covered and refrigerated.

Confetti Black Bean Salad

Makes 8 to 10 servings

If you like black bean salsa, you'll love this salad. Dark green, heart-shaped poblano peppers have a mild smokiness, but you can substitute another green pepper if they aren't available. This is a great make-ahead dish for a potluck or picnic, and it only gets better if made ahead.

I cup dried black beans, sorted over
    for stones, soaked overnight in
    cold water and drained
2 red bell peppers, roasted (see page 40)
    and cut into ¼-inch-thick strips
2 poblano peppers (or use Anaheim,
    Hungarian, or green bell peppers),
    ribs and seeds discarded, finely diced
2 large ripe tomatoes, seeded and
    cut into ½-inch cubes
3 cups fresh corn kernels
I red onion, thinly sliced
I cup chopped fresh cilantro
⅓ cup plus I tablespoon olive oil
2 tablespoons balsamic vinegar
2 tablespoons red wine vinegar
I teaspoon cumin seeds, roasted in a dry
    skillet (see page 25)
Salt and freshly ground pepper, to taste

Place the beans in a medium saucepan and add enough cold water to cover by I inch. Bring to a boil over high heat. Reduce the heat to low and simmer until the beans are tender, about I hour. Drain and rinse under cold water. Spread the beans on a clean kitchen towel to remove excess moisture.

In a large bowl, preferably a wooden salad bowl, mix the beans, bell and poblano peppers, tomatoes, corn, onion, and cilantro.

In a medium bowl, whisk the oil, balsamic and red wine vinegars, and cumin to combine. Pour over the salad and mix well. Season with the salt and pepper. Let stand at room temperature for at least I hour and up to 2 hours. Or cover and refrigerate for up to I day. Serve at room temperature.

Autumn Vegetable Antipasto

Makes 6 servings

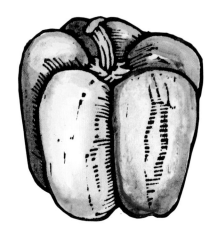

The last harvest from the garden makes a flavorful medley to serve as a first course (or as a side dish for fish). Use this recipe to show off the more unusual Italian vegetables, such as Romanesco broccoli with its spiral turrets, dramatic purple cauliflower, or the flat-topped cipolline onions. Serve the marinated vegetables with a wedge of your favorite cheese and lots of crusty bread.

½ cup basil herb–infused or red wine vinegar

½ cup olive oil

¼ cup fresh lemon juice

2 tablespoons sugar

2 tablespoons chopped fresh basil

2 cups cauliflower florets

2 cups broccoli florets

2 red or green bell peppers, seeded, ribbed, and thinly sliced

1 small fennel bulb, trimmed, cored, fronds removed, and cut into thin slices

1 cup (about 8) cipolline or white boiling onions, peeled (cut large onions in half crosswise so they cook evenly)

1 cup thinly sliced daikon (white radish)

2 hot chiles, such as cayenne, serrano, or jalapeño, seeded and thinly sliced

Salt and freshly ground pepper, to taste

Mix the vinegar, oil, lemon juice, ¼ cup water, sugar, and basil in a large nonreactive (stainless steel or enameled) saucepan. Add the cauliflower, broccoli, peppers, fennel, onions, daikon, and chiles and cover. Bring to a boil over high heat. Reduce the heat to medium low and simmer for 5 minutes. Transfer to a large glass or stainless steel bowl and cool. Season with the salt and pepper. Cover tightly and refrigerate to marinate overnight.

To serve, remove the vegetables from the marinade with a slotted spoon, and place on a lettuce-lined platter. Serve chilled. Store, covered, in the refrigerator for up to 1 week.

Celeriac Rémoulade

Makes 4 servings

Celeriac is a knobby root vegetable with thin sparse leaves that resemble a celery top. The tough outer skin is pared away to reveal the creamy white center. This crisp interior soaks up other flavors well, and celeriac rémoulade is justly famous as one of the all-time great appetizers. It is also a fantastic picnic salad, and can be served as a side dish to grilled tuna.

2 medium celeriac (celery root)
   (about 2 pounds)
½ cup mayonnaise
¼ cup chopped cornichons
1 tablespoon finely chopped fresh
   tarragon
1 teaspoon Dijon mustard
1 teaspoon finely chopped fresh thyme
2 garlic cloves, minced
Salt and freshly ground pepper,
   to taste

Using a sharp paring knife, trim off the top and bottom of each celeriac. Stand the root on end and pare off the thick skin. Cut into wedges, trim any spongy areas, and shred (the food processor fitted with a shredding disk does the quickest job). You should have about 4 cups. Transfer to a large bowl.

Mix the mayonnaise, cornichons, tarragon, mustard, thyme, and garlic. Pour over the celeriac and mix. Season with the salt and pepper. Cover and refrigerate until well chilled, at least 2 hours. Serve chilled.

Grilled Radicchio and Gorgonzola Salad

Makes 4 servings

In Italy, all "head" chicories are called *radicchio*. In America, the term is applied only to the red varieties, which are often named after the region where the particular variety originated. The exotically beautiful Treviso radicchio, shaped like a slender Romaine lettuce, has deep burgundy leaves and white central stems. When you find it, it is particularly good in this salad.

3 heads radicchio, preferably Treviso
Extra virgin olive oil, as needed
Salt and freshly ground pepper, to taste

⅓ cup toasted and coarsely chopped walnuts
    (see page 12)
½ cup crumbled Gorgonzola cheese
3 tablespoons Basic Vinaigrette (page 35)
3 tablespoons heavy cream
1 teaspoon finely chopped fresh thyme

Build a charcoal fire in an outdoor grill and let burn until the coals are covered with white ash. Let the fire burn down to medium hot. (You should be able to hold your hand at the grill level for about 3 seconds.) For a gas grill, preheat on High, then turn to Medium.

Cut each radicchio head into quarters, lengthwise, through the stem. Brush the wedges with oil and season with the salt and pepper.

Grill, with the smooth outer side of the radicchio facing down over the coals, until the leaves are charred and the heart is tender, about 10 minutes. Don't worry about overcooking the radicchio, as it should be tender. Round radicchio will take longer than thin Treviso radicchio. Cut the radicchio, including the charred leaves, crosswise into thin strips. Transfer the warm radicchio strips to a large bowl, preferably a wooden salad bowl.

Mash the Gorgonzola in a small bowl with a fork, and gradually work in the vinaigrette, heavy cream, and thyme. Pour over the radicchio, add the walnuts, and toss. Serve warm.

Three-Pepper Salad with Fontina

Makes 6 servings

~

This salad is typically served at the end of the hot Piedmontese summer, when sweet peppers are plentiful and the olive oil is freshly pressed. In Vermont, we make this with Golden Summer, Marconi, or Corno di Toro red, and Lilac or Sweet Chocolate purple peppers. Use a fine extra virgin olive oil for this salad, as it will add the proper note of authenticity.

6 bell peppers (2 yellow, 2 red,
   and 2 purple), roasted (see page 40)
   and cut into ¼-inch-thick strips
12 black olives, such as Kalamata,
   pitted and coarsely chopped
6 ounces Fontina d'Aosta cheese, rind
   removed, cut into ½-inch cubes
   (about 1½ cups)
2 tablespoons heavy cream
1 teaspoon fresh lemon juice
1 teaspoon Dijon mustard
1 teaspoon finely chopped fresh tarragon
¼ cup extra virgin olive oil
Salt and freshly ground pepper, to taste

Combine the peppers, olives, and cheese. Mix the cream, lemon juice, mustard, and tarragon in a small bowl, and gradually whisk in the oil. Season with the salt and pepper. Pour over the peppers and mix. Serve immediately.

Warm Swiss Chard Salad

Makes 4 servings

~

To serve greens with a slightly softer constitution as a salad, cook them briefly and serve them warm with a garlicky lemon vinaigrette. The ribs can be saved to be layered with cheese and smothered with a béchamel sauce as in Cardoons au Gratin, page 153. If you wish, use spinach or beet greens, or a combination.

2 large bunches of Swiss chard (2 pounds)
3 tablespoons olive oil
1 tablespoon fresh lemon juice
2 garlic cloves, minced
Salt and freshly ground pepper, to taste
Dark Asian sesame oil or hot sesame oil,
   for serving

Wash the Swiss chard well in a sink of cold water. Lift the leaves out of the water to leave the grit at the bottom of the sink. Drain and remove the thick ribs, reserving them for another use.

Bring a large pot of lightly salted water to a boil over high heat. Add the leaves and cook until tender, about 8 minutes. Drain and cool slightly. If desired, coarsely chop the leaves.

Transfer the warm chard to a large bowl. Mix the oil, lemon juice, and garlic in a small bowl. Pour over the chard and mix. Season with the salt and pepper. Serve warm, drizzling each serving with the sesame oil.

Lunches and Light Meals

*F*requently, a simple meal is much more appropriate than a big spread. After a hot morning in the garden, we need a relaxing lunch in the shade. This chapter is about all the ways to break from the sandwich habit at lunch, and discover how easy it is to bring fresh flavors to the table. We'll nibble on crisp vegetables served with a tasty dip, some whole grain bread, and an iced tea. Healthy grain salads, sometimes made the night before from dinner's leftovers, also fill the bill.

Dinner doesn't always have to be an appetizer followed by a main course with two side dishes. As an alternative, I often serve a hearty vegetarian entrée accompanied by a green salad. There seems to be no end to the possibilities of a savory pie: carrots, Brussels sprouts, leeks, fennel, chard, and spinach all find their way into a first course or light lunch. I also look for ways to add variety to pastry crusts with fresh herbs and nuts, or use phyllo dough for an extra-flaky effect.

Grains are useful for creating satisfying meals without a lot of meat. Rice, polenta, bulgur, and couscous all provide light meals with international flavors. Cuisines from around the world have influenced many of these recipes, because gardens play a major role in the universality of cooking. One of the best reasons for growing a garden is to bring other cultures into our lives.

Edible Flowers

At The Cook's Garden, flowers and food are partners in the garden and on the dinner table. Flowers are used as bouquets on the dinner table and edible blooms often end up on the plate as well. My mother taught me the importance of garnishes, and she always had a jar of fresh parsley in the refrigerator for this purpose. I have moved beyond parsley, using edible flowers as colorful, delicate accents that also spark the appetite.

Many flowers from our cutting garden can be used in the kitchen. The first criterion, of course, is that they are recognized as safe to eat. Also, be sure that the flowers are unsprayed. Our choice of flowers is based not only on flavor, but also on appearance, and ability to stay fresh-looking out of water and to complement food in some striking way. Most flowers can be used whole; some look better when only their petals are used.

The flowers in this list are a mix of annuals and perennials, and all are easy to grow from seed in a small garden or in flowerpots. To preserve edible flowers, the easiest method is to dry the blooms in a flower press (available at craft stores), then store them in an envelope inside an airtight bag or jar in a cool, dry place. I keep dried flowers in my spice drawers, so they are nearby when I need them to garnish a birthday cake or winter soup.

ANISE HYSSOP. In our gardens, this member of the mint family is a self-sowing annual, but in other parts of the country it is a perennial. Anise hyssop is usually covered with honey bees sucking on the 2-inch-long pink and mauve flower spikes. The tiny flowers and leaves have a flavor reminiscent of licorice. Both work well in baked goods and desserts, and can be brewed into a marvelous tea. For a delicate flavor, strip the tiny flowers from the calyx. In recipes such as infused custards, where a more pronounced flavor is desired, chop whole blossoms.

ARUGULA. Arugula quickly goes to seed when it is not harvested or in hot weather, and tiny white flowers will appear. The peppery flavor of white blossoms resembles that of the leaves, and they can be added to salads or used as a garnish on deviled eggs.

CHIVES

BORAGE. One of the prettiest of all edible flowers, the blue star-shaped blossoms seem incongruous against the hairy foliage of the sprawling borage plant, but they hold up remarkably well after picking. For drinks, float borage flowers in punch bowls or glasses of iced tea, or freeze them in ice cubes.

CALENDULA. Also known as pot marigold, calendula grows in a range of orange and yellow colors. The daisylike petals are edible, and can be used to color and flavor butter, cheese, and rice dishes, or sprinkled in a salad. Dry the petals to use as a garnish for winter soups—they look especially nice on top of butternut squash soup.

CHIVES. We love to grow members of the Allium family, and the common chive has been with us since the beginning, a hardy perennial that happily blooms in the early spring. The purple flower heads are made up of individual florets that can be broken off and added to salads, dips, butters, and infused in vinegar. They are easy to dry—just cover the blossoms and part of the stems with a paper bag and hang the bunch upside down in a dry, airy place.

BERGAMOT. The nectar of this aromatic plant, otherwise known as beebalm, is attractive to bees and hummingbirds. The native tribes of the Oswego River in New York made the leaves into a beverage, giving bergamot another name, Oswego tea. The blooms are strongly flavored, and best used sparingly in fruit salads and jams. For a special treat, infuse the flowers in custard and use to make a fragrant ice cream. (This plant should not be confused with citrus bergamot, a mint that is a major flavor component in Earl Grey tea.)

LAVENDER. Aromatic lavender has long been used as an ingredient in perfumes and potpourri, but it also has magical effects as a culinary herb. Removed from the stem, the blossoms can be used sparingly in desserts and fruit. A small amount of lavender is used to heighten the flavor of *herbes de Provence,* a blend of dried basil, thyme, savory, and fennel.

LEMON GEM MARIGOLD. All marigold blossoms are edible, but the Lemon Gem is one of our favorites, and we grow it just for this purpose. A popular annual grown from seed, Signet marigolds grow in a range of lemon yellow, orange, and bicolor blossoms, with a citrus-scented foliage making a fernlike backdrop. The small flowers can be used whole in salad.

NASTURTIUM. The common name of this bright colored annual, which originated in Peru, is Indian cress. It grows quickly and easily from seed, and the bright, pungently flavored blossoms make it a favorite with gardeners and cooks. The green lily pad–shaped leaves can be used in small quantities in green salads.

VIOLA. Wild violas spring up as weeds in many gardens, but keep them in mind for a bright garnish in salads, soups, or cakes—the tiny purple and yellow flowers look fantastic on a chocolate-glazed torte. Pick violas and keep their stems in water until ready to use. Pinch off the flower heads and use the whole flower. Dry the flowers in a press, or paint them with sugar water for a candied effect.

Vegetable and Cheddar Quiche

Makes 6 servings

Classic quiche Lorraine is simply a savory bacon custard pie. Once you've learned the basic recipe, all kinds of seasonal variations will come to mind.

1 recipe Pastry Dough (page 74)

1 cup heavy cream or half-and-half
4 large eggs
½ teaspoon chopped fresh thyme or
   ¼ teaspoon dried thyme
¼ teaspoon chopped fresh sage or ⅛ teaspoon
   dried sage
¼ teaspoon fine sea salt
A grinding of black pepper
1 cup shredded sharp Cheddar cheese,
   preferably Vermont Cheddar
2 bacon strips, cooked and crumbled
   (optional)
1 cup cooked chopped vegetables,
   combinations such as broccoli,
   leeks, asparagus, or spinach
   (squeeze spinach dry to
   remove excess moisture)
1 tablespoon finely chopped
   fresh parsley or chervil

Position a rack in the center of the oven and preheat to 375°F. Roll out the dough on a lightly floured work surface into an 11- to 12-inch-wide circle about ⅛ inch thick. Fit into a 9-inch pie plate, trimming the overhang to ½ inch over the sides. Fold the edges under and crimp the edge of the dough. Prick the dough in several places with a fork. Line the dough with a piece of aluminum foil, and fill with dried beans, raw rice, or commercial pie weights.

Bake until the dough looks set but not browned, about 12 minutes. Lift up and remove the foil with the beans. Transfer the pie shell to a wire cake rack and let stand until ready to fill.

Whisk the cream, eggs, thyme, sage, salt, and pepper until combined. Sprinkle the cheese (and bacon, if using) over the bottom of the pastry, then top with the vegetables. Pour in the custard, and then sprinkle with the parsley.

Bake until a knife inserted in the center of the filling comes out clean, about 35 minutes. Let stand for 10 minutes before serving warm.

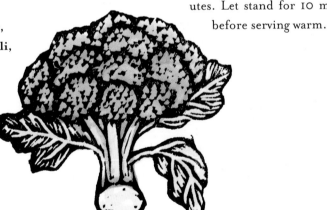

Pastry Dough

Makes one 9-inch tart

Butter provides flavor and vegetable shortening contributes tenderness to make this a perfect pastry for your pies and tarts.

- 1¼ cups unbleached all-purpose flour
- ¼ cup cake flour
- 1½ tablespoons sugar
- ¼ teaspoon fine sea salt
- 9 tablespoons (1 stick plus 1 tablespoon) unsalted butter, chilled, cut into ½-inch cubes
- 3 tablespoons vegetable shortening
- ⅓ cup ice water, as needed

Mix the all-purpose and cake flours, sugar, and salt in a medium bowl. Using a pastry blender or a large fork, cut the butter into the flour until the mixture resembles coarse cornmeal with a few pea-sized pieces. Gradually stir in the water until the dough holds together. (Or, pulse the dry ingredients in a food processor to combine, add the butter and shortening and pulse until crumbly. With the machine running, add water just until the dough comes together. Do not overmix.) Gather up the dough into a thick disk, wrap in waxed paper, and refrigerate for 30 minutes to 2 hours. The dough can be prepared up to 2 days ahead. If well chilled and hard, let stand at room temperature for about 10 minutes to soften slightly before rolling out.

Herbed Lemonade

Makes 4 to 6 servings

Fresh-squeezed lemonade is a harbinger of summer. At the Vermont State Fair, we line up at the stand that sells fresh lemon juice pressed over a cup of ice and a big scoop of sugar. Our more refined recipe is sweetened with a homemade syrup, and fragrant with spearmint and a good grating of fresh ginger. If you wish, freeze tiny borage flowers into ice cubes, and use them to chill your drink, and play up the herb connection.

I cup sugar

8 to 10 large sprigs of fresh mint
   or lemon balm

I tablespoon shredded fresh ginger
   (use the large holes on a box grater)

4 lemons

Thinly sliced lemon, and fresh mint
   or lemon balm sprigs, for garnish

Bring the sugar and I cup water to a boil over high heat, stirring just until the syrup comes to a boil. Add the mint and ginger and reduce the heat to medium low. Cook at a slow boil until the syrup is slightly thickened, about 8 minutes. Strain through a wire strainer into a bowl, pressing hard on the herbs to extract the flavor. Cool completely.

Grate the zest from the lemons; squeeze and strain their juice. You should have ¾ cup of juice. Add to the pitcher, along with the syrup and 3 cups water. Stir well.

Serve over ice, garnished with the lemon slices and herb sprigs.

Carrot Quiche

Makes 6 to 8 servings

〜

This bright orange quiche is a feast for the eyes and the palate. We grow plenty of Touchon carrots, a French heirloom variety that consistently wins in our tasting trials. Use the best farm stand carrot you can find for this quiche, and you will be amply rewarded by the additional flavor. The dough in this recipe is wonderfully pliable and can be rolled out right away or chilled for later.

PASTRY

1 cup unbleached all-purpose flour

½ cup whole wheat flour

1 tablespoon finely chopped fresh herbs, such as a combination of thyme, chives, and parsley

½ teaspoon fine sea salt

8 tablespoons (1 stick) unsalted butter, chilled, cut into ½-inch cubes

½ cup yogurt or sour cream

2 tablespoons Dijon mustard, for brushing the shell

FILLING

4 medium carrots, scrubbed but unpeeled, shredded (2½ cups)

2 tablespoons dry sherry

1 tablespoon unsalted butter or olive oil

1 medium red onion, thinly sliced into half-moons

½ cup shredded sharp Cheddar cheese, preferably Vermont Cheddar

1 cup half-and-half

2 large eggs

1 large egg yolk

1 tablespoon finely chopped fresh tarragon

¼ teaspoon fine sea salt

⅛ teaspoon freshly ground pepper

Position a rack in the center of the oven and preheat to 400°F.

To make the dough, pulse the all-purpose and whole wheat flours, herbs, and salt in a food processor to combine. Add the butter and pulse until the mixture resembles coarse cornmeal with a few pea-sized pieces. Turn off the machine and add the yogurt. Pulse just until the dough comes together into a ball. Roll out the dough on a lightly floured work surface into a 12-inch round about ⅛ inch thick. Transfer to a lightly buttered 9-inch tart pan. Prick the dough in several places with a fork. Line the dough with a piece of aluminum foil, and fill with dried beans, raw rice, or commercial pie weights.

Bake until the dough looks set but not browned, about 12 minutes. Lift up and remove the foil with the beans. Transfer the pan to a wire cake rack to cool slightly.

Bring a medium saucepan of lightly salted water to a boil over high heat. Add the carrots and cook until they are bright orange and tender, about 1 minute. Drain well. Transfer to a medium bowl and toss with 1 tablespoon of the sherry.

Melt the butter in a medium skillet over medium heat. Add the onion and cook until tender, about 5 minutes. Stir in the carrots and cook for 1 minute to combine the flavors. Cool slightly.

Using the back of a spoon, paint the mustard inside of the pastry shell. Sprinkle with the cheese, and top with the carrots. Whisk the half-and-half, eggs, yolk, tarragon, remaining 1 tablespoon sherry, and the salt and pepper in a medium bowl until combined. Pour into the pastry shell.

Place the quiche on a baking sheet. Bake until the custard seems set when you give the pan a gentle shake, about 30 minutes. Cool for about 10 minutes, then slice and serve warm or at room temperature.

Fall Harvest Pie with Leeks, Brussels Sprouts, and Horseradish

Makes 6 servings

Seasonal recipes are at the heart of any kitchen garden. This combination of fall vegetables works like a piece of well-orchestrated music. Fresh horseradish is a great condiment and can add zest to a host of cold-weather dishes. Wash the harvested roots well, then peel and shred in a food processor. Transfer to a jar with a tight lid, and pour in cider vinegar to cover. Refrigerated, the mixture will keep for practically forever.

I recipe Pastry Dough (page 74)
2 cups Chicken Stock (page 29)
6 medium leeks, well rinsed, white and pale
   green parts, coarsely chopped into ¼-inch
   dice
I pint Brussels sprouts, trimmed and cut into
   halves lengthwise
4 tablespoons (½ stick) unsalted butter
¼ cup unbleached all-purpose flour
½ cup heavy cream
I tablespoon freshly grated horseradish root
   or use prepared horseradish
I tablespoon finely chopped fresh parsley
I teaspoon finely chopped fresh rosemary
   or ½ teaspoon dried rosemary
Salt and freshly ground pepper, to taste

Position a rack in the center of the oven and preheat to 375°F. Roll out the dough on a lightly floured work surface into an 11-inch wide circle about ⅛ inch thick. Fit into a 9-inch pie plate, trimming the overhang to ½ inch over the sides. Fold the edges under and crimp the edge of the dough. Prick the dough in several places with a fork. Line the dough with a piece of aluminum foil and fill with dried beans, raw rice, or commercial pie weights.

Bake until the dough looks set, about 12 minutes. Lift up and remove the foil with the beans and continue baking the pastry until beginning to brown, about 8 minutes. Transfer the pie to a wire cake rack and let stand until ready to fill.

Bring the stock, leeks, and Brussels sprouts to a simmer in a large saucepan over medium heat. Adjust the heat to medium low and simmer until the sprouts are just tender when pierced with the tip of a sharp knife, 10 to 15 minutes. Drain over a bowl to reserve the stock.

Melt the butter in the saucepan over medium-low heat. Whisk in the flour. Whisking often, let the roux bubble without browning for 2 minutes. Gradually whisk in the reserved stock and bring to a simmer. Cook, stirring often, until thick, about 10 minutes. Stir in the heavy cream, then the horseradish, parsley, and rosemary. Fold in the vegetables and season with the salt and pepper. Pour into the pastry shell.

Place the pie pan on a baking sheet and bake until the top is lightly browned, about 25 minutes. Let stand for 10 minutes then slice and serve hot.

Fresh Spinach Phyllo Pie

Makes 8 servings

❧

Our spinach adores the cool climate of Vermont, and it is easy to find ourselves facing a mountain of harvested leaves. That's when we make spinach pie in phyllo crust, an impressive dish that is great for dinner guests. You won't use the entire box of phyllo, but the remaining sheets can be refrigerated for a week or so.

FILLING

2 tablespoons olive oil

2 tablespoons unsalted butter

1 medium red onion, chopped

2 pounds fresh spinach, stems removed,
    well rinsed but not dried, coarsely chopped
    (8 packed cups)

3 large eggs

½ cup ricotta or small-curd cottage cheese

¼ teaspoon freshly grated nutmeg

½ teaspoon fine sea salt

⅛ teaspoon freshly ground pepper

12 sheets phyllo dough, defrosted (see Note)

8 tablespoons (1 stick) unsalted butter,
    melted

½ cup wheat germ or dried bread crumbs

To make the filling, heat the oil and butter in a large skillet over medium heat. Add the onion and cook, stirring often, until golden, about 7 minutes. A large handful at a time, stir in the spinach with the water still clinging to the leaves. Cover and cook until the spinach is wilted, about 1 minute, then add the remaining spinach in the same manner until you have used it all. Uncover the skillet and cook the spinach to evaporate some of the accumulated liquid, about 5 minutes. Drain in a colander and cool until easy to handle. A handful at a time, squeeze the excess liquid from the spinach.

In a food processor, blend the eggs until combined. Add the spinach, cheese, nutmeg, salt, and pepper and pulse until the spinach is finely chopped.

Position a rack in the center of the oven and preheat to 375°F. Lightly butter the inside of a 9- × 13-inch baking dish with some of the melted butter. Line the pan with two sheets of phyllo, letting the excess hang over the sides, and brush the phyllo with melted butter. Add two more sheets, butter, and continue to stack a total of six sheets, buttering the top sheets. Spread the filling in the pan. Repeat with another six phyllo sheets, buttering every other sheet. Tuck the excess dough into the pan, and butter the top of the phyllo.

Bake until the phyllo is crisp and golden, about 45 minutes. Let stand for 10 minutes. Cut into squares and serve hot, or cool and serve at room temperature.

NOTE: Defrost phyllo in the refrigerator overnight, then let stand at room temperature for 2 hours before unrolling. While working with the dough, keep it covered with a damp kitchen towel or a large sheet of plastic wrap to prevent its drying out.

Caramelized Onion Tart

Makes 6 servings

We always grow about six types of onions because they are all different. For a mild flavor in salads, we're partial to the sweet Walla Walla. When we want more gusto in our greens, we go for the Italian Red Torpedo. The petite, round flat cippolline are perfect for roasting or pickling. But for this recipe, you need a well-flavored yellow onion that is neither too sharp nor too sweet. Most supermarket onions are okay, but try this with the lovely Giallo di Milano, a superior Italian variety. Slow cooking brings out every drop of sweetness in an onion, which is balanced here by the sherry or balsamic vinegar.

PASTRY

1½ cups unbleached all-purpose flour

½ teaspoon salt

8 tablespoons (1 stick) unsalted chilled butter, cut into ½-inch pieces

½ cup sour cream

FILLING

3 tablespoons olive oil

3 large sweet onions, thinly sliced

2 teaspoons light brown sugar

½ teaspoon sea salt

⅛ teaspoon freshly ground pepper

⅛ cup Marsala sherry or balsamic vinegar

1 teaspoon finely chopped fresh thyme

1 teaspoon finely chopped fresh rosemary

1 large egg

½ cup ricotta cheese

½ cup shredded sharp Cheddar cheese, preferably Vermont Cheddar

¼ cup pine nuts, lightly toasted (see page 55) and coarsely chopped

Blend together the flour and salt in the bowl of a food processor fitted with a steel blade. Work the flour and salt until mixed, and with the machine on, add the butter one piece at a time. Add the sour cream and blend until the dough forms a ball, less than a minute. Roll out the dough onto a lightly floured work surface into an 11- to 12-inch wide circle about ⅛ inch thick. Fit into a 9-inch pie plate, trimming the overhang to ½ inch over the sides. Fold the edges under and crimp the edge of the dough. Refrigerate while making the filling.

Melt the oil in a large skillet over medium-high heat. Add the onions and cook, stirring often, until they soften. Stir in the sugar, salt, and pepper. Reduce the heat to low and cook, stirring often, until the onions are deeply browned and have a sticky texture, about 30 minutes. Remove from the heat, stir in the sherry or vinegar, thyme, and rosemary, and gently cook for another 2 minutes. Remove from the heat and set aside.

Position a rack in the center of the oven and preheat to 400°F. Beat the egg in a medium bowl, then stir in the ricotta, Cheddar cheese, and the pine nuts to blend. Spread the mixture evenly in the pastry shell and spread the onions on top.

Bake until the pastry is golden brown, 35 to 40 minutes. Let stand for 10 minutes. Slice and serve warm or at room temperature.

"Sweet" Vegetable Tart with Almond Crust

Makes 6 to 8 servings

Throughout Provence and Italy, cooks use chard, zucchini, or fennel as the basis for a sweet tart that is served as a first course or light meal guaranteed to pique the appetite. Rather than choose one vegetable, I combine all three. The almond crust beautifully accents the ricotta-honey filling. For a real show-stopper, use Rainbow Swiss chard, which has the same flavor as green chard, but yellow, red, orange, white, and chartreuse stems. This variety has lots of stamina, and will grow all summer long to provide plenty of good eating.

ALMOND CRUST

2 cups unbleached all-purpose flour

1/4 cup sugar

12 tablespoons (1 1/2 sticks) unsalted butter, chilled, cut into 1/2-inch pieces

1 large egg yolk

1 tablespoon olive oil

1/2 cup coarsely chopped fennel bulb

3 large eggs

1 1/2 cups ricotta cheese

1/4 cup honey

1/3 cup raisins, plumped in hot water for 10 minutes, drained and patted dry

2 cups ribbed and finely chopped chard leaves, preferably Rainbow chard

1 medium golden zucchini, trimmed and shredded

To make the crust, grind the almonds, flour, and sugar together in a food processor into a very fine powder. Add the butter and egg yolk and pulse until the mixture is the texture of coarse cornmeal. Gather into a thick disk and wrap in waxed paper. Refrigerate for 30 minutes.

Position a rack in the center of the oven and preheat to 400°F. Roll out the dough on a lightly floured work surface to a 12-inch round about 1/8 inch thick. Fit into a 9-inch tart pan, fitting the dough snugly into the corners of the pan. Trim the dough so 1/4 inch rises above the edge of the pan. Press the dough firmly against the sides of the pan. Prick the dough all over with a fork. Line the dough with aluminum foil and fill with dried beans.

Place on a baking sheet and bake until the dough looks set, about 12 minutes. Lift up and remove the foil with the beans. Set the pastry shell aside while making the filling. Reduce the oven temperature to 375°F.

Heat the oil in a medium skillet over medium heat. Add the fennel and cook, stirring often, until softened, about 5 minutes. Cool slightly.

Whisk the eggs in a medium bowl. Stir in the cheese, honey, and raisins. Add the chard, zucchini, and fennel and mix well. Spread into the pastry shell.

Bake until the filling is set in the center when you give the tart a gentle shake, about 50 minutes. Let stand for 10 minutes on a wire cake rack before serving warm.

NARCISSUS

Curried Vegetable Strudel

Makes 8 servings

If you are looking for a way to dress up your vegetables, this exotically spiced strudel is the answer. Add eight ounces of ground lamb, cooked and drained, to the mixture for a very tasty nonvegetarian version.

2 tablespoons olive oil

I medium leek, white and pale green parts only, coarsely cut into ¼-inch-thick rounds

I garlic clove, minced

I teaspoon curry powder

½ teaspoon ground turmeric

½ teaspoon ground cumin

2 cups broccoli florets

2 cups cauliflower florets

2 tart apples, peeled, cored, and cut into ½-inch cubes

⅓ cup raisins

¼ cup sliced almonds, toasted (see page 12)

2 large eggs, beaten

½ cup shredded sharp Cheddar cheese, preferably Vermont Cheddar

8 tablespoons (½ stick) unsalted butter, melted

8 sheets phyllo dough

Heat the oil in a large skillet over medium heat. Add the leek and garlic, curry powder, turmeric, and cumin and cook, stirring often, until the leek softens, about 5 minutes. Add the broccoli, cauliflower, and apples, ¼ cup water, and cover tightly, reduce the heat to medium and cook until the vegetables are tender, about 5 minutes. If any liquid remains in the skillet, uncover and cook until it evaporates. Transfer to a bowl, stir in the raisins and almonds, and cool slightly. Stir in the eggs, then the cheese.

Position a rack in the center of the oven and preheat to 375°F. Brush a large baking sheet with some of the melted butter.

Place a phyllo sheet on a large kitchen towel and brush lightly with melted butter. Repeat to make a stack of eight phyllo sheets, leaving the top sheet unbuttered. Spread the vegetable mixture in a thick log about ½ inch from the bottom of the dough, leaving a ½-inch border on each side. Using the towel as an aid, roll up the pastry from the long side to enclose the filling. Transfer the strudel, seam down, to the baking sheet, and tuck the ends under the roll. Brush the strudel with melted butter.

Bake until the strudel is crisp and golden, about 45 minutes. Cool on the baking sheet for 10 minutes. Slice on the diagonal into 8 pieces and serve.

Bulgur and Sugar Snap Salad

Makes 4 servings

A basic pilaf gets a lift from summer's sweet onions, cucumbers, and sugar snap peas. Serve chilled as a main course salad, or warm as a side dish.

2 tablespoons olive oil

1 medium sweet onion, such as Walla Walla or Vidalia, chopped

½ cup peeled and seeded cucumber, chopped into ½-inch dice

1¾ cup Chicken Stock (page 29)

1 cup medium-grain bulgur

¼ cup raisins

1 teaspoon finely chopped fresh mint

Grated zest of 1 orange

1 teaspoon finely chopped fresh mint

1 cup sugar snap peas, cut on the diagonal into ½-inch pieces

⅓ cup plus 1 tablespoon pine nuts, toasted (see page 55)

¼ cup thinly sliced scallions (green tops only)

Lemon wedges, for serving

Heat the oil in a medium pan over medium heat. Add the onion and cook, stirring often, until softened, about 3 minutes. Add the cucumber, and cook until crisp-tender, about 2 minutes. Stir in the stock, bulgur, raisins, mint, and orange zest. Bring to a boil.

Reduce the heat to low and cover tightly. Simmer until the bulgur is tender and the liquid is absorbed, about 10 minutes. Remove from the heat, fluff with a fork, and stir in the sugar snap peas, pine nuts, and scallions. Transfer to a bowl and cool to room temperature. Cover and refrigerate until chilled, about 1 hour. Serve chilled, with the lemon wedges.

Couscous and Lentil Salad
with Arugula

Makes 8 to 10 servings

There's enough here to feed a crowd, so it is a great dish to take to a potluck or picnic. Vary the greens according to what's available—arugula will add a nice peppery kick and mesclun provides a mellower flavor.

I cup green lentils

½ teaspoon fine sea salt, plus more to taste

I cup couscous

¼ cup lemon juice

3 tablespoons red wine vinegar

¼ cup olive oil

2 garlic cloves, minced and mashed
    into a paste with a sprinkle of salt

6 scallions, white and green parts,
    chopped

2 cups packed coarsely
    chopped arugula or
    mesclun

I pint cherry tomatoes,
    cut into halves

I cup crumbled feta cheese or
    rindless chèvre

Place the lentils in a medium saucepan and add enough water to cover by 2 inches. Bring to a boil over high heat. Reduce the heat to medium low and simmer until the lentils are just tender, about 45 minutes. Drain, rinse under cold water, and transfer to a bowl.

In the meantime, bring 1¼ cups water and the salt to a boil over high heat. Stir in the couscous, remove from the heat, and cover tightly. Let stand until the couscous is tender and has absorbed the water, about 10 minutes. Fluff with a fork and stir into the lentils.

Whisk the lemon juice, vinegar, oil, and garlic in a small bowl to combine. Pour over the lentils and couscous and mix well. Add the scallions, arugula, and cherry tomatoes and mix. Season with the salt. Cover and refrigerate until chilled, at least 2 hours and up to 8 hours. Just before serving, mix in the cheese. Serve chilled.

Polenta with Tuscan Kale

Makes 6 to 8 servings

This hearty, rustic dish of polenta mixed with garlicky kale is an Italian classic. Tuscan kale, with slender leaves, is becoming more available outside of the kitchen garden—you will find it at many farmers' markets, where it is sometimes called *cavolo nero* or black kale. The Tuscan variety isn't really black, just a darker green than the typical kale, and it has an earthier flavor. It cooks to melting tenderness in less time than its sturdier American cousin, so if you use the latter, cook it for a few minutes longer. The traditional method for cooking polenta takes at least thirty minutes, but we use instant polenta with excellent results.

½ pound black Tuscan kale, stems discarded, leaves well rinsed, and coarsely chopped (6 cups)
1 teaspoon fine sea salt, plus more for cooking the kale
1 cup instant polenta
4 tablespoons olive oil, plus more for serving
2 garlic cloves, finely chopped
½ cup coarsely chopped reconstituted sun-dried tomatoes
¼ cup pine nuts, toasted (see page 55)
Freshly grated Parmesan cheese, for serving

Bring a large pot of lightly salted water to a boil over high heat. Add the kale and reduce the heat to medium. Cook until the kale is tender, about 15 minutes. Drain, reserving 6 cups of the cooking water.

Bring the reserved cooking water and 1 teaspoon salt to a boil in a medium saucepan over high heat. Whisk in the polenta and return to a boil. Reduce the heat to medium low and cook at a low boil, whisking often, until the polenta is tender, about 3 minutes.

Heat the oil over medium heat in a medium skillet. Add the garlic and cook until barely golden brown, about 2 minutes. Transfer the cooked garlic into the pot along with the polenta. Add the kale, sun-dried tomatoes, and pine nuts. Return to low heat and stir until well combined. Serve hot, sprinkled with Parmesan cheese, and additional oil passed on the side.

Wild Mushroom Risotto

Makes 4 to 6 servings

Risotto is not a meal for when you are in a hurry. The creamy starch needs to be coaxed from the rice with gentle cooking and almost constant stirring. Let the selection of seasonal wild mushrooms at the market inspire your choice, and don't be afraid to try something unfamiliar, as new varieties are showing up all the time.

6 cups Vegetable Broth (page 27)
2 tablespoons unsalted butter
1 tablespoon olive oil
½ cup chopped shallots
½ pound mixed wild mushrooms, such as chanterelle, stemmed shiitake, or portobello caps, finely diced
2 garlic cloves, minced
1½ tablespoons fresh lemon juice
1½ cups Arborio rice
½ cup dry Marsala or dry white wine
⅓ cup freshly grated Parmesan cheese
¼ cup heavy cream
2 tablespoons finely chopped fresh parsley
Salt and freshly ground pepper, to taste

Bring the broth to a simmer in a medium saucepan over medium heat. Reduce the heat to very low and maintain the broth at the barest simmer.

Melt the butter with the oil in a large, heavy-bottomed saucepan over medium heat. Add the shallots and cook, stirring often, until softened, about 3 minutes. Add the mushrooms and garlic, and cook until the mushrooms begin to give off their liquid, about 5 minutes. Stir in the lemon juice, then the rice. Cook the rice, stirring often, until it changes to a chalky white, about 2 minutes. Add the wine and stir until it is absorbed by the rice.

Stir 1 cup of the hot broth into the rice. Cook, stirring almost constantly, until the rice absorbs almost all of the broth, about 3 minutes. Stir in another cup of broth, and stir until it is almost completely absorbed. Repeat, keeping the risotto at a steady simmer and adding more broth as it is absorbed, until you use all of the broth and the rice is barely tender, about 20 minutes. If you run out of broth and the rice isn't tender, use hot water.

Remove from the heat and stir in the Parmesan, cream, and parsley. Season with the salt and pepper. Serve immediately.

Wild Rice Salad with Butternut Squash and Dried Cranberries

Makes 6 servings

Grains are the earth's seeds and, as important sources of food around the world, are adaptable to a wide range of ethnic seasonings. In this dish, American wild rice, butternut squash, and cranberries are mixed with yogurt and Indian spices for an unusual salad. Rather than prepare wild rice just for this salad, cook up extra for dinner the night before, and use the leftovers. The cooking time will vary, depending on the variety of rice, so be flexible.

I cup wild rice, rinsed

$\frac{1}{2}$ teaspoon fine sea salt, plus more to taste

$\frac{1}{2}$ butternut squash, seeded, peeled, and cut into $\frac{1}{2}$-inch cubes

I tablespoon olive oil

I poblano chile or small green bell pepper, seeds and ribs discarded, cut into $\frac{1}{4}$-inch dice

I cup yogurt

$\frac{1}{2}$ cup dried cranberries, plumped in hot water to cover for 10 minutes, drained

I teaspoon ground cumin

I teaspoon ground cardamom

$\frac{1}{2}$ teaspoon ground coriander

$\frac{1}{2}$ cup chopped fresh cilantro

$\frac{1}{4}$ cup chopped fresh mint

Freshly ground pepper, to taste

Bring the wild rice, 3 cups water, and $\frac{1}{2}$ teaspoon salt to a boil in a medium saucepan over high heat. Cover tightly and reduce the heat to low. Simmer until the rice is tender, 45 minutes to 1 hour, and drain if necessary. Transfer to a bowl and cool.

Meanwhile, position a rack in the center of the oven and preheat to 450°F. Lightly oil a baking sheet. Toss the squash and oil on the sheet. Bake, stirring occasionally, until the squash is lightly browned and tender, about 30 minutes. Cool. Add to the wild rice, with the poblano chile.

Purée the yogurt, drained cranberries, cumin, cardamom, and coriander in a blender. Pour over the wild rice mixture, add the cilantro and mint, and mix. Season with the salt and pepper. Serve at room temperature.

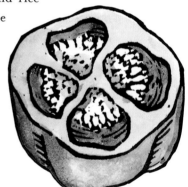

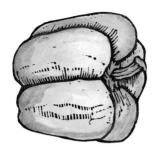

Roasted Caponata

Makes 8 servings

The secret to this delicious caponata is the roasted vegetables and a sweet-sour accent of balsamic vinegar (the classic recipe uses stewed vegetables, sugar, and red wine vinegar). Heap the caponata on lettuce leaves and serve with a platter of assorted cheeses and lots of grilled crusty bread or crackers for a Mediterranean-style lunch. It also doubles as a great vegetarian sandwich spread or side dish with grilled fish.

1 medium eggplant, peeled and cut into
   ¾-inch cubes
4 medium zucchini, cut into
   ¼-inch thick rounds
4 medium summer squash, cut into
   ¼-inch thick rounds
2 medium celery ribs, cut into ½-inch dice
1 large red onion, cut into ½-inch dice
1 large red bell pepper, seeded, ribbed,
   and cut into ½-inch dice
1 large yellow bell pepper, seeded, ribbed, and
   cut into ½-inch dice
½ cup olive oil, as needed
3 garlic cloves, crushed under a heavy knife
1 teaspoon fine sea salt, plus more to taste
½ teaspoon freshly ground pepper,
   plus more to taste

½ cup balsamic vinegar, plus more to taste
¼ cup pitted and coarsely chopped black
   oil-cured olives
¼ cup pitted and coarsely chopped green
   olives, preferably Sicilian
¼ cup tomato paste
3 tablespoons drained and rinsed capers
1 tablespoon finely chopped fresh oregano

Position the racks in the top third and center of the oven and preheat to 400°F. Lightly oil two large roasting pans or rimmed baking sheets.

Spread the eggplant, zucchini, summer squash, celery, red onion, and red and yellow peppers in the roasting pans. Mix the oil and garlic in a measuring cup, and drizzle over the vegetables. Season the vegetables with 1 teaspoon salt and ½ teaspoon pepper. Bake, stirring occasionally, until the vegetables are barely tender, about 30 minutes. The vegetables on the top rack may cook more quickly than those on the center rack.

Whisk the balsamic vinegar, black and green olives, tomato paste, capers, and oregano in a large bowl to dissolve the tomato paste. Add the roasted vegetables and mix well. Return the caponata to one roasting pan (the vegetables will have shrunk). Bake on the center rack, stirring occasionally, until the vegetables are tender, about 30 minutes. Season with the salt and pepper, and a dash of balsamic vinegar, if you wish. Cool completely. (The caponata can be made up to 3 days ahead, cooled, covered, and refrigerated.) Serve at room temperature.

Asparagus with Lemon Chive Sauce

Makes 4 servings

For the best quick lunch, I'll put some water on to boil and go out to the garden to harvest asparagus. Homegrown asparagus spears are never uniform, so it is best to cook them lying flat in a skillet, removing the thinner pieces as they cook. It is worthwhile to make a double batch of the creamy sauce because leftovers can be used as a dip, sandwich spread, or sauce for grilled salmon.

LEMON CHIVE SAUCE

4 ounces cream cheese,
    at room temperature
¼ cup yogurt
Grated zest of 1 lemon
1 tablespoon finely chopped
    fresh chives
⅛ teaspoon ground cumin
⅛ teaspoon sugar
Salt, to taste

1 pound asparagus

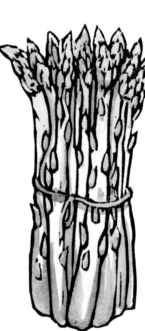

To make the sauce, mash the cheese and yogurt together in a medium bowl until smooth. Whisk in the lemon zest, chives, cumin, and sugar. Season with salt.

Snap off the tough stems of the asparagus. Remove the tough skin of thick spears up to the bud with a vegetable peeler.

Fill a large skillet halfway with lightly salted water and bring to a boil over high heat. Add the asparagus spears, laying them flat in the water. Cook until the spears are just tender when pierced with the tip of a knife, 5 to 8 minutes, depending on the size. As the spears become tender, transfer with tongs to a colander. Rinse the asparagus under cold water and drain well. If you wish, refrigerate the asparagus until chilled.

Arrange equal portions of the asparagus on dinner plates, and top with a spoonful of the sauce. Serve, passing the remaining sauce on the side.

Herbed Cheese Spread

Makes about 1 cup

The best time to make this savory cheese spread is, of course, in the summer, when fresh herbs are abundant. This is a family favorite, and we find many uses for it. Served with a mound of crisp fresh vegetables and crackers, it is a light and tasty lunch. At other times, it does duty as a filling for cherry tomatoes or snow peas, or even as a spread on a roast beef sandwich. Try to make it a day before to allow the flavors to meld. If you have them, garnish the spread with nasturtium flowers—not only are they pretty, but they also add a dash of mild spiciness to the cheese.

2 garlic cloves, peeled
2 tablespoons finely chopped fresh basil
2 tablespoons finely chopped fresh dill
1 tablespoon finely chopped fresh chives
8 ounces cream cheese, at room temperature
2 tablespoons unsalted butter,
    at room temperature
2 tablespoons pitted and chopped black olives
    (optional)

With the machine running, drop the garlic through the feed tube of a food processor. Add the basil, dill, and chives and pulse to blend. Add the cream cheese, butter, and olives, if using. Pulse a few times to combine, scraping down the sides of the bowl as needed. Transfer to a small bowl and cover tightly. Refrigerate to blend the flavors, at least 2 hours or up to 1 week. Serve at room temperature.

DRIED FLOWERS AND HERBS HANG FROM
BEAMS-A SWEET SCENTED CANOPY THAT
PROLONGS THE PLEASURES OF A GARDEN.

Baba Ganoush

Makes 2 cups, about 4 servings

We grow eggplants to use in centerpiece tabletop arrangements as much as we do to eat them. The beautiful Italian Violetta di Firenze is our favorite for both purposes. Here's our recipe for the classic Middle Eastern eggplant spread. Serve with pita bread and olives as a cooling lunch on a hot summer day.

I large eggplant, unpeeled
½ cup pine nuts or pecans, toasted
    (see pages 55 and 12)
¼ cup finely chopped fresh parsley
3 tablespoons tahini (sesame paste)
3 tablespoons fresh lemon juice
I garlic clove, minced and mashed into a paste
    with a pinch of salt
Salt, to taste

Position a rack in the center of the oven and preheat to 400°F.

Prick the eggplant a few times with a fork and place on a baking sheet. Bake until the eggplant collapses, about 40 minutes. Cool until easy to handle.

Scrape the flesh from the skin into a food processor; discard the skin. Add the nuts, parsley, tahini, lemon juice, garlic paste, and salt to taste and process until smooth. Transfer to a serving bowl. Serve immediately, or cover and refrigerate for up to 3 days.

Cilantro Guacamole

Makes 1½ cups, 6 to 8 servings

Avocados do not grow in Vermont, but we wish they did. To make our guacamole, which is great served with sliced tomatoes for a fast and satisfying lunch, we start with the California variety. Most of the other ingredients come from our garden for the best "gwack" this side of the border.

2 ripe avocados, peeled and pitted
2 scallions, white and green parts,
    chopped
2 ripe plum tomatoes, seeded and finely
    chopped
I jalapeño chile, seeded and minced,
    or more or less to taste
3 tablespoons finely chopped fresh cilantro
2 tablespoons Maple Tomato Salsa
    (page 243) or use store-bought salsa
1½ tablespoons fresh lime juice
I garlic clove, minced
Salt, to taste
Tortilla chips or warm corn tortillas,
    for serving

Mash the avocados in a medium bowl with a fork. Mix in the remaining ingredients, keeping the guacamole chunky. Transfer to a serving bowl. (The guacamole can be made up to I day ahead, with a piece of plastic wrap pressed directly on its surface.) Serve with the tortilla chips.

Main Courses

*W*hen it comes to dinner, I let my garden dictate my choice for the main course. Very often, that means that the meal will be vegetarian because it is a healthier choice and, to my mind, a whole lot more fun to cook. If the asparagus is ready, rather than turn them into a salad or side dish, I let them star as the entrée, perhaps rolled into crêpes with ramps and wild mushrooms. Or I will turn a mound of greens into a savory pie or simmer summer vegetables into a chili.

The recipes in this chapter are not necessarily meatless, but they do reflect how I, and many other people, cook. I don't eat a lot of red meat, and when I do, it is organically raised, and I serve it in small quantities with lots of vegetables and grains. When I eat poultry, it is from free-range birds, and I remove the skin to reduce the fat content. A lot of the protein in my family's diet comes from fish, and I've learned how to make wonderful dishes from commonly available seafood such as salmon and cod.

Main courses usually fall into two categories—everyday meals and dishes fit for company. Both are well represented here, but in this book, they actually have more in common than most. I am not a fussy cook, and the simplest recipes are often better than more complicated fare because the cook can then enjoy the time spent in the kitchen. It is amazing how something as effortless as fresh herbs can make a familiar dish special. I have learned to trust the pure flavors of our homegrown produce to make my meals the best they can be.

Asparagus Crêpes with Wild Mushroom and Ramp Sauce

Makes 4 to 6 servings

These crêpes are so sophisticated that you could find them on the menu of a good restaurant, but the main ingredients are wild plants (or cultivated varieties thereof) that could have been foraged from the woods. Ramps are wild leeks that grow in certain areas of the Northeast in early spring and can be purchased during their short season in farmers' markets. They look like a leafy scallion and have a very strong, almost garlicky flavor.

CRÊPES
I cup unbleached all-purpose flour

I cup half-and-half

3 large eggs

½ cup water

6 tablespoons (¾ stick) unsalted butter, melted

½ teaspoon fine sea salt

FILLING
1½ pounds asparagus, peeled and tough stems removed

I cup shredded smoked Cheddar cheese, preferably Vermont Cheddar

SAUCE
4 tablespoons (½ stick) unsalted butter

I cup finely chopped fresh mushrooms, such as chanterelles, morels, or stemmed shiitakes

4 ramps, trimmed, white roots and leafy tops finely chopped, or substitute 4 scallions, white and green parts, finely chopped

I garlic clove, minced (optional, if using scallions)

½ cup heavy cream

To make the crêpes, whisk together the flour, half-and-half, eggs, water, I tablespoon of the melted butter, and salt until smooth. Transfer to a bowl and cover. Let stand at room temperature for 2 hours.

Over medium-high heat, heat a nonstick 8-inch skillet until it is hot. Brush lightly with some of the remaining melted butter. Pour a scant ¼ cup of the batter into the bottom of the skillet, and immediately tilt and swirl the skillet so the batter coats the bottom in a thin layer. Fill in any holes with dribbles of batter from the measuring cup. Cook until the edges look dry and the top is set, about I minute. Using a spatula to lift up one edge, turn the crêpe and cook until the other side is splotched with golden brown spots, about 30 seconds. Transfer to a plate. Repeat with the remaining batter, separating the crêpes with pieces of waxed paper, to make 12 crêpes.

To make the filling, bring a large skillet of lightly salted water to a boil over high heat. Add the asparagus, laying the spears flat in the pan.

Cook until the asparagus is tender, transferring the thinner spears with tongs to a colander as they become tender, 5 to 8 minutes, depending on the thickness of the spears. Rinse under cold water, drain, and pat dry. Cut the spears in half crosswise.

Position a rack in the center of the oven and preheat to 350°F. Lightly butter a 9- × 13-inch baking dish.

Place a crêpe on the work surface. Sprinkle a tablespoon or so of the cheese in the center and top with a few asparagus pieces. Fold in the right and left sides about 1 inch, then roll up from the bottom to make a cylinder. Place, seam side down, in the baking dish. Repeat with the remaining ingredients. Lightly brush the tops of the crêpes with melted butter.

Bake until the crêpes are heated through and the cheese is melted, about 20 minutes.

Meanwhile, to make the sauce, melt the butter in a medium saucepan over medium heat. Add the mushrooms, ramps, and garlic, if using. Cook, stirring occasionally, until the mushrooms are tender, about 15 minutes. Stir in the cream, bring to a boil, and cook until the sauce is lightly thickened, about 5 minutes.

Serve the hot crêpes on plates, topped with a generous spoonful of the sauce.

Savory Vegetables in Polenta Crust

Makes 6 to 8 servings

This polenta crust is a flavorful alternative to the familiar flaky pastry. Stuffed with an Italian-style vegetable and herb filling, and topped with mozzarella, this pie is really a polenta pizza. Call it what you will—it is satisfying.

CRUST

1 teaspoon fine sea salt
1/2 cup yellow cornmeal
1 teaspoon olive oil

FILLING

1 tablespoon olive oil
1 medium onion, cut into 1/4-inch-thick half-moons
1 medium red bell pepper, seed and ribs removed, cut into 1/4-inch-thick slices
1 medium zucchini, cut into 1/4-inch-thick rounds
2 garlic cloves, minced
3 tablespoons balsamic vinegar
2 tablespoons finely chopped fresh basil
1 teaspoon finely chopped fresh oregano
1/4 pound grated mozzarella cheese
Salt and freshly ground pepper, to taste
2 large ripe tomatoes, cut into 1/4-inch-thick rounds

Position a rack in the center of the oven and preheat to 375°F. Lightly oil a 10-inch pie pan.

To make the crust, bring 1 cup water and the salt to a boil in a medium saucepan over high heat. Whisk the cornmeal into 2 cups cold water in a medium bowl, and whisk into the boiling water. Bring to a boil, then reduce the heat to low. Cook, whisking often, until the cornmeal is very thick, 15 to 20 minutes. Cool slightly. Spread evenly in the pie pan to make a thick crust. Brush the crust lightly with the oil. Bake until the crust is firm and set, about 45 minutes. Remove the crust from the oven and increase the oven temperature to 450°F.

To make the filling, heat the oil in a large skillet over medium-high heat. Add the onion, red pepper, zucchini, and garlic and cook, stirring occasionally, until the vegetables are barely tender, about 5 minutes. Stir in the vinegar, basil, and oregano, and cook until the vinegar is evaporated, about 1 minutes. Season with the salt and pepper.

Sprinkle the crust with half of the cheese. Spread over it half of the vegetables and top with half of the tomato slices. Repeat with the remaining vegetables and tomatoes, and sprinkle with the remaining cheese.

Bake until the cheese is melted, about 10 minutes. Let stand for 5 minutes. Slice into wedges and serve hot.

Black Bean and Vegetable Chili

Makes 6 to 8 servings

A hearty one-dish meal is always welcome at the end of a busy day, and this one is a family favorite. Almost any combination of summer vegetables will taste wonderful together as long as they are not overcooked, so the trick is to simmer the black beans in a separate pot. Serve with Cheddar, Chile, and Corn Muffins (page 178), or spoon over soft polenta.

2 cups dried black beans, soaked overnight in
    cold water to cover

1 medium eggplant, cut into 1-inch cubes

1 teaspoon fine sea salt, plus more to taste

1/2 cup olive oil

2 medium onions, chopped

4 garlic cloves, minced

2 medium zucchini, cut into 1/2-inch dice

2 medium carrots, cut into 1/2-inch dice

1 medium green bell pepper, seeds and ribs
    discarded, cut into 1/2-inch pieces

1 small fennel bulb, trimmed, fronds
    removed, and thinly sliced

2 serrano chiles, seeded and minced

8 ripe plum tomatoes, cut into 1/2-inch cubes

1 cup Vegetable Broth (page 27) or water

1/2 cup finely chopped fresh parsley

1 cup fresh or frozen and defrosted corn
    kernels

1/2 cup finely chopped fresh basil

1/2 cup finely chopped fresh dill

Drain the beans and place in a large saucepan with enough cold water to cover them by 2 inches. Bring to a boil over high heat. Reduce the heat to low and simmer until the beans are tender, about 45 minutes. Drain and set aside.

Meanwhile, toss the eggplant with 1 teaspoon salt in a colander. Let stand in a sink to drain off the bitter juices, about 30 minutes. Rinse well under cold water and pat dry with kitchen towels.

Heat 1/4 cup of the oil in a large skillet over medium-high heat. Add the eggplant and cook, stirring occasionally, until golden brown, about 10 minutes. Set aside.

Heat the remaining 1/4 cup of the oil in a large saucepan over medium heat. Add the onion and garlic and cook, stirring occasionally, until softened, about 5 minutes. Add the zucchini, carrots, bell pepper, fennel, and chiles and cook, stirring occasionally, until crisp-tender, about 10 minutes. Stir in the eggplant, beans, tomatoes, broth, and parsley. Bring to a boil over high heat. Reduce the heat to low and simmer for 30 minutes. Stir in the corn, basil, and dill and simmer until the vegetables are tender, about 15 minutes. Season with the salt. Serve hot.

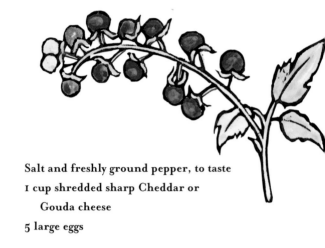

Spring Green Pie

Makes 8 servings

In Vermont, the warmer spring weather encourages the maple sap to flow, the trees to bud, and the salad greens in the cold frame to come back to life. The perennial chicories in the garden also begin to appear, along with the wild greens like dandelion. Italian cooks make a stuffed pie with bitter spring greens as an Easter specialty, and it is an idea that is easily translated to New England. A few ounces of chopped cooked pancetta or bacon are a nice option, especially if the greens are bitter.

DOUGH

One ¼-ounce package (2¼ teaspoons)
  active dry yeast
1 teaspoon sugar
¼ cup warm (105° to 110°F) water
1 cup milk
1 large egg
2 tablespoons olive oil
1 teaspoon fine sea salt
2 cups unbleached all-purpose flour
1 cup whole wheat flour

FILLING

1 tablespoon olive oil
1 medium onion, coarsely chopped
1 garlic clove, minced
6 cups packed assorted spring greens,
  such as chicory, spinach, dandelion,
  and escarole, well rinsed but not dried
2 tablespoons finely chopped sun-dried
  tomatoes

Salt and freshly ground pepper, to taste
1 cup shredded sharp Cheddar or
  Gouda cheese
5 large eggs

To make the dough, stir the yeast and sugar into the warm water in a small bowl. Let stand until foamy, about 5 minutes. Pour into a large bowl, and whisk in the milk, egg, oil, and salt. Combine the all-purpose and whole wheat flours in a separate bowl. Gradually stir enough of the flour mixture into the wet ingredients to make a dough that is too stiff to stir. Turn out onto a lightly floured work surface. Knead, adding the flour mixture as required, to make a smooth, elastic dough, about 10 minutes.

Gather the dough into a ball. Place in an oiled bowl and turn to coat the dough with oil. Cover with a damp kitchen towel and let stand in a warm place until doubled in volume, about 1 hour.

Meanwhile, make the filling. Heat the oil in a large skillet over medium heat. Add the onion and garlic and cook, stirring often, until golden, about 5 minutes. Add a large handful of the greens with any water left clinging to the leaves, and cover. Cook until the greens are wilted, about 2 minutes. Continue adding the greens, a handful at a time, and covering until all of the greens are wilted. Reduce the heat to low and cook until the greens are tender, about 10 minutes. Drain and let cool until easy to handle. A handful at a time, squeeze the excess liquid out of the greens. Coarsely chop the greens. Transfer to a bowl and mix in the sun-dried tomatoes. Season with the salt and pepper.

Position a rack in the center of the oven and preheat to 375°F.

Punch down the dough and divide into two balls, one slightly larger than the other. Cover the smaller ball with a damp kitchen towel. Roll out the larger ball of dough into an 11-inch circle. If the dough retracts, cover with a damp kitchen towel, let stand for a few minutes, then try again.

Fit the dough into a lightly oiled 9-inch pie pan.

Sprinkle the bottom of the dough with the cheese, then top with the greens. Spacing them evenly apart with one egg in the center, crack the five eggs over the greens. Roll out the remaining dough into a 9-inch circle, and center over the bottom crust. Roll the edges together and pinch decoratively to seal, leaving a 1-inch-wide open space on one side. Blow through this hole to make the top crust puff, and pinch the dough to close.

Bake until the crust is golden brown, about 45 minutes. Cool for 10 minutes. Cut into wedges and serve hot.

Spinach Enchiladas with Three Peppers

Makes 6 servings

It is ironic that the hottest peppers are the most innocent looking. My daughter, Molly, learned this at an early age, when she popped a tiny Thai chile into her mouth—and has been wary of chiles ever since. Nonetheless, chiles are so nutritious that I do try to sneak them onto our menu. These spinach enchiladas, spiked with three different peppers, are so good that even Molly likes them.

10 cups packed fresh spinach leaves, well rinsed to remove grit (equivalent to two 12-ounce bags)

2 tablespoons olive oil

2 medium onions, chopped

1 medium red bell pepper, seeded and chopped into ½-inch dice

1 Anaheim chile or green bell pepper, seeded and chopped into ½-inch dice

1 or 2 jalapeño chiles, seeded and minced, to taste

12 corn tortillas

Vegetable oil, for the tortillas

2 cups shredded sharp Cheddar cheese, preferably Vermont Cheddar

1½ cups Maple Tomato Salsa (page 243), or use store-bought salsa

Bring a large pot of lightly salted water to a boil and add the spinach. Cook just until tender, about 5 minutes. Drain and rinse under cold water. A handful at a time, squeeze out the excess moisture and chop the spinach coarsely.

Heat the oil in a large skillet, preferably nonstick, over medium heat. Add the onions and cook, stirring occasionally, until golden, about 8 minutes. Add the bell pepper, Anaheim chile, and jalapeños and cook until softened, about 3 minutes. Stir in the spinach and cook, stirring often to prevent sticking, until the mixture is quite dry, about 5 minutes.

Position a rack in the center of the oven and preheat to 375°F. Lightly oil a 9- × 13-inch baking dish. Brush a medium skillet with oil and heat over medium heat. One at a time, heat the tortillas, turning once, until soft and pliable, about 30 seconds. Place a warmed tortilla on a work surface. Spoon about ¼ cup of the spinach filling in the center of the tortilla, and top with about 2 tablespoons of cheese. Roll up and place seam side down in the baking dish. Repeat with the remaining tortillas, filling, and cheese. Spread the salsa over the top and sprinkle with any remaining cheese.

Bake until the salsa is bubbling and the cheese is melted, about 25 minutes. Serve hot.

GREEN MOUNTAIN GRUN SALSA

Baked Scrod with Fennel and Garlic Croutons

Makes 4 servings

Fennel is one of the best friends a fish can have in the kitchen. This enticing dish, which can be adapted to other firm-fleshed fish fillets, can be ready to cook in less time than it takes for the oven to preheat. Licorice basil will add another scented accent to the fish, but if unavailable, use regular basil or even the fennel fronds. Serve this with steamed brown rice and broccoli florets.

4 tablespoons (½ stick) unsalted butter

1 medium fennel bulb, trimmed, fronds removed, halved, cored, and cut crosswise into ¼-inch-thick slices

1 medium red bell pepper, seeds and ribs discarded, cut into ½-inch dice

1 small onion, chopped

Salt and freshly ground pepper, to taste

1 cup dry white wine

Four 6-ounce skinless scrod or cod fillets

2 tablespoons finely sliced licorice basil leaves, plus more for garnish

2 tablespoons olive oil

3 slices firm white bread, cut into ¼-inch cubes (1 cup)

2 garlic cloves, minced

Position a rack in the center of the oven and preheat to 350°F. Lightly butter a 9- × 13-inch baking dish.

Melt the butter in a large skillet over medium-high heat. Add the fennel, red pepper, and onion and cook, stirring often, until softened, about 5 minutes. Season with the salt and pepper. Spread in the baking dish, and pour in the wine. Arrange the fish in the dish, and sprinkle with the basil and season lightly with salt and pepper.

Heat the oil in the skillet over medium-high heat. Add the bread cubes and garlic and cook, stirring often, until the croutons are golden, about 3 minutes. Spread equal quantities on the fish fillets.

Bake until the fish looks opaque when flaked with a fork, about 20 minutes.

Cod Fillets with Herb-Parmesan Crust

Makes 4 servings

One of the joys of growing your own herbs is using them fresh in the summer, but don't forget to harvest and dry the plants to supply superior flavor later. Because essential oils in dried herbs evaporate with age, it is useful to know when the herb was harvested. Harvest herbs in the summer before their flowers appear, and hang the branches upside down in a well-ventilated room to dry out. Remove the dried leaves from the stems and store in airtight jars in a cool, dry place. Even dried herbs will add flair to the simplest dish, and these golden, crusty fish fillets are a perfect example. To keep the crust intact during cooking, refrigerate the prepared fish fillets for an hour so that the coating can set.

I large egg

½ cup milk

½ cup unbleached all-purpose flour

¼ cup dried bread crumbs

2 tablespoons freshly grated Parmesan cheese

I teaspoon finely chopped fresh thyme or ¼ teaspoon dried thyme

I teaspoon finely chopped fresh tarragon or ¼ teaspoon dried tarragon

I teaspoon finely chopped fresh summer savory or ¼ teaspoon dried summer savory

¼ teaspoon salt

⅛ teaspoon freshly ground pepper

Four 6-ounce skinless cod or scrod fillets

¼ cup olive oil

Whisk the egg and milk in a medium bowl. Mix the flour, bread crumbs, Parmesan cheese, thyme, tarragon, savory, salt, and pepper in another medium bowl. Dip each fillet in the milk, then into the herbed flour, patting the flour onto the fish to make it adhere. Transfer to a waxed paper-lined baking sheet. Refrigerate for I hour to set the crust.

Heat the oil in a large skillet over medium heat until hot. Add the fish fillets and cook until the crust on the underside is set but not browned, about 2 minutes. Turn the fillets and cook until the undersides are golden brown, about 4 minutes. Turn again and cook until the other side finishes cooking to golden brown and the fish looks opaque when flaked in the center, about 2 minutes. Using a slotted spatula, transfer to paper towels to drain briefly. Serve hot.

Grilled Scrod with Mammoth Basil Wrap

Makes 4 servings

Mammoth basil leaves are the size of your hand, and well suited for wrapping fish fillets or other quick-cooking foods for the grill. The leaves will impart a delicate flavor to the fish and help keep the flesh moist, too. Soak the leaves in cold water to keep the basil from scorching on the grill. This dish is especially nice with Lemon-Basil Brown Rice (page 168).

8 mammoth basil leaves

1½ pounds skinless scrod fillets

¼ teaspoon salt

¼ teaspoon freshly ground pepper

4 tablespoons Basil Pesto (page 170),
   or use ½ stick softened unsalted butter

1 lemon, cut into 8 thin slices

Wooden toothpicks or small bamboo skewers,
   soaked in water for 30 minutes and drained

Light a charcoal fire on one side of an outdoor grill and let burn until the coals are covered with white ash. Or preheat a gas grill on High, then switch the burner on one side to Off.

While the fire is heating, soak the basil leaves in a bowl of cold water.

Cut the scrod fillets vertically into eight strips each about 2 inches wide. Season the strips with the salt and pepper. Spread with the pesto and top with a slice of lemon. Drain the basil leaves, shaking off most of the water. Wrap each strip in a wet basil leaf, and secure with a toothpick.

Lightly oil the grill. Place the fish on the empty or Off side of the grill and cover. Grill until the fish is completely cooked in the center when cut with a sharp knife, about 10 minutes. Serve hot, removing the basil leaves before eating.

Salmon in Phyllo Packets with Tomato and Ginger

Makes 4 servings

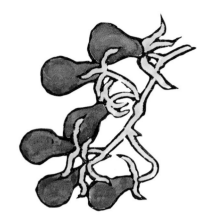

The next time company comes for dinner, consider these phyllo-wrapped salmon fillets. They can be made well ahead of serving and refrigerated until ready to bake. Serve with your favorite hollandaise or aïoli.

> 2 ripe plum tomatoes, seeded and cut into
>   fine dice
> 1 tablespoon peeled and grated fresh ginger
> Grated zest of 1 lemon
> ½ teaspoon fennel seeds, crushed in a mortar
>   or under a heavy saucepan
> Salt and freshly ground pepper, to taste
> 8 sheets defrosted phyllo
> 4 tablespoons (½ stick) unsalted butter, melted
> 1½ pounds skinless salmon or scrod fillets,
>   cut into eight 2-inch-wide strips

Mix the tomatoes, ginger, lemon zest, and fennel in a small bowl, and season with the salt and pepper.

Lightly oil a baking sheet. Lightly brush a phyllo sheet with melted butter, then fold in half lengthwise. Place a salmon strip at one short end of the phyllo, about 1 inch from the edge and the bottom of the dough. Spread about 1 tablespoon of the tomato mixture over the salmon. Fold the short end of the phyllo over the salmon, then fold the bottom edge up and the top edge down. Starting at the short end, roll up the salmon in the phyllo to make a cylinder. Place on the baking sheet, seam side down. Repeat with the remaining phyllo, salmon, tomatoes, and butter, reserving 1 tablespoon melted butter for brushing the tops of the phyllo packets. (The packets can be prepared up to 4 hours ahead, covered, and refrigerated.)

Position a rack in the center of the oven and preheat to 450°F. Brush the tops of the packets with the reserved melted butter. Bake until the phyllo is golden brown, 12 to 15 minutes. Serve immediately.

Red Snapper and Sugar Snap Peas en Papillote

Makes 6 servings

Cook your food in a parchment paper wrap, and you are entitled to use the fancy French term *en papillote*, which means "in an envelope." This method allows the ingredients to cook in their own juices, exchanging flavors in the process. When the diners open their packets at the table, the room will be filled with the fragrant aroma. In this light but utterly delicious recipe, snapper is melded with sugar snap peas and baby carrots—vary it with vegetables of the season and available fish fillets.

½ teaspoon fine sea salt

¼ teaspoon freshly ground pepper

2 tablespoons unsalted butter, cut into 12 very thin slices

Six 8-ounce red snapper fillets

4 tablespoons finely chopped shallots

1 cup sugar snap peas, cut into halves on the diagonal

18 baby carrots, trimmed

1 lemon, sliced into 6 thin rounds

12 sprigs fresh thyme or lemon thyme

6 tablespoons dry white wine

Position the racks in the top third and center of the oven and preheat to 400°F. Cut six 9- × 12-inch pieces of baking parchment paper. Mix the salt and pepper together.

Place a piece of parchment on the work surface with one short end facing you. Fold the paper crosswise in half to make a crease, and unfold. Place two pieces of butter on the bottom half of the paper. Place a snapper fillet on the butter, and season lightly with the salt and pepper mixture. Sprinkle with 2 teaspoons of the shallots. Top with about 3 tablespoons of the sugar snap peas, 3 baby carrots, 1 lemon slice, and 2 sprigs of thyme. Sprinkle with 1 tablespoon of the wine. Fold the paper over to enclose the fish and vegetables, and tightly fold the open sides closed. Repeat with the remaining parchment paper and ingredients. Place the packets on 2 large baking sheets. (The packets can be prepared up to 4 hours ahead and refrigerated.)

Bake, switching the position of the sheets from top to bottom halfway through baking for even cooking, until the paper is well browned, 15 to 20 minutes. Transfer each packet to a dinner plate and serve, allowing each guest to cut open the packet at the table.

With an astonishing ninety-five percent of the peas grown in the United States on commercial farms ending up canned or frozen, it is hard to find fresh peas in the pod. Look for a farm stand that picks the peas often, and choose crisp, bright green pods. To see if they're really fresh, break open a pod or two—they should have a clean snap. Of course, for the best fresh peas, grow your own. Never wash peas for storage, but keep them refrigerated in perforated plastic bags for up to 4 days, or no longer than a day or so for snow peas.

Gardeners and cooks now have several types of peas to choose from, each with its own characteristics.

SHELLING PEAS. These are the peas with inedible pods. The leafy green vines are trellised, and some of the heirloom varieties can grow to a height of 6 feet. To shell the peas, snap the stem end, and pull it, with the attached string, down the side of the pod. Push open the resulting seam in the pod and scrape the peas into a bowl. To cook and serve in the classic method, place the peas in a saucepan and cover with an inch of water. Bring to a boil over high heat and cook for 2 minutes. Drain the peas, and toss with butter, salt, and pepper. One pound of peas in the pod will yield 1 cup shelled peas, or enough for 2 servings.

SUGAR SNAP PEAS. One of the earliest types of edible-pod peas and wildly prolific, the pods of sugar snap peas are deliciously edible. In fact, the raw pods are often devoured in the short trip between the garden and the kitchen. To cook them, trim the stem end, pulling off the string. The best cooking methods are the easiest: sauté the peas or steam them over boiling water until crisp-tender, then serve with minted butter. One pound of sugar snap peas equals 4 cups, or enough for 4 servings.

SNOW PEAS. Peas with edible, flat pods, snow peas are popular in stir-fries because they cook quickly. They are so thin that they don't store moisture well, and they wilt quickly. Snow pea tendrils can also be harvested for garnishing soups or stir-fried on their own or in a vegetable mixture. If you don't grow your own, they can sometimes be found at Asian grocers. 1 pound of snow peas equals 4 cups, or enough for 4 servings.

Salmon with Sorrel Sauce

Makes 4 servings

Sorrel is a well-behaved perennial that supplies a wealth of greens from early spring to late fall. But be aware that the leaves change their flavor and texture as they get older. Young, tender spring leaves have a lemony tartness that works well in salads; the more mature, large leaves benefit from being cooked for a soup or sauce. New potatoes with butter and chives and fresh sugar snap peas would be excellent side dishes.

SORREL SAUCE

2 cups packed finely chopped sorrel leaves, washed and thoroughly towel dried

1 cup dry white wine

3 tablespoons chopped shallots

3 garlic cloves, coarsely chopped

6 whole black peppercorns

1 bay leaf

1 cup heavy cream

Salt, to taste

1 tablespoon unsalted butter

Four 6-ounce skinless salmon fillets

$\frac{1}{2}$ teaspoon fine sea salt

$\frac{1}{4}$ teaspoon freshly ground pepper

Chopped fresh parsley, for garnish

To make the sauce, bring the sorrel, wine, shallot, garlic, peppercorns, and bay leaf to a boil over high heat in a medium, non-reactive saucepan. Cook until the wine is reduced by half, about 10 minutes. Add the cream and bring to a boil again, being careful that the sauce doesn't boil over. Cook until the sauce is thick enough to coat a wooden spoon, about 15 minutes. Rub the sauce through a wire sieve into a small bowl. Season with the salt. Cover and keep warm.

Melt the butter in a large skillet over medium-high heat. Season the salmon with the salt and pepper. Cook in the skillet, turning once, until the flesh is barely opaque when flaked in the center, about 10 minutes.

Place each salmon fillet on a dinner plate, top with a spoonful of the sauce, and sprinkle with the parsley. Serve immediately, with the remaining sauce passed on the side.

Chicken Breasts with Tomatoes, Olives, and Garlic

Makes 4 to 6 servings

Boneless, skinless chicken breast has become one of the most popular ingredients in today's kitchen, and cooks need as many good recipes for it as possible. Covered in a garlic and olive-studded tomato sauce, these breasts soak up a lot of flavor. If you have the time, marinate them in the uncooked tomato mixture in the refrigerator for a few hours before baking. Couscous is the perfect bed for the chicken and its sauce.

2 tablespoons extra virgin olive oil

6 garlic cloves, coarsely chopped

$^{1}/_{3}$ cup pitted and coarsely chopped green olives

I jalapeño chile, seeded and sliced into thin rounds

3 ripe red tomatoes, peeled (see Note), seeded, and coarsely chopped

3 ripe yellow tomatoes, peeled (see Note), seeded, and coarsely chopped

$^{3}/_{4}$ teaspoon fine sea salt

$^{1}/_{4}$ teaspoon freshly ground pepper

$^{1}/_{2}$ cup dry white wine

Six 6- to 7-ounce boneless, skinless chicken breast halves

6 sprigs fresh thyme

Lemon wedges, for serving

COUSCOUS

$^{1}/_{4}$ teaspoon fine sea salt

$1^{1}/_{2}$ cups couscous

Position a rack in the center of the oven and preheat to 350°F. Oil a 10- × 15-inch baking dish with I tablespoon of the oil.

Scatter the garlic, olives, and jalapeño over the bottom of the dish. Top with the tomatoes and season with $^{1}/_{4}$ teaspoon salt and $^{1}/_{8}$ teaspoon pepper. Pour in the wine. Arrange the chicken breasts on the tomatoes and season with the remaining $^{1}/_{2}$ teaspoon salt and $^{1}/_{8}$ teaspoon pepper. Place a thyme sprig on top of each breast. Cover tightly with aluminum foil.

Bake until the chicken is cooked through when pierced with the tip of a knife, 40 to 45 minutes.

Meanwhile, make the couscous. Bring 2 cups water and salt to a boil in a medium saucepan over high heat. Stir in the couscous. Cover tightly and remove from the heat. Let stand until the couscous absorbs the water and is tender, about 5 minutes.

To serve, spoon the couscous onto plates, and top with the chicken and sauce. Serve immediately, with the lemon wedges.

NOTE: To peel tomatoes, drop them into a large pot of boiling water and cook just until the skin loosens, about I minute. Drain, rinse under cold water, and use a sharp paring knife to remove the skin.

To seed tomatoes, cut crosswise in half. Use your finger to poke out the pockets of seeds.

Herbed Chicken with Cider Sauce

Makes 4 servings

≈

You already have a garden full of herbs, so the only question is what to make as an entrée? Here is an exquisite but simple dish with ample flavor provided by fresh herbs and apple cider. Try to make this with Herbed Sea Salt to accentuate the herbal qualities even more. The sauce calls out for something to soak it all up, such as rice or couscous.

⅔ cup unbleached all-purpose flour
1 teaspoon finely chopped fresh thyme
1 teaspoon finely chopped fresh tarragon
1 teaspoon finely chopped fresh chives
1 teaspoon finely chopped fresh parsley
½ teaspoon Herbed Sea Salt (page 43)
    or fine sea salt, plus more to taste
¼ teaspoon freshly ground pepper,
    plus more to taste
Four 6- to 7-ounce boneless, skinless
    chicken breasts
2 tablespoons unsalted butter
2 tablespoons olive oil
1 cup apple cider
Chopped fresh parsley, for garnish

Mix the flour, thyme, tarragon, chives, parsley, herbed salt, and pepper in a medium bowl. Coat each breast in the flour, patting to help the flour adhere, and shaking off the excess.

Melt the butter with the oil in a large skillet and heat until hot. Add the chicken and cook, turning once, until lightly browned on both sides, about 5 minutes. Add the cider and bring to a boil. Cover tightly and reduce the heat to medium-low.

Simmer until the chicken is cooked through when pierced with the tip of a sharp knife and the sauce has thickened, about 20 minutes. Season the sauce with the salt and pepper. Serve hot, sprinkled with the parsley.

Herb Marinade for Lamb

Makes 1 cup, enough to coat an
8-pound leg of lamb

⇒

Lamb is a special occasion food, which makes it the perfect choice for a Christmas or New Year's dinner. This is my favorite recipe. It is best when there is time to allow the marinade to smother the leg of lamb for at least 12 hours before cooking. Serve with scalloped potatoes and baked tomatoes.

5 garlic cloves, peeled

⅛ cup crystallized ginger, coarsely chopped

¼ cup Dijon mustard

¼ cup balsamic vinegar

½ cup olive oil

¼ cup fresh or 1 tablespoon dried rosemary

1 teaspoon dried thyme

1 teaspoon dried marjoram

3 tablespoons tamari sauce

In a food processor fitted with a steel blade, blend all the ingredients together until a smooth paste forms. Cut 1-inch slits all over into the leg of lamb with a sharp knife. Using a small spoon, insert the garlic herb paste. Rub the rest of the marinade all over the leg of lamb. Place in a roasting pan large enough to hold the leg, and cover tightly with plastic wrap and refrigerate for up to two days.

Preheat the oven to 300°F.

Remove the plastic wrap and cook the lamb for about 1½ hours. Lamb will cook even more when it is removed from the oven, so do not overcook. Allow 15 minutes per pound for medium-rare meat, 18 minutes for well-done, and 12 minutes for rare. Remove to a carving board and loosely cover with a tea towel to keep warm. Allow the roast to sit for 30 minutes before carving into thin slices.

Tarragon Chicken

Makes 4 servings

Tarragon is a favorite perennial herb and a mainstay of the herbal garden. True culinary tarragon does not grow from seed and is propagated only from cuttings. To be sure that you have the real thing, break off a leaf and taste it—it should have a licorice-flavored bite. For the best results in this dish, marinate the chicken overnight.

1 cup dry vermouth

2 tablespoons fresh lime juice

6 garlic cloves, minced

2 tablespoons finely chopped fresh tarragon or 1 tablespoon dried tarragon

8 boneless, skinless chicken thighs

2 tablespoons olive oil

Fresh tarragon sprigs, for garnish

SAUCE

1 cup dry vermouth

½ cup heavy cream

2 scallions, white and green parts, finely chopped

2 tablespoons fresh lime juice

2 tablespoons finely chopped fresh tarragon or 1 tablespoon dried tarragon

½ cup Chicken Stock (page 29)

4 tablespoons (½ stick) unsalted butter, cut into 4 slices

4 large egg yolks

Salt and freshly ground pepper, to taste

To marinate the chicken, mix the vermouth, lime juice, garlic, and tarragon in a medium stainless-steel or glass bowl. Add the chicken thighs and mix well. Cover and refrigerate for at least 4 hours or overnight.

To make the sauce, bring the vermouth, cream, scallions, lime juice, tarragon, and stock to a boil over high heat. Boil until the liquid is reduced by one-third, about 15 minutes. Reduce the heat to low. One piece at a time, whisk in the butter. Beat the egg yolks in a small bowl. Whisk about ½ cup of the hot sauce into the yolks, then stir back into the saucepan. Whisk just until thickened, but do not boil. Season with the salt and pepper. Place the saucepan in a large skillet of hot, but not simmering, water to keep warm.

To cook the chicken, remove it from the marinade and shake off the excess. Heat the oil in a large skillet over medium-high heat. Add the chicken and weight it on top with another skillet or a pot. Cook until the underside is crisp and golden, about 7 minutes. Turn and weight again and cook until the other side is golden and the chicken looks cooked through when pierced with the tip of a sharp knife, about 7 minutes.

Transfer each piece of chicken to a plate and top with a few spoonfuls of the sauce. Garnish with the tarragon sprigs and serve hot.

Vietnamese Salad Rolls with Chicken and Shrimp

Makes 8 rolls, 4 to 6 servings

Vietnamese cuisine has many variations of these rice paper–wrapped rolls, and this recipe is just a hint of what can be made from lettuce, savory herbs, and bit of meat. If you make the rolls ahead of serving, do not refrigerate them or the rice paper will toughen. Besides, it is fun to bring all of the ingredients to the table and roll them up as needed. You will find rice papers, rice sticks, hoisin sauce, and chili paste at your natural foods store or Asian market.

I teaspoon vegetable oil

Two 6-ounce boneless, skinless chicken
    breasts

12 medium shrimp

4 ounces rice vermicelli (also called rice
    sticks)

Eight 12-inch rice paper rounds

I small head red leaf lettuce, leaves separated,
    washed and dried, cut in half lengthwise
    (cut away any thick ribs)

I cup mung bean sprouts

½ cup fresh mint leaves

I cup hoisin sauce, for serving

¼ cup chopped roasted peanuts, for serving

2 tablespoons chili paste, for serving

Heat the oil in a nonstick skillet over medium-high heat. Add the chicken breasts and cook, turning once, until browned on both sides, about 5 minutes. Reduce the heat to medium low and cook, turning occasionally, until the chicken is cooked through when pierced with the tip of knife, about 7 minutes. Cool slightly, then cut crosswise on the diagonal to make 16 thin slices each about 1-inch wide.

Bring a medium saucepan of lightly salted water to a boil. Add the shrimp and cook just until the shells turn pink, about 3 minutes. Drain. Peel and devein the shrimp. Cut each shrimp in half lengthwise.

Bring another medium saucepan of water to a boil. Add the rice vermicelli and boil until tender, about 4 minutes. Drain, rinse under cold water. Place in a bowl, and randomly snip the vermicelli into shorter lengths.

Make a roll-up station to make two rolls at a time: Place a large kitchen towel on the work surface. Fill a large bowl with hot tap water. Place rice papers nearby, along with the chicken, rice vermicelli, shrimp, lettuce, sprouts, and mint. Have a damp second towel ready for cleaning your hands.

Dip 1 rice paper round in the hot water, edge first, and submerge until moistened and pliable, about 10 seconds. Spread out on the towel. Repeat with a second round, and spread it out next to the first.

On the bottom edge of the first round, place a neat row of 3 shrimp halves, and top with 2 chicken slices, a folded piece of lettuce, about 1 tablespoon vermicelli, 1 tablespoon sprouts, and 4 mint leaves. Fold in the right and left sides about 1 inch, then roll up from the bottom to make a roll. Transfer to a platter. Repeat with the second round. The rolls can be made up to 2 hours ahead and stored at cool room temperature in an airtight container lined with a damp kitchen towel.

Cut each roll into 2 or 4 slices. Serve with small bowls of the hoisin sauce, peanuts, and chili paste, for dipping.

Letter from the Garden

A characteristic autumn display on our front porch starts with a big Blue Hubbard squash. Balanced on its backside with its stem end curved back on its belly, it resembles a teetering sea otter. Next to it, I might arrange a few flat-topped, burnt umber colored Rouge Vif d'Etampes pumpkins. To balance the picture, a tubular Tromboncini spirals around a bevy of Swan's Neck gourds.

Everywhere is a cascading cornucopia of fall colors. Inside the front hall, tucked under the main table, you'll find round baskets full of brilliant orange Hokkaido, pine green Table Ace, striped Delicata, and Gold Nugget squash.

Winter squash is a quiet performer in a cook's garden. Although it requires a considerable amount of space, maintenance is relatively low compared with other crops. Harvest is easy, and if cured in the sun for a few days, squash will last most of the winter in a cool room.

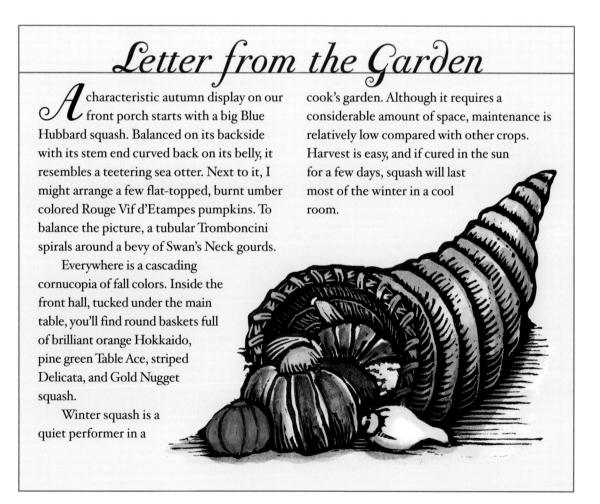

The Cook's Garden's Favorite Squash

*W*hat we call zucchini, the French call *courgettes* and the Italians *zuccette*; the final *-ette* they have in common means "small." French and Italian gardeners discovered long ago that the best way to keep summer squash from growing into the size of a boat is to harvest them while they're small.

Summer squash was discovered in the Americas, and will grow like a native plant if you give it the chance. It is endlessly productive. No matter how many young squash you harvest, there will always be more. In fact, if you cut off the little zucchini when they're 3 inches long, you will have true baby zucchini at a much lower price than that of the specialty produce shop. This will solve any potential zucchini glut, and give you some of the best squash you've ever eaten.

Winter squash should be allowed to grow to full size so it can develop its full flavor. A mainstay in pioneer and homestead gardens, winter squash has only recently been discovered by culinary gardeners, who appreciate the way its delightfully sweet taste and creamy texture lends a special touch to winter meals.

Glancing at the squash in the supermarket, you may think that all squash are the same, but there is a wide variety of tastes, shapes, and colors. At The Cook's Garden we grow a large assortment of both summer and winter squashes. That way, we'll have some for stuffing, others for grilling and roasting, and even some for tempura (battered and deep-fried baby zucchini are wonderful). In fact, because we can easily get them at the local market, we rarely grow traditional zucchini and acorn squash anymore. But here are some examples of summer and winter squashes that we are growing.

Summer Squash

ELITE. Of all the green zucchini we have grown over the years, this one wins our taste trials as the best. A super-early hybrid, it is both high yielding and easy to pick. Harvest them small with the flowers still attached, then slice them lengthwise and sauté in a bit of oil with garlic.

SUNBURST. A golden yellow patty pan squash that is both vigorous and productive. Harvest at silver-dollar size and deep-fry for a tempura treat, or allow to grow to 4 to 6 inches in diameter, and stuff with ricotta cheese and herbs.

RONDE DE NICE. This French heirloom variety is distinguished by its round shape. Cut in halves, remove the seeds, stuff with a savory sauce or tomato, rice, and sausage, and bake.

TROMBONCINO. The fruits of this vine grow long and thin, curving to a bell at the flower end. For the best quality, trellis the vines and harvest when the squash are 8 to 18 inches long. The fine, sweet flavor is unlike any other summer squash. If you let them grow throughout the summer, they can be harvested as gourds.

GOLD RUSH. Shoppers at our garden market often mistake this for a yellow summer squash, but it is a true zucchini with excellent flavor. It is great combined with green zucchini.

Winter Squash

GOLD NUGGET. This heirloom has been a favorite for generations. The compact, bushy plants bear a large number of 1-pound, deep golden fruit. Among their best features is their size, which is just right for 2 portions, their long storage capability, and their good looks.

RED KURI. Also known as Orange Hokkaido, this prime Japanese squash is a great choice for soups and pies. The teardrop-shaped, bright orange fruits weigh in at an average of 5 pounds.

Especially rich in vitamin A, they are traditionally considered the best choice for macrobiotic diets.

MARINA D'CHIOGGIA. Italian cooks often use the flesh of this big, deep green beauty as the base for gnocchi. A staple of Venetian markets, these squash can be stored in a root cellar or cool basement and sliced as needed.

DELICATA. Otherwise known as the sweet potato squash, this distinctive-looking squash is cylindrical with green and ivory ridges. Common in supermarkets, it is worth baking like any winter squash, but the flesh will need less butter and sugar. Its long boat shape makes it useful for stuffing with a heap of seasoned wild rice.

SUGAR PUMPKIN. My own favorite of all our pumpkinlike squash, this is the one to grow for pumpkin pie. The thin skin makes it easy to cut open and the interior flesh is moist but not too watery. Harvest when they weigh about 2 pounds, and you'll get enough purée for the best pies ever, along with pumpkin seeds for snacks.

Calzone with Broccoli-Mozzarella Filling

Makes 4 servings

Winter is "high carb" time in the North Country, and calzone is on our dinner menu at least once a week, usually with a seasonal vegetable filling. It's a good idea to make a double batch and freeze some for a quick meal during busy times. With lots of fragrant herbs in this dough, you won't find any crusts left behind on the plate.

DOUGH

1 cup warm (105° to 115°F) water

One ¼-ounce package (2¼ teaspoons) active dry yeast

1 tablespoon sugar

2 tablespoons olive oil

1 tablespoon finely chopped fresh basil or 1 teaspoon dried basil

1 tablespoon finely chopped fresh oregano or 1 teaspoon dried oregano

2 teaspoons seeded and finely chopped hot chile pepper, such as serrano

1 garlic clove, minced

½ teaspoon salt

2 cups unbleached all-purpose flour

1 cup whole wheat flour

FILLING

2 tablespoons olive oil, plus more for brushing the calzone

1 medium onion, chopped

1 medium red bell pepper, seeds and ribs removed, cut into ½-inch dice

1 garlic clove, minced

2 cups coarsely chopped broccoli florets

2 ripe plum tomatoes, seeded and chopped into ½-inch dice or ¼ cup diced sun-dried tomatoes

½ cup Parmesan cheese

½ cups grated mozzarella cheese

To make the dough, pour the warm water into a large bowl and stir in the yeast and sugar. Let stand until the mixture looks foamy, about 10 minutes. Stir in the oil, basil, oregano, chile pepper, garlic, and salt. Combine the all-purpose and whole wheat flours. One cup at a time, gradually stir the flour into the liquid until the dough is too stiff to stir. Now knead the dough in the bowl until the dough comes together.

Turn the dough out onto a floured work surface. Knead by hand, adding more flour as necessary, until the dough is smooth and elastic, about 8 minutes. If you run out of flour, use more all-purpose flour. Form the dough into a ball. Place in a large, lightly oiled bowl, and turn the dough to coat it with oil. Cover the bowl with a damp kitchen towel. Let stand in a warm place until doubled in volume, about 1 hour.

To prepare the filling, heat the oil in a large skillet over medium heat. Add the onion, red pepper, and garlic and cook, stirring often, until softened, about 5 minutes. Add the broccoli and cover. Cook just until beginning to soften, about 3 minutes. Stir in the tomatoes. Cool. Drain in a colander to remove any collected juices.

Punch down the dough, turn out onto a lightly floured work surface, and knead briefly. Cut the dough into four equal pieces and form into balls. Working with one piece at a time (keeping the other pieces covered with a damp kitchen towel), roll out the dough into a 10- ×

12-inch rectangle. Leaving a $1/2$-inch border on the bottom and sides, sprinkle the bottom half of the rectangle with 2 tablespoons Parmesan cheese and $1/2$ cup mozzarella, then top with one-quarter of the filling. Fold the dough down to cover the filling and pinch the open sides closed. Place the calzone on 2 lightly oiled baking sheets, and cover with damp kitchen towels. Let stand in a warm place until the dough looks puffy, about 40 minutes.

Position two racks in the top and center of the oven and preheat to 425°F.

Slash a small slit in the top of each calzone, and brush the tops with oil. Bake until the dough is golden brown, about 30 minutes, switching the sheets from top to bottom halfway through baking. Let cool for 5 minutes before serving.

Spinach Fettuccine with Winter Vegetables and Herbed Cream

Makes 4 to 6 servings

We usually leave our parsnips and carrots in the ground until spring. During the winter, anything from the garden is a treat, but these root vegetables are actually sweeter after a siege of cold weather. Here they are combined with leek, pear, and butternut squash in a luxurious cream sauce to make a hearty pasta dish that is as beautiful to look at as it is to eat.

HERBED CREAM

2 cups dry white wine
2 sprigs fresh thyme
2 sprigs fresh parsley
4 sprigs fresh rosemary
3 tablespoons coarsely chopped shallots
3 garlic cloves, coarsely chopped
6 whole black peppercorns
1 bay leaf
2 cups heavy cream
Salt and freshly ground pepper, to taste

4 ounces sliced pancetta or bacon
2 tablespoons unsalted butter
1 cup peeled and seeded butternut squash, cut into ½-inch dice
4 medium carrots, cut into thin matchsticks
2 medium parsnips, cut into thin matchsticks
1 tablespoon olive oil
1 firm pear, such as Bosc, peeled, cored, and cut into ½-inch dice

1 medium leek, white and pale green parts only, coarsely chopped into ¼-inch dice
1 tablespoon chopped fresh sage
Salt and freshly ground pepper, to taste
1 pound dried spinach fettuccine

To make the herbed cream, bring the wine, thyme, parsley, rosemary, shallots, garlic, peppercorns, and bay leaf to a boil in a medium, stainless-steel or enameled saucepan over high heat. Cook until the wine is reduced to 1 cup, about 15 minutes. Add the cream and bring to a boil, being careful that the cream does not boil over. Cook until the sauce is thick enough to coat a wooden spoon, about 15 minutes. Season with the salt and pepper. Strain through a wire sieve. Return to the saucepan, cover, and keep warm. (The herbed cream can be made up to 1 day ahead, cooled, covered, and refrigerated. Reheat before using.)

Place the pancetta in a large skillet, then cook over medium heat until crisp and browned, about 5 minutes (starting the pancetta in a cold skillet reduces splattering). Transfer to paper towels to drain, keeping the fat in the skillet. Cool and coarsely chop the pancetta.

Add the butter to the fat in the skillet and melt over medium heat. Add the squash and cook for 5 minutes. Add the carrots and parsnips and cook until the squash is tender, about 10 minutes. Transfer to a bowl.

Heat the oil in the same skillet over medium heat. Add the pear and leek and cook, stirring often, until the leek is golden, about 7 minutes. Stir in the sage. Add the squash mixture and pancetta and cook just until hot. Season with the salt and pepper. Remove from the heat and cover to keep warm.

Meanwhile, bring a large pot of lightly salted water to a boil over high heat. Add the fettuccine and cook just until tender, about 9 minutes. Drain well, and return to the pot. Add the hot herbed cream and toss well.

Serve the pasta in bowls, topped with the vegetables.

Herbed Ricotta Gnocchi with Spinach-Arugula Pesto

Makes 4 to 6 servings

There is something so satisfying about making gnocchi, tender pillows of dough that do not require a pasta machine. Other recipes use mashed potatoes or semolina, but our family is partial to the ricotta cheese version. For the best results, use fresh ricotta (as distinguished from the commercial brands), which is available at cheese stores and Italian grocers. The bright green pesto proves that you don't have to use basil to get a terrific herb sauce for pasta.

PESTO SAUCE

2 garlic cloves, peeled

2 tablespoons pine nuts,
   toasted (see page 55)

1½ cups packed arugula leaves,
   well rinsed and towel dried

1½ cups packed fresh spinach leaves,
   well rinsed and towel dried

¼ cup freshly grated Parmesan cheese

½ cup olive oil

Salt and freshly ground pepper,
   to taste

GNOCCHI

1 cup unbleached all-purpose flour

1 tablespoon finely chopped fresh chives

1 tablespoon finely chopped fresh sage

1 tablespoon finely chopped fresh
   chervil or 1½ teaspoons fresh
   tarragon

½ teaspoon ground fennel seeds

½ teaspoon fine sea salt

¼ teaspoon freshly grated nutmeg

⅛ teaspoon freshly ground pepper

1 pound whole milk ricotta cheese, drained

To make the pesto, with the machine running, drop the garlic through the feed tube of a food processor to mince. Add the pine nuts, arugula, spinach, and Parmesan and pulse until the greens are finely chopped. With the machine running, gradually add the oil to make a thick paste. Season with the salt and pepper. Transfer to a small bowl and cover tightly with plastic wrap. (The pesto can be made up to 2 hours ahead and kept at room temperature.)

To make the gnocchi, pulse the flour, chives, sage, chervil, fennel, salt, nutmeg, and pepper in the food processor until the herbs are very finely minced and blended into the flour. Transfer to a medium bowl. Add the ricotta and mix well (your hands may work better than a spoon). Flour your hands, and knead the dough in the bowl until it holds together. The dough will be sticky, but do not add more flour or the gnocchi will be heavy.

Line a baking sheet with waxed paper (not plastic wrap) and dust with flour. Working with about ⅓ cup of dough at a time, place on a lightly floured work surface and roll underneath your palms to make a ½-inch-thick rope. Cut into ¾-inch-long pieces. Using the tines of a fork, press indentations into each piece, and place the gnocchi on the baking sheet. Repeat until all the dough is used.

Bring a large pot of lightly salted water to a simmering boil over medium heat. Add the gnocchi and cook until they rise to the surface. Boil for 30 seconds, until the gnocchi are set but tender. Drain carefully. (The gnocchi can be made up to 4 hours ahead, rinsed under cold water, and drained well. Toss them with olive oil and store at room temperature. To reheat, cook in a large nonstick skillet over low heat.)

Toss the hot gnocchi with the pesto and serve immediately.

Fettuccine with Brussels Sprout Sauce

Makes 4 to 6 servings

Brussels sprouts are hardly a common ingredient for a pasta sauce, but this dish, with a hint of heat supplied by fresh horseradish and Dijon mustard, has become one of our fall favorites. A bit of soppressata or pancetta will round out the flavor, but leave it out if you prefer a vegetarian meal.

1½ pints Brussels sprouts, root ends trimmed, discolored leaves discarded
4 tablespoons (½ stick) unsalted butter
2 tablespoons olive oil
½ cup soppressata or pancetta in ¼-inch dice
1 large onion, finely chopped
2 garlic cloves, minced
1 medium red bell pepper, roasted (see page 40), seeded, and coarsely chopped
2 cups packed chopped fresh spinach leaves, well rinsed to remove grit
1½ cups shredded sharp Cheddar cheese, preferably Vermont Cheddar
1 cup half-and-half
½ cup freshly grated Parmesan cheese
1 tablespoon Dijon mustard
2 teaspoons freshly grated horseradish root, or use prepared horseradish
2 tablespoons finely chopped fresh dill (optional)
1 teaspoon dried tarragon
Salt and freshly ground pepper, to taste
1 pound dried fettuccine

Bring a medium saucepan of lightly salted water to a boil over high heat. For even cooking, cut a shallow X in the bottom of each sprout, and cut the largest ones in half lengthwise. Add the Brussels sprouts to the water and cook until tender, 6 to 8 minutes. Remove from the water with a slotted spoon (the water can be used to cook the pasta).

Melt 2 tablespoons of the butter with the oil in a large skillet over medium heat. Add the soppressata or pancetta and cook until lightly browned, about 3 minutes (cook pancetta until browned and crisp, about 5 minutes). Add the onion and garlic and cook, stirring often, until the onion softens, about 5 minutes. Stir in the roasted pepper and spinach, cooking until the spinach wilts, about 2 minutes. Add the Brussels sprouts, Cheddar cheese, half-and-half, Parmesan, mustard, horseradish, dill, if using, and tarragon and stir to melt the cheese. Season with salt and pepper. Remove from the heat and cover to keep warm.

Meanwhile, cook the fettuccine in a large pot of lightly salted water over high heat just until tender. Drain and return to the pot. Toss with the remaining 2 tablespoons butter. Serve the hot fettuccine in bowls topped with the sauce.

Side Dishes

*I*t wasn't too long ago (I think of that time as the Vegetable Dark Ages) when almost *all* vegetables were considered side dishes. One had the occasional "vegetable main dish," such as stuffed zucchini or bell peppers, but it was usually stuffed with meat. Not that there is anything wrong with side dishes. In fact, most main courses need to be bolstered by harmonious side dishes. Many meals are simply unthinkable without a mound of creamy mashed potatoes or crisp home fries.

Most of the side dishes recommended here are fast and easy, allowing the cook to concentrate on the main course. The asparagus stir-fry with sesame seeds and the radish and arugula sauté will be done before you know it. Other recipes are so special that you might consider serving them as entrées—the beet and goat cheese soufflé and the ricotta-stuffed pattypan squash come to mind.

Whenever you cook with fresh, flavorful vegetables, be they pulled from your garden or brought home from a farmers' market, the results will be extraordinary. Even the most humble side dish will taste better. So get ready to rethink the side dishes on your menu. They might not remain so humble for long.

Herb Butters

Each makes about ¾ cup

Herb butters are one of the best ways to preserve the flavor of fresh herbs. Stir a good-sized nugget into steamed vegetables or cooked grains, melt onto grilled fish, chicken, or chops, or toss with pasta instead of pesto for a quick meal. For a decorative touch, spread softened herb butter in a layer in a small baking dish, refrigerate until firm, and cut out shapes with miniature cookie cutters. Freeze the butter shapes or place in ice water to firm up.

BASIL GARLIC BUTTER

8 tablespoons (1 stick) unsalted butter, softened

⅓ cup finely chopped fresh basil

1½ tablespoons fresh lemon juice

2 garlic cloves, minced

CHIVE BUTTER

8 tablespoons (1 stick) unsalted butter, softened

3 tablespoons minced shallots

2 tablespoons finely chopped fresh chives

1½ tablespoons fresh lemon juice

1 tablespoon finely chopped fresh parsley

FINES HERBES BUTTER

8 tablespoons (1 stick) unsalted butter, softened

1½ tablespoons minced shallots

1 tablespoon tarragon vinegar

2 teaspoons finely chopped fresh parsley

2 teaspoons finely chopped fresh tarragon

2 teaspoons finely chopped fresh chives

2 teaspoons finely chopped fresh chervil

Mash the butter with all of the other ingredients in a medium bowl until well combined. Transfer to a 12-inch square of waxed paper, spooning the butter into a 6-inch-long strip. Use the waxed paper to help roll the butter into a log, and wrap tightly in the waxed paper. Refrigerate until firm, at least 2 hours, or overnight. Store the herb butter in the refrigerator for up to 4 weeks. (Herb butter can also be frozen for up to 6 months. Use a sharp knife to cut off pieces as needed.)

Steamed Artichokes with Herb Butter

Makes 4 servings

We appreciate artichokes for the beauty of their silver-green leaves as much as for their flavorful flowers. Admittedly, Vermont has such a short growing season that we have to start the plants in a greenhouse before transferring them outside, and if we are lucky there will be a few buds by the end of the summer. But California artichokes have two major seasons, from February to May, and then a shorter one in October.

4 large artichokes
1 recipe Herb Butter (page 136) of your
    choice, melted

Trim off the stem of each artichoke. Cut off the top ¼ inch from each artichoke to remove the thorny end. Using scissors snip off the thorny tips from the leaves.

Stand the artichokes in a large saucepan and add enough lightly salted water to come 2 inches up the sides. Cover tightly and bring to a boil over high heat. Reduce the heat to medium low and cook, covered, until the artichokes are tender when the bases are pierced with a sharp knife, about 30 minutes. Drain well.

Place each artichoke on a plate and serve with a small bowl of melted herb butter for each person for dipping.

Roasted Asparagus with Sun-Dried Tomatoes

Makes 4 servings

Everyone knows how to steam asparagus, but roasting brings out a different kind of flavor. Sun-dried tomatoes contrast nicely with the green spears. To serve as a warm salad, place on a bed of tender lettuce or a radicchio leaf.

1 pound asparagus, peeled and tough stem
    ends trimmed
2 tablespoons chopped sun-dried tomatoes
2 tablespoons chopped shallots
1 tablespoon olive oil
Salt and freshly ground pepper, to taste
Lemon wedges, for serving

Position a rack in the center of the oven and preheat to 450°F.

Spread the asparagus in a single layer in a shallow baking dish. Sprinkle the sun-dried tomatoes, shallots, and oil evenly over the asparagus, and season with the salt and pepper. Roast for 10 minutes. Turn the asparagus and roast until tender, about 5 minutes. Serve hot, with the lemon wedges.

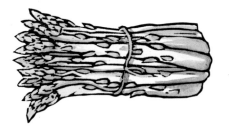

Stir-Fried Asparagus with Sesame Seeds

Makes 4 servings

One of the most exciting rewards for a gardener is witnessing the first firm spears of asparagus shooting out of the ground—few garden delicacies are more prized by cooks. This dish cooks quickly, so have everything ready to go before you start.

1 tablespoon sesame seeds

2 teaspoons olive oil

1 pound asparagus, peeled and tough ends trimmed, tender spears cut diagonally into 1-inch lengths

1 scallion, white and green parts, thinly sliced into rounds

1 tablespoon soy sauce

2 teaspoons dark Asian sesame oil

½ teaspoon sugar

Heat a large skillet or wok over high heat. Add the sesame seeds and stir almost constantly until they are toasted a light golden brown, about 2 minutes. Transfer to a plate.

Add the oil to the skillet and heat over high heat until hot. Add the asparagus and scallion and cook, stirring occasionally, just until the asparagus is crisp-tender and golden brown around the edges, about 3 minutes. Stir in the soy sauce, sesame oil, and sugar. Cover and cook until the asparagus is tender, about 2 minutes. Serve hot.

Baby Carrots with Tarragon

Makes 4 servings

Because carrots are at the height of their flavor and nutritional value when pulled straight from the garden, we are always sure to grow plenty. We especially love the Touchon, a French heirloom variety that has been bred for the home gardener. Their roots are sweet, but their tops are so weak that they can be harvested only by hand, making them an impossible crop for commercial growers who pull up their carrots with machines.

1 pound young baby-sized carrots with tops, scrubbed but unpeeled, with tops trimmed to 1-inch lengths

4 tablespoons (½ stick) unsalted butter

¼ teaspoon sugar

¼ teaspoon fine sea salt

1 teaspoon finely chopped fresh tarragon

Place the carrots in a medium saucepan with ½ cup of water. Add 3 tablespoons of the butter, and the sugar and salt. Cover tightly and bring to a boil over high heat. Reduce the heat to medium low and simmer for 10 minutes. Uncover and cook until the carrots are tender and the liquid has evaporated (keep a close watch to be sure the saucepan doesn't run dry, and add a bit more water if needed), about 10 minutes. Drain, if necessary. Transfer to a serving dish, and toss with the remaining 1 tablespoon butter and the tarragon. Serve hot.

Baby Beets with Horseradish Butter

Makes 4 servings

＝

Several rows of mixed beets in the garden will guarantee a variety of colors and sizes through the summer. We especially enjoy baby beets in this dish. Luckily, horseradish can be harvested any time of the year, and the two make a great summer combination.

12 small beets, scrubbed and trimmed
(leave the top 1 inch of stem attached)
2 tablespoons unsalted butter
1 tablespoon finely grated fresh horseradish
root, or use prepared horseradish
1 tablespoon cider vinegar
1 tablespoon chopped fresh dill
Salt, to taste

Bring a medium pot of lightly salted water to a boil over high heat. Add the beets and cover. Reduce the heat to medium and cook until the beets are tender when pierced with the tip of a knife, about 30 minutes. Drain, rinse under cold water, and slip off the skins.

Melt the butter in a medium saucepan over medium heat. Add the horseradish, vinegar, and dill. Add the beets and stir gently to coat with the butter. Season with the salt to taste. Serve hot.

Garlicky Broccoli Raab

Makes 4 servings

Broccoli raab (also called rapini) looks like long, thinner stems of broccoli with loose heads. It has a pleasantly bitter flavor that comes through after a slow simmer in olive oil and garlic. Add some sun-dried tomatoes and pine nuts to make a great pasta sauce.

> 1 pound broccoli raab
> ¼ cup olive oil
> 2 garlic cloves, finely chopped

Rinse the broccoli raab well in cold water to remove any grit. Do not dry. Chop into 2-inch pieces.

Heat the oil in a large, heavy-bottomed saucepan over medium heat. Stir in the garlic, then the broccoli raab. Cover tightly and reduce the heat to low. Cook, stirring occasionally, until the broccoli is wilted and tender, about 20 minutes. Serve hot.

Round Carrots and Apples with Maple Glaze

Makes 4 servings

Round carrots are quite a novelty, even for experienced gardeners. When we first cooked with them, we'd slice them into rounds and deep-fry them tempura-style. Now we stew them with apples to make a comforting side dish, which is equally good hot or cold.

1 pound small round carrots (about 15), scrubbed but unpeeled

4 tablespoons (½ stick) unsalted butter

¼ teaspoon fine sea salt

1 tablespoon olive oil

1 cooking apple, such as Cortland or McIntosh, peeled, cored and cut into 1-inch cubes

1 tablespoon pure maple syrup

½ teaspoon freshly grated ginger

Place the carrots in a medium saucepan with ½ cup water, 3 tablespoons of the butter, and the salt. Cover tightly and bring to a boil over high heat. Reduce the heat to low and simmer, until the carrots are tender (check to be sure that the water doesn't run dry, and add more water if necessary), about 15 minutes. Drain.

Meanwhile, heat the oil in a large skillet over medium-high heat. Add the apple and cook, stirring occasionally, until golden, about 5 minutes. Stir in the remaining 1 tablespoon butter and the maple syrup and ginger. Add the carrots and reduce the heat to low. Cook, stirring often, until the carrots are glazed, about 2 minutes. Serve hot, or cool to room temperature, cover and refrigerate until cold, and serve chilled.

Radish with Arugula Sauté

Makes 4 servings

In the spring, many an overzealous kitchen gardener is faced with an abundance of radishes and arugula, so it makes sense to combine the two. This simple dish may surprise you, as cooking will mellow the usually spicy arugula until it resembles spinach. Easter Egg radishes are a favorite in our garden, as they grow in a variety of colors from deep purple to bright red.

2 tablespoons unsalted butter
8 radishes, preferably Easter Egg, or use
    traditional red radishes, cut into
    thin rounds
2 cups coarsely chopped arugula, well
    rinsed and towel dried
Salt and freshly ground pepper, to taste

Melt the butter in a large skillet over medium heat. Add the radishes, and cook, stirring often, until barely tender, about 4 minutes. Transfer to a bowl.

Add the arugula to the skillet and cook, stirring often, until wilted, about 3 minutes. Return the radishes to the skillet and mix. Season with the salt and pepper. Serve hot.

Herbed Zucchini Pancakes

Makes 12 to 14 pancakes

The zucchini in these delicate pancakes are just a jumping-off point for other vegetable additions, so feel free to add a handful of shredded carrots, parsnips, or onions to the batter. Cooking will go much more quickly if you use two skillets or a large griddle. Serve the pancakes with Savory Green Sauce (page 164), or make a batch of your favorite hollandaise sauce.

2 medium green zucchini, scrubbed and
    grated (2 cups)
2 medium golden zucchini, scrubbed and
    grated (2 cups)
2 teaspoons fine sea salt
4 large eggs
½ cup unbleached all-purpose flour
4 tablespoons (½ stick) unsalted butter,
    melted
1 tablespoon finely chopped fresh basil
1 tablespoon finely chopped fresh chives
⅛ teaspoon freshly ground pepper
1 cup shredded sharp Cheddar cheese,
    preferably Vermont Cheddar
¼ cup olive oil
Savory Green Sauce (page 164)

Toss the zucchini in a colander with the salt. Let stand in a sink to draw out the juices, about 30 minutes. Rinse well with cold water. A handful at a time, squeeze out the excess moisture from the zucchini.

Position a rack in the center of the oven and preheat to 200°F.

Beat the eggs in a medium bowl. Add the zucchini, flour, melted butter, basil, chives, and pepper and mix well. Fold in the cheese.

Heat the oil in a large skillet over medium heat. Using ¼ cup for each pancake, drop the batter into the skillet, using a spatula to spread the thick batter into ½-inch-thick pancakes. Cook, turning once, until the pancakes are golden brown, about 5 minutes on each side. Using a slotted spatula, transfer to a baking sheet and keep warm in the oven while making the remaining pancakes. Serve hot, with the sauce.

Rainbow Beet and Chèvre Soufflé

Makes 4 to 6 servings

~

This elegant soufflé, with sweet beets and a hint of orange, is so rich that I have considered serving it as a dessert. The crimson of the beets will bleed into the green-flecked yellow soufflé to create a beautiful rainbow effect. At your most elegant dinners, this could also be served as a first course.

4 medium beets with tops

Grated zest of 1 large orange

$\frac{1}{3}$ cup fresh orange juice

$\frac{1}{2}$ teaspoon sugar

$\frac{1}{2}$ teaspoon fine sea salt

$\frac{1}{8}$ teaspoon freshly ground pepper

4 tablespoons ($\frac{1}{2}$ stick) unsalted butter, softened

2 tablespoons freshly grated Parmesan cheese

$\frac{1}{2}$ cup crumbled rindless goat cheese

3 tablespoons unbleached all-purpose flour

1 cup milk

4 large eggs, separated

Trim the tops off the beets. Wash the tops well in cold water. Scrub the beets.

Place the beets in a medium saucepan and add enough lightly salted water to cover. Bring to a boil over high heat. Reduce the heat to medium and cook until the beets can be pierced with a knife, about 30 minutes. Drain and rinse under cold water until easy to handle. Slip off the skins, and cut into $\frac{1}{8}$-inch-thick rounds. Transfer to a medium bowl, and mix in the orange zest and juice, sugar, salt, and pepper.

Place the beet tops and enough lightly salted water to cover in another medium saucepan and bring to a boil over high heat. Reduce the heat to medium and cook just until the tops are tender, about 5 minutes. Drain, rinse under cold water, and squeeze out the excess moisture. Pat the greens dry with paper towels and chop coarsely.

Position a rack in the center of the oven and preheat to 375°F. Butter a 1-quart soufflé dish with 1 tablespoon of the butter. Sprinkle the bottom of the dish with the Parmesan cheese. Layer the sliced beets with their juices in the bottom of the dish, then sprinkle with the goat cheese.

Melt the remaining 3 tablespoons of butter in a medium saucepan over medium-low heat. Whisk in the flour and let bubble without browning for a couple of minutes. Gradually whisk in the milk. Increase the heat to medium and bring to a boil, whisking constantly. Remove from the heat and cool slightly. One at a time, whisk in the yolks, then stir in the beet tops.

Beat the egg whites in a medium bowl until they form soft peaks. Stir about one-quarter of the whites into the sauce, then fold in the remainder. Pour over the beets in the dish. Bake until puffed and golden brown, about 30 minutes. Serve immediately, while the soufflé is still puffed.

Brussels Sprouts with Glazed Pecans

Makes 6 servings

⌒

Brussels sprouts are at their best after a few hard, late fall frosts. The cold weather smoothes out the rough edges of flavor and gives the sprouts a mellow sweetness. As a change of pace to buttered sprouts, this festive dish is very appropriate for a holiday dinner.

½ cup pecans, toasted (see page 12)

4 tablespoons (½ stick) unsalted butter

1 tablespoon sugar

½ teaspoon ground cumin

⅛ teaspoon cayenne pepper

1 pound Brussels sprouts, root ends
   trimmed, discolored leaves
   discarded, and a shallow X cut
   into the bottom of each sprout

Zest of 1 large orange

Salt and freshly ground pepper,
   to taste

Toast the pecans, remove from the oven, and toss with 1 tablespoon of the butter, the sugar, cumin, and cayenne. Set aside.

Meanwhile, bring a large pot of lightly salted water to a boil over high heat. Add the sprouts and cook until barely tender, about 8 minutes. Drain well. Return to the pot and toss with 3 tablespoons of the butter. Add the spiced nuts and mix. Season with the orange zest and the salt and pepper. Serve hot.

Pattypan Squash with Ricotta Stuffing

Makes 4 servings

⌒

Pattypan squash are easy to find at the local summer farm stand or farmers' market. If you want some to grow in your kitchen garden, the Sunburst variety has the best flavor. Here squash is stuffed with a light cheese filling that is accented with corn, radishes, and scallions—they'll look like large flowers with puffy centers.

**4 medium pattypan squash, preferably
   Sunburst variety**
1 cup ricotta cheese
**½ cup grated sharp Cheddar cheese,
   preferably Vermont Cheddar**
**1 cup fresh or frozen corn kernels,
   cooked**
2 tablespoons finely chopped radishes
**2 tablespoons finely chopped scallions
   or fresh chives**
1 tablespoon chopped fresh parsley
**Salt and freshly ground pepper or cayenne
   pepper, to taste**

Position a rack in the center of the oven and preheat to 400°F.

Meanwhile, place a collapsible vegetable steamer in a large pot. Add enough water to reach the bottom of the steamer. Place the squash in the steamer, cover tightly, and bring to a boil over high heat. Steam the squash for 5 minutes until tender when pierced with the tip of a sharp knife, yet still firm. If squash are particularly small, be sure not to overcook them. Remove the squash from the pot and rinse under cold water until easy to handle. Using a spoon or a melon baller, scoop out a 2-inch-wide opening from the center of each squash, like a doughnut hole, out of the middle.

Mix the ricotta and Cheddar in a medium bowl, then stir in the corn, radishes, scallions, and parsley. Season with the salt and pepper. Stuff each squash with a heaping mound of the cheese mixture.

Place in shallow baking dish and tent with foil, being sure that the foil doesn't touch the cheese. Bake for 20 minutes. Uncover and continue baking until the squash are tender and the stuffing is lightly browned, about 20 minutes. Serve hot.

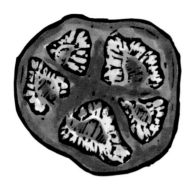

Sweet Baked Tomatoes

Makes 4 servings

Baking brings out the sugar in tomatoes, giving them a natural sweetness. Make this dish at the end of tomato season when the tomatoes are bursting with flavor and the weather is beginning to turn cool enough that you won't mind turning on the oven. For a striking and delicious presentation, bake a variety of colored tomatoes in the same dish. We use heirloom varieties like the orange and yellow Big Rainbow and the striped Green Zebra, which remains green even when fully ripe.

¼ cup olive oil

¾ cup cubed French or Italian bread, cut into ¼-inch dice

4 large ripe tomatoes, preferably a combination of colors

1 tablespoon unsalted butter, cut into small cubes

1 garlic clove, cut into slivers

Salt and freshly ground pepper, to taste

6 fresh basil leaves, finely sliced

Position a rack in the center of the oven and preheat to 350°F.

Heat the oil in a large skillet over medium-high heat. Add the bread cubes and cook, stirring often, until lightly browned, about 5 minutes.

Slice the tops off the tomatoes. Gently poke out and discard the seed pockets with their juice. Place the tomatoes in a small baking dish, just large enough to hold them. Distribute the butter and garlic evenly among the tomatoes, pressing them deep in the cavities. Season with the salt and pepper. Top with the bread cubes.

Bake until the tomatoes are tender and lightly browned around the edges, about 30 minutes.

Fried Green Tomatoes in Cornmeal-Thyme Crust

Makes 4 servings

Every gardener is familiar with the problem of green tomatoes at the end of the summer and with the temptation to toss them into the compost pile. The ones that have a hint of color can be allowed to ripen on a sunny windowsill, but that still usually leaves plenty of hard, completely green tomatoes to be fried up for breakfast or lunch. This method uses the traditional cornmeal crust, enlivened by a dash of fresh thyme. These are best served piping hot from the skillet, so cook and serve in batches, or set yourself up with an extra skillet.

6 medium green tomatoes, cored and cut into
   ½-inch thick rounds
1½ cups milk
1 cup yellow cornmeal
½ cup unbleached all-purpose flour
2 teaspoons finely chopped fresh thyme
1 teaspoon fine sea salt
¼ teaspoon freshly ground pepper
½ teaspoon cayenne pepper
½ cup olive oil

Soak the tomato slices in the milk in a shallow dish for a few minutes. Combine the cornmeal, flour, thyme, salt, pepper, and cayenne in another shallow dish. Dip the tomatoes on both sides in the cornmeal mixture, patting to help the crust adhere, and place on waxed paper. Let stand while the oil heats to help set the crust.

Heat the oil in a large skillet, preferably cast iron, over medium-high heat. In batches without crowding, add the tomatoes and cook, turning once, until golden, about 2 minutes per side. Using a slotted spatula, transfer the tomatoes to paper towels to drain. Serve hot.

Vegetarian Egg Rolls with Savoy Cabbage Filling

Makes about 20 egg rolls

Savoy cabbage is surely one of the most beautiful vegetables in the garden. It is so attractive that I find it hard to harvest. Usually sliced and served in a slaw, Savoy cabbage is also a great substitute for the traditional Chinese cabbage in egg rolls. Although they will no longer be vegetarian, add 1 pound ground pork or beef, cooked and well drained, to the filling with the bean sprouts.

FILLING

2 tablespoons vegetable oil, plus more for deep-frying

1 medium leek, white and pale green parts only, coarsely chopped

2 garlic cloves, minced

3 medium celery ribs, coarsely chopped

1 medium red bell pepper, seeded and cut into ¼-inch-thick strips

1 tablespoon grated fresh ginger (use the large holes on a box grater)

1 small head shredded Savoy cabbage (6 cups)

2 tablespoons rice wine or sherry vinegar

2 tablespoons soy sauce

3 cups fresh mung bean sprouts, rinsed and drained

20 egg roll wrappers

2 tablespoons cornstarch mixed with water to make a thin paste, for closing the rolls

Plum sauce, duck sauce, and hot mustard, for dipping

To make the filling, heat the 2 tablespoons of oil in a large skillet or wok over high heat. Add the leek and garlic and stir-fry until the leeks are golden, about 4 minutes. Add the celery, red pepper, and ginger and stir-fry until softened, about 2 minutes. Add the cabbage and cook, stirring often, until tender, about 7 minutes. Mix in the vinegar and soy sauce. Transfer to a large colander and let stand to drain and cool. Mix in the bean sprouts.

Position an egg roll on a work surface with the points at 12, 3, 6, and 9 o'clock. Place about ¼ cup of the cooled filling just below the center of the wrapper. Fold in the points at 3 and 9 o'clock, and roll up from the bottom to form a cylinder, moistening the top point with the cornstarch paste to make it adhere. Place the egg roll seam side down on a wire cake rack. Repeat with the remaining filling and wrappers. Let stand for 10 minutes before frying.

Pour enough oil into a large saucepan to come 2 inches up the sides and heat over high

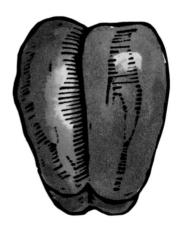

heat to 350°F. Preheat the oven to 200°F. Place a metal colander on a rimmed baking sheet and have ready next to the stove.

In batches without crowding, deep-fry the egg rolls until crisp and golden, 1 to 2 minutes. Using a slotted spoon, carefully transfer the fried rolls to the colander to drain. Place the drained rolls on a baking sheet and keep warm in the oven while frying the remaining rolls. Serve hot, with small bowls of the plum sauce, duck sauce, and hot mustard for dipping.

BAKED EGG ROLLS. Arrange the egg rolls on a lightly oiled baking sheet and brush lightly with vegetable oil. Bake in a preheated 375°F oven until golden brown, about 30 minutes.

Sweet Onions Stuffed with Parsnip Purée

Makes 4 servings

You will find sharp-flavored onions for cooking every day of the year in the market, but true sweet onions are harvested only in the summer. Sweet onions, such as the famous Vidalia and Walla Walla varieties, are low in sulfur and tear-free, and their mild personality really shines in salads. They are also great stuffed, and here they are paired with parsnips, another vegetable famous for sweetness. This dish is a stunning showcase for the beauty of the vegetable form.

4 tablespoons (½ stick) unsalted butter
2 pounds parsnips, peeled and cut into
    ½-inch-thick rounds
1 cup Vegetable Broth (page 27) or
    Chicken Stock (page 29)
Salt and freshly ground pepper, to taste
4 large sweet onions, such as Vidalia, Walla
    Walla, Maui, or Texas Sweet, peeled
½ teaspoon finely chopped fresh sage
½ teaspoon finely chopped fresh thyme
Olive oil, as needed
½ cup shredded sharp Cheddar cheese,
    preferably Vermont Cheddar

Trim the root end from each onion so it sits flat. Cut off the top inch from each onion and reserve. Using a paring knife or a grapefruit spoon, scoop out the inside of each onion to make a ¾-inch-thick shell.

Melt 2 tablespoons of the butter in a medium saucepan over medium-high heat. Add the parsnips and cook, stirring often, until softened, about 5 minutes. Add the broth, cover, and bring to a boil. Cook until the parsnips are tender and have absorbed most of the liquid, about 20 minutes. Transfer to a food processor and purée. Season with the salt and pepper.

Position a rack in the center of the oven and preheat to 350°F. Lightly oil a baking sheet.

Arrange the onions on the baking sheet. Cut the remaining 2 tablespoons of butter into small cubes and dot the onion cavities with the butter. Sprinkle with equal amounts of the sage and thyme. Fill the cavities with the purée.

Bake until the onions are tender when pierced with the tip of a sharp knife, about 1 hour. During the last 10 minutes of baking, top each onion with the shredded cheese. Serve hot.

Cardoons au Gratin

Makes 4 servings

Cooks grow cardoons for the stalks, which have a subtle artichoke flavor. But they are also outstanding, four-foot-tall ornamental plants with magnificent notched, silvery leaves that form a massive backdrop to fall asters and the hardier perennials. Outside your own kitchen garden, cardoons can be found in the cooler months at well-stocked grocers and markets with an Italian clientele, who often serve cardoons baked in a creamy cheese sauce. Thick Swiss chard ribs can also be prepared in this way, blanched just until tender.

1 pound cardoon stalks, rinsed clean and towel dried

3 tablespoons unsalted butter

2 tablespoons unbleached all-purpose flour

1 cup milk, heated

½ cup grated sharp Cheddar cheese, preferably Vermont Cheddar

Salt and freshly ground pepper, to taste

¼ cup freshly grated Parmesan cheese

¼ cup dried bread crumbs

Position a rack in the center of the oven and preheat to 375°F. Lightly butter an 11½- × 8-inch baking dish.

Trim off the leaves from the cardoons. If the stalks have tough strings, pull them off. Cut into 4-inch lengths. Bring a large pot of lightly salted water to a boil over high heat. Add the cardoons and cook until tender, about 10 minutes. Drain and pat dry.

Melt the butter in a small saucepan over medium-low heat. Whisk in the flour and let bubble without browning for about 2 minutes. Gradually whisk in the milk and bring to a simmer. Remove from the heat and stir in the Cheddar cheese. Season with the salt and pepper.

Spread the bottom of the baking dish with a tablespoon or so of the sauce. Arrange half of the cardoons in the dish, spread with half the sauce, and sprinkle with half of the Parmesan cheese. Repeat with the remaining cardoons, sauce, and Parmesan. Sprinkle with the bread crumbs.

Bake until the top is golden brown, about 20 minutes.

Creamy Kohlrabi

Makes 4 servings

To many good cooks, kohlrabi is an odd vegetable. The green knobs look like turnips, but its sweet flavor is its own, although it might remind some people of broccoli. Young tender kohlrabi can be sliced or shredded and served raw in salads; larger ones do well when creamed. But I have to warn you—this dish is supposed to serve four people, but it is so delicious is just might serve only two.

2 large kohlrabi

I teaspoon fine sea salt, plus more to taste

4 tablespoons (½ stick) unsalted butter

I small onion, sliced into thin half-moons

3 tablespoons heavy cream

⅛ teaspoon dried marjoram

Freshly ground pepper, to taste

Strip the top and root ends from the kohlrabi. Using a paring knife, remove the skin. Grate the kohlrabi on the large holes of a box grater or in a food processor fitted with the grating disk. You should have about 4 cups. Toss in a colander with the salt. Let stand in a sink to drain off juices, about 30 minutes. Rinse well under cold water. A handful at a time, squeeze out the excess liquid.

Melt the butter in a medium skillet over medium heat. Add the kohlrabi and the sliced onion and cover. Cook, stirring occasionally, until the onion is softened, about 5 minutes. Uncover and cook, stirring occasionally, until the kohlrabi is golden brown, about 5 minutes. Stir in the cream and marjoram and cook until the cream is absorbed, about I minute. Season with the salt and pepper, being careful with the salt. Serve hot.

Glazed Cipolline Onions

Makes 4 to 6 servings

Serve a spoonful of these tasty onions alongside roast chicken or even grilled salmon. The small, flat cipolline onions are attractive and unusual, but familiar white boiling onions can be substituted.

2 dozen cipolline or white boiling onions
3 tablespoons unsalted butter
Salt, to taste
2 tablespoons brown sugar
1 tablespoon balsamic vinegar

Bring a large pot of water to a boil over high heat. Add the onions and cook to loosen the skins, about 3 minutes. Drain and rinse under cold water. Trim the tops and root ends from the onions, and remove the peel.

Mix ½ cup water, 1 tablespoon of the butter, and a pinch of salt in a skillet large enough to hold the onions in one layer. Add the onions and bring the mixture to a boil over high heat. Cover tightly and reduce the heat to low. Simmer, adding a bit more water if needed, until the liquid has evaporated and the onions are tender when pierced with the tip of a sharp knife, about 15 minutes. If any liquid remains, uncover and cook until it does evaporate.

Stir the brown sugar, remaining 2 tablespoons butter, and the vinegar in a medium saucepan over medium heat until the mixture is melted and smooth, about 2 minutes. Add the onions and mix gently to coat. Serve warm.

Mashed Turnips with Apples

Makes 4 servings

Gilfeather turnips, named by the Vermont family who has handed the variety down through several generations, are the biggest and best available. The large white roots have green shoulders, a fine texture, and a sweet flavor—it has become our favorite turnip. No matter what variety you use, this easy dish is a wonderful addition to the holiday table. In fact, in New England, it isn't Thanksgiving without a bowl of turnips!

1 large Gilfeather turnip or 2 large
    traditional white turnips, peeled,
    and cut into 1½-inch chunks
1 tablespoon olive oil
2 large McIntosh apples, peeled,
    cored, and cut into 1-inch chunks
¼ teaspoon freshly grated nutmeg
    or ground cinnamon

Place a collapsible vegetable steamer in a large saucepan and add enough cold water to reach the bottom of the steamer. Add the turnip, cover tightly, and bring to a boil over high heat. Reduce the heat to medium and cook until the turnip is very tender, about 30 minutes. Drain well. Transfer to a food processor and purée.

Meanwhile, heat the oil in a large skillet over medium-high heat. Add the apple and cook, stirring occasionally, until golden brown and tender, about 5 minutes. Add the turnip purée and the nutmeg, and mix well. Serve hot.

Caramelized Shallot Timbales

Makes 8 servings

Deeply colored and intensely flavored, caramelized shallots give these individual custards the color and texture of a pâté and an extraordinary flavor that is hard to identify at the first taste. Serve them with rich game birds, such as roast duck or goose.

1 tablespoon olive oil

12 shallots (about 12 ounces),
    peeled but whole

1 cup Vegetable Broth (page 27)
    or water

1 teaspoon finely chopped fresh sage

1 tablespoon sugar

1½ tablespoons dry sherry

1½ cups heavy cream

4 large eggs

4 large egg yolks

¼ teaspoon fine sea salt

⅛ teaspoon freshly ground pepper

Small sprigs of fresh parsley,
    for garnish

Heat the oil in a medium skillet over low heat. Add the shallots and cook, stirring often, until the shallots are golden brown on all sides, about 30 minutes. Add the broth and sage and increase the heat to medium. Cook at a rapid simmer, stirring occasionally, until the liquid has evaporated and the shallots are tender, about 10 minutes. Sprinkle with the sugar and cook, occasionally shaking the pan, until the shallots are glazed, about 1 minute. Sprinkle in the sherry. Scrape the shallots and their juices into a blender and purée. You should have about ½ cup shallot purée.

Position a rack in the center of the oven and preheat to 350°F. Lightly butter eight 4-ounce ramekins.

Process the cream, eggs, yolks, shallot purée, salt, and pepper until well combined. Pour equal quantities of the mixture into the ramekins. Place the ramekins in a large roasting pan. Pour enough hot water to come halfway up the sides of the ramekins. Cover the entire pan loosely with aluminum foil. Bake until the custards are set when given a slight shake, about 20 minutes. Let stand 5 minutes. Run a knife around the inside of each ramekin and invert to unmold. Garnish each ramekin with parsley, and serve hot.

Spinach and Vermont Cheddar Custard

Makes 4 servings

As you must have noticed by now, I am a big fan of our local Vermont cheese. This high-quality cheese adds so much flavor to the simplest dishes. Cheddar and spinach are old friends, and are beautifully combined in this delicate custard. A lovely side dish, it would also make a fine brunch entrée. For a custard that is intensely rich in color and flavor, use farm-fresh eggs from free-range chickens.

8 ounces fresh spinach leaves, stemmed and
    well rinsed (3 cups packed)
1 cup heavy cream
4 large egg yolks
1 cup shredded sharp Cheddar cheese,
    preferably Vermont Cheddar
¼ teaspoon salt
⅛ teaspoon freshly ground pepper
⅛ teaspoon freshly grated nutmeg

Position a rack in the center of the oven and preheat to 325°F. Lightly butter four 4-ounce ramekins.

Bring a large pot of lightly salted water to a boil over high heat. Add the spinach and cook until tender, about 5 minutes. Drain and rinse under cold water. A handful at a time, squeeze out the excess moisture from the spinach. Chop coarsely. You should have about 1 cup chopped spinach.

Whisk the cream and yolks in a medium bowl until well combined. Stir in the spinach, cheese, salt, pepper, and nutmeg. Ladle or pour equal quantities of the custard into the ramekins. Place the ramekins in a large roasting pan. Add enough hot water to come about halfway up the sides of the ramekins.

Bake until the custards are set when given a slight shake, about 25 minutes. Let stand 5 minutes. Run a knife around the inside of each ramekin and invert to unmold. Serve hot.

The Dirt on Potatoes . . .

You've heard about comparing apples and oranges, but it's time to compare apples and potatoes. The average apple and potato each contains 100 calories, but the potato has twice as much iron, the same amount of calcium, and thirteen times as much ascorbic acid. Yet no one ever says "a potato a day keeps the doctor away."

Cooks are careful to choose just the right apple for their pies and apple sauce. What about the potato? It also comes in many varieties and in a kaleidoscope of colors, flavors, textures, and cooking requirements. It is important to choose the right potato for the recipe.

There are two main categories for potatoes, starchy and waxy. A few varieties have intermediate qualities and show up on both lists.

HIGH-STARCH POTATOES. Perfect for baking, sautéing, and deep-frying, high-starch potatoes hold together well, with a dry, mealy flesh when cooked. Most have a thick skin, but some thin-skinned varieties exist—just don't try to boil them or they will fall apart.

WAXY POTATOES. With a low starch content and a flesh that remains moist and cohesive after cooking, waxy potatoes are best for boiling. Thin-skinned varieties (often erroneously called "new" potatoes, a term that should apply to the small, young potatoes of a harvest) are always a good choice for boiling and salads. They are also good for tossing with olive oil and roasting, or sautéing as home fries.

It used to be that growing your own was the only way to try some of the fascinating range of potatoes, but now many specialty markets stock a range of heirloom potatoes. Some of our favorites are All-blue, Yukon Gold, Fingerling and Banana types, Yellow Finns, and any kind of red-skinned new potato. The best way to tell what kind of potato you have is to cut it in half and if the knife retains a gluey foamy substance, it most likely is a high starch and good for baking, while the boilers would retain a cleaner cut.

- Leftover mashed potatoes are not only good for breakfast, heated up with a bit of butter in a skillet, but they also can be used in bread making and to thicken soup.
- Beat leftover mashed potatoes with an egg and dip in bread crumbs for a delicate and elegant potato pancake.

- Mashed potatoes can be the base for wonderful combinations with other cooked and puréed vegetables such as carrot, parsnip, turnips, celeriac, and roasted garlic (page 38). Boil the vegetables separately and combine while hot.

Mashed Potatoes

Makes 4 to 6 servings

Mashed potatoes, a mainstay in any house with small children, are best made with starchy potatoes, yet any potato will do. Scrub them clean and cook with skins on in order to maintain optimum nutrients. Potato water can be reused to thin the potatoes as a low-fat substitute for milk, or reserve as stock for soups or other sauces. While there is not much flavor left in the potato water, the vitamin and mineral content is high. All kinds of variations for mashed potatoes exist, so use the following as a basic formula.

2 to 3 pounds potatoes

2 teaspoons fine sea salt

4 to 6 tablespoons (¼ to ¾ stick) unsalted butter

1 cup milk or half-and-half

¼ teaspoon freshly ground pepper

Scrub the potatoes clean and place in a kettle with water to cover. Sprinkle with 1 teaspoon of the salt, cover the pot, and bring to a boil. Simmer for 30 minutes, until the potato skins crack open and a sharp knife can easily pierce through a potato. Drain in a colander. If the potatoes are unusually moist, transfer back to the pan and stir for a few minutes over medium heat.

Heat the milk to just below boiling, pour over the potatoes, along with the butter, salt, and the remaining pepper. Mash with a pronged potato masher, a hand-held blender, or a large wooden spoon until smooth and then whip until creamy. (Do not use a food processor, which will result in gluey potatoes.) Serve hot.

Warm Fingerling Potato and Snap Bean Salad

Makes 6 to 8 servings

〰

Fingerling potatoes are highly prized culinary treasures with a tight, creamy flesh. Growing no bigger than an average-sized finger, they are the perfect salad potato. They can be found at farmers' markets, but any red-skinned potato will do. We think the salad works best as a side dish, served warm with, perhaps, grilled or poached fish. It is also very appetizing if allowed to chill overnight. It will surely become a favorite in your family, too.

6 slices bacon

2 pounds Fingerling or small red-skinned potatoes, scrubbed but unpeeled

4 ounces green beans, preferably snap beans, trimmed

⅓ cup basil-flavored vinegar

1 teaspoon Dijon mustard

1 teaspoon whole-grain mustard, such as Moutarde de Meaux

1 garlic clove, minced

½ cup olive oil

¼ cup finely minced fresh herbs, preferably a combination of parsley, summer savory, and chives

1 medium red bell pepper, roasted (see page 40) and cut into ¼-inch-wide strips

¼ cup finely chopped fresh basil, for garnish

Salt and freshly ground pepper, to taste

Cook the bacon in a skillet over medium heat until crisp and brown, about 8 minutes. Using a slotted spatula, transfer to paper towels to drain and cool. Crumble the bacon.

Bring a medium saucepan of lightly salted water to a boil over high heat. Add the potatoes and reduce the heat to medium. Cook until the potatoes are tender, about 10 minutes. Using a skimmer or wire sieve, remove the potatoes from the water. Rinse the potatoes under cold water and set aside to cool slightly. Cut the potatoes into ¼-inch-thick rounds.

Add the green beans to the water and cook until barely tender, about 3 minutes. Drain and rinse under cold water. Cut the beans on the diagonal into 1-inch lengths.

Whisk the vinegar, mustards, and garlic in a wooden salad bowl. Gradually whisk in the oil, add the herbs. Add the potatoes, green beans, and red pepper strips and mix. Mix in the bacon, sprinkle with the basil, and season with the salt and pepper. Serve warm.

Tips for Potato Salad

- For best results, make potato salad with low-starch, waxy potatoes, especially the red-skinned type or a Fingerling type. High-starch baking potatoes will be mealy and crumbly in a salad.

- Don't overcook potatoes for salad. Stick the potatoes with a sharp knife, and if tender, remove from the heat. Try to catch the potatoes just before the skins split, or they could end up mushy. Dress the potatoes while still warm to absorb the dressing.

- To retain the best flavor and nutrients, do not peel the potatoes. If combining different colored potatoes, it's a good idea to boil them separately as they cook at different rates.

- Potatoes can take a lot of seasoning, especially salt. Keep in mind that the potatoes will taste different once they have cooled. Keep tasting and season to taste.

Twice-Baked Potatoes with Savory Green Sauce

Makes 4 servings

⌒

Baked potatoes are a favorite in our family, so we plant four times as many starchy baking potatoes as any other type. Even though they store well in our root cellar, we have usually gone through our entire crop by spring. There may be nothing quite as satisfying as a buttered potato, but this tangy sauce is exceptionally good, and can be served with Herbed Zucchini Pancakes (page 144) or put into service as a dip for crudités. Use whatever greens are abundant in your garden— the combination below is only a suggestion.

6 large baking potatoes, scrubbed, patted dry, and poked several times with a fork
3 tablespoons unsalted butter
½ cup milk or half-and-half
Salt and freshly ground pepper, to taste

SAVORY GREEN SAUCE
2 garlic cloves, peeled
½ cup yogurt or sour cream
1 teaspoon freshly grated horseradish root, or use prepared horseradish
2 cups mixed cooking greens and herbs, such as a combination of fresh spinach, young kale, or mustard greens

Position a rack in the center of the oven and preheat to 450°F. Place the potatoes on a baking sheet. Bake until the potatoes are tender, about 1 hour. Cut each potato in half lengthwise, and scoop out the flesh into a bowl, leaving potato-skin shells. Mash the potato flesh with the butter and milk, and season with the salt and pepper. Refill the shells and, if necessary, return to the oven to keep warm.

In the meantime, make the sauce. Fit a food processor with the metal blade. With the machine running, drop the garlic through the feed tube to mince the garlic. Add the yogurt and horseradish and pulse to combine. Add the greens and process until the greens are puréed. Serve the potatoes hot, with the sauce passed on the side.

Tips for Baked Potatoes

- After digging up potatoes, let them rest on top of the soil in the sun for a day to harden their skins, which helps them keep longer. Do not leave them in the sun for more than a day, or they will turn green and become inedible. Keep some of the soil on the potatoes to retain moisture, and store them in a cool, dark, and dry place. Scrub the potatoes just before cooking.

- Potatoes are one of the best sources of potassium, most of which is found in the skin. Cook potatoes in their skins whenever possible. When potatoes are boiled in their skins, some of the potassium will leach into the water, but most of the vitamins inside the potato will be retained. Save the potato water to add to soups or to cook other vegetables in.

- Leftover baked potatoes make excellent home fries. Chop into small chunks, season with salt, pepper, and rosemary, and sauté in olive oil until golden.

- A timesaving tip for baking potatoes—boil the potato for 10 minutes, drain, and then bake at 400°F for 30 minutes. The flavor won't be affected.

- To avoid soggy potato flesh, prick the skins of potatoes before baking, which allows the steam to escape. Never wrap a potato in aluminum foil, which also holds in the steam. The only time a potato should be wrapped in foil is when it is being roasted on a campfire.

- To reheat a whole baked potato, dip it in water and bake at 350°F for 20 minutes.

Crisp Potato Wedges
with Rosemary

Makes 4 servings

No matter how many of these I make, there are never any leftovers. They can be served at breakfast or brunch with eggs, or as a side dish for poached fish or grilled chops. Choose a potato with moderate starch, such as a Yukon Gold or one of the thin-skinned varieties, and allow two medium-sized potatoes per person.

2 pounds potatoes, such as Yukon Gold
   or red-skinned, scrubbed but not peeled
4 tablespoons olive oil
2 tablespoons unsalted butter
2 garlic cloves, coarsely chopped
1 tablespoon finely chopped fresh rosemary
Salt and freshly ground pepper, to taste

Cut the potatoes into quarters lengthwise, and then into 1-inch chunks. Wrap in a kitchen towel to remove the excess surface moisture.

Heat the oil in a large skillet over medium-high heat. Add the potatoes and cook, stirring often, until the potatoes are golden brown all over, about 25 minutes. Transfer to a serving bowl.

Melt the butter in the skillet. Add the garlic and cook until crisp and golden, about 2 minutes. Mix in the rosemary and pour over the potatoes. Season with the salt and pepper. Serve hot.

Tips for Sautéed Potatoes

- For crispy results, sautéed potatoes should be completely dry before being added to the hot olive oil. Pat them with a kitchen towel before adding to the skillet.
- Add salt and other seasonings near the end of the cooking, as salt will pull moisture from the potatoes and make them soggy.
- For fast and simple potato pancakes, grate high-starch potatoes in a food processor and mix in a beaten egg. Heat olive oil in a large skillet, and add the potato mixture, forming thin pancakes. Fry for about 5 minutes on each side until crisp. Kids love them and they are healthier than French fries.
- Leftover boiled or baked potatoes make excellent crisp home fries for breakfast because their excess moisture has been removed.
- Make amusing sautéed potatoes by cutting out animal or geometric shapes from ½-inch-thick raw potato slices with a miniature cookie cutter. Your kids will love to help.

Tricolor Scalloped Potatoes

Makes 6 servings

The blue potato, a direct descendant of the original potato from the Andes Mountains, is rugged and hardy, and kids love them mashed. In truth, their flavor isn't as good as that of other varieties. To remedy this drawback, we often match them up with their cousins as in this new version of a classic dish with blue, white, and yellow potatoes. Use a food processor, a mandoline, or a plastic slicer to cut the potatoes into rounds of an even thickness.

> 6 tablespoons (¾ stick) unsalted butter, melted
>
> 3 garlic cloves, crushed through a press
>
> 4 medium new potatoes, peeled and cut into ⅛-inch-thick rounds
>
> 2 medium Yukon Gold potatoes, peeled and cut into ⅛-inch-thick rounds
>
> 4 small blue potatoes, peeled and cut into ⅛-inch-thick rounds
>
> 1 teaspoon chopped fresh thyme
>
> 1 teaspoon fine sea salt
>
> ¼ teaspoon freshly ground pepper
>
> 1 cup heavy cream, heated to boiling
>
> 1 cup shredded Gruyère cheese

Position a rack in the center of the oven and preheat to 425°F. Lightly butter a 13- × 9-inch baking dish.

Mix the melted butter with the garlic. Arrange a layer of potatoes, alternating the colors, in the dish. Drizzle with half of the garlic butter and season with half of the thyme, salt, and pepper. Repeat with the remaining potatoes, garlic butter, thyme, salt, and pepper. Pour the heavy cream over the potatoes and sprinkle with the cheese. Cover with foil and bake for 30 minutes.

Uncover and continue to bake until the potatoes are tender when pierced with a fork and the top is a deep golden brown, another 15 minutes. Let stand for a few minutes, then serve hot.

Lemon-Basil Brown Rice

Makes 4 servings

≈

With scented lemon basil in the garden, you will be looking for ways to add its citrus fragrance and gentle flavor to your favorite dishes. This aromatic rice dish can be served alongside many main courses but it really shines with the Grilled Scrod with Mammoth Basil Wrap (page 110). If the combination of lemon and basil appeals to you, but you don't have lemon basil, substitute ¼ cup chopped sweet basil and the grated zest of 1 lemon.

> 2 tablespoons unsalted butter
> ½ cup finely chopped onion
> ½ cup finely chopped red bell pepper
> 1 cup brown rice
> 1 bay leaf
> 2½ cups Chicken Stock (page 29) or water
> ¼ teaspoon fine sea salt
> ½ cup finely chopped fresh lemon basil

Melt the butter in a medium saucepan over medium heat. Add the onion and red pepper and cook until the onion is golden, about 6 minutes. Add the rice and cook, stirring often, until the rice turns a lighter shade, about 3 minutes. Stir in the bay leaf, then the stock and the salt. Bring to a boil.

Cover tightly and reduce the heat to medium low. Simmer until the rice is tender, about 45 minutes. Stir in the chopped lemon basil. Serve hot.

A Passion for Pesto

My deep, unwavering love for pesto is sustained by a large plot of sweet Genovese basil, a European variety renowned for its refined flavor and consistent yield. There are numerous varieties of basil throughout the world, all members of the mint or Lamiaceae family, which includes most of the culinary herbs. In fact, other herbs in the same family, many of which are distinguished by their square stems, include mint, sage, lemon balm, thyme, rosemary, and oregano. There are five distinct categories of basil.

SWEET BASIL. The most familiar and widely grown variety, sweet basil has slightly ridged, bright green leaves that are smooth and shiny. Sweet basils have a strong flavor with an occasional touch of bitterness. It is also easy to harvest by picking leaf clusters from the tops of the stems. Most American seed companies sell common sweet basil, but elite European strains, such as my beloved Genovese, are worth searching out. These are slower to bolt and less likely to become bitter after long cooking in sauces.

BUSH BASIL. Characterized by a bushy plant with tiny aromatic leaves, bush basil is very ornamental, and looks like a dwarf shrub. It is especially suited to container gardening. To harvest, snip off branches and strip off the miniature leaves. The aroma and flavor are exceptional, and many chefs consider bush basil to be the basil of choice for pesto.

PURPLE BASIL. So striking is purple basil that some gardeners grow it purely as an ornamental; it does look great as a contrast to gray-leafed plants such as artemisia in a garden border. Opal basil, with dark purple leaves and soft lavender flowers, was the first to make a double impression in the garden and the kitchen. Use the leaves and flowers in salads, or steep the leaves to make a colorful basil vinegar.

LETTUCE-LEAF BASIL. Otherwise known as mammoth basil. With large, wide leaves and a milder flavor than other basils, this variety is useful for salads or to wrap around fish fillets before grilling (see Grilled Scrod with Mammoth Basil Wrap on page 110). Lettuce-leaf basil needs lots of space, as much as 12 inches between plants. Cold water can cause black spots on the leaves, so take care in watering.

SCENTED BASIL. These basils have a distinct perfumed aroma that is often reminiscent of other edible plants. Cinnamon basil, lemon basil, and anise basil all smell strongly of their eponymous foods, but the flavors remain basil-like. Use scented basil in place of regular basil whenever you want a hint of something different.

Basil Pesto

Makes about 1½ cups

⸙

The first time I made pesto was a pivotal moment in my cooking life. I have been hooked on sweet basil ever since. I have added a bit of lemon juice to the classic recipe, which brightens the flavor even more. Pesto has many uses that go beyond pasta. Spoon it over steamed vegetables, turn it into a marinade for chicken or fish, or use it as a dip for crudités or crusty bread. Use this basic recipe for your own variations, adding a bit of scented basil, oregano, rosemary, or other herbs as you wish.

This makes enough pesto for one pound of pasta. When draining the pasta, reserve a few tablespoons of the cooking water. When tossing the pasta with the pesto, add the cooking water to dilute the pesto and make it cling better to the pasta.

> 4 garlic cloves
> 2 cups packed fresh basil leaves,
>   well rinsed and towel dried
> 1 cup packed fresh Italian flat-leaf parsley
> ¼ cup pine nuts, toasted (page 55)
> ¼ cup fresh lemon juice
> ¾ cup extra virgin olive oil
> ¼ cup freshly grated Parmesan cheese
> Salt and freshly ground pepper,
>   to taste

With the machine running, drop the garlic through the feed tube of a food processor fitted with the metal blade to chop the garlic. Add the basil, parsley, pine nuts, and lemon juice and purée. With the machine running, slowly add the oil to make a creamy paste. Add the cheese and pulse to combine. Season with the salt and pepper. (The pesto can be made up to 2 weeks ahead, transferred to a covered container, topped off with a thin layer of olive oil to cover the surface, and refrigerated. Use at room temperature.)

Letter from the Garden

After twenty years of gardening in Vermont, we thought we understood the rhythms of the seasons. Then, one autumn, the first frost simply refused to come. When it did arrive, it was a full month later than the usual first nip, later than anyone in our valley could recall. Oddly, the previous spring was also the latest in memory, so cold and rainy that we couldn't even plant our peas until mid-May.

Yet, in the end, we had an average season. The whole affair showed us that the observations of gardeners who are working outside in the elements are much more important than records of average seasonal temperatures. By the time the tomatoes started to roll in during the short, hot days of August, we had forgotten the long weeks of spring, waiting for the ground to dry out. Folks in Vermont still talk about the summer of 1816, when the weather was so cold summer *never* arrived.

When global warming truly takes place, it will sneak up on us. It will not be so much an actual warming of the earth as a reshuffling of the climatic deck, an overall increase in the craziness and variability of the seasons.

The year of our late frost was also one of the wettest on record, but that followed one of the driest years. A gardener can easily forget that he can't really count on any monthly or yearly weather pattern; gardening is a constant gamble.

Breads, Pizzas, and Muffins

*P*lanting a garden and baking bread are excellent ways to express creativity and establish an individual style. A gardener begins with seeds, plants, and soil; a baker with flour, yeast, and water, materials available to everyone. But it is the individual talents of each gardener or baker, usually gained through experience, that transform the basic components into something extraordinary.

With their colorful display cases, bakeries may tempt us away from baking our own yeast breads and even quick breads, muffins, and other goodies. The tactile pleasure of baking, combined with the aromas that fill the kitchen, are treats that go beyond the wholesome flavors that settle in your mouth. Home-baked bread is one of the best ways to bring your garden into your kitchen. Just about any bread recipe is enhanced with the produce of a garden: a snip of fresh herbs, a cup of puréed winter squash substituted for an equal amount of liquid, or a helping of pesto swirled through a yeast bread.

Tips for Breads, Pizzas, and Muffins

Rolling up your sleeves and kneading soft, pliable dough is one of the great joys of baking. There is nothing to making bread by hand—mix the liquids and dissolved yeast in a big bowl, stir in flour until the dough is too stiff to add any more, and knead on a work surface until the dough is smooth and springy. Some people may prefer to use a heavy-duty electric mixer or a food processor, which is what I use to mix small-batch doughs such as pizza, but the bowls of most processors are too small to hold the ingredients for most recipes.

- Unbleached all-purpose flour has a high gluten content that makes it my first choice for yeast breads. Gluten is the protein combination in wheat that gives structure to baked goods, and unbleached flour helps make crusty bread with a chewy crumb. Some cooks suggest flour with moderate or low gluten content for sweet baked goods, such as pies, muffins, and cakes, but these flours are almost always chemically bleached. I prefer the superior wheat flavor and nutritional value of unbleached flour for my baking. I also like to bake with spelt flour, milled from an ancient strain of wheat, which is an alternative for those with wheat intolerance.

- Active dry yeast, if properly stored in a tight-fitting container in the refrigerator, can keep for up to one year, but to be certain, proof your yeast before baking, especially in warm water.

- Some markets now carry only quick-rising yeasts. To take advantage of the rapid rise, follow the instructions on the package. But the more slowly a bread rises, the better it tastes. So, if you must use quick-rising yeast but wish to slow down the process, simply reduce the amount of the yeast you use by about one-third. For example, if a recipe calls for $2\frac{1}{4}$ teaspoons of quick-rising yeast, use $1\frac{1}{2}$ teaspoons of active dry yeast.

- The "warm place" for bread means an ideal temperature of 78°F. This temperature can usually be found near a turned-on stove or in a furnace room with a hot water heater.

- How can you tell when a dough has "doubled in volume"? Poke a finger about $\frac{1}{2}$ inch into the dough. If the indentation stays, the dough is ready.

- Cover the dough with a moist kitchen towel to keep it from drying out.

- Preheat the oven thoroughly before baking. Most ovens take at least 20 minutes to reach the correct temperature. A good oven thermometer is a worthwhile purchase and will give a more accurate reading.

Letter from the Garden

One thing that makes The Cook's Garden different is that we aren't just a catalogue company, but gardeners first and last. We maintain both trial gardens and display gardens just to give our customers an opportunity to see some of the more unusual vegetables and flowers we offer.

The trial gardens are located in Burlington, Vermont, near where the Winooski River empties into Lake Champlain. If you are in the Burlington area anytime between April and October, please stop by for a look around. Each year the garden looks a little different, partly due to the weather conditions, but more likely because there are so many new vegetables and flowers we want to try. Visitors will always find a maze for the children (and the young at heart) made from bamboo trellis as the basic structure. The entrance is indicated by the vine plants (such as tomatoes, morning glories, hyacinth beans, and sunflowers) we've tucked into the portal. It's a good spot to find shade on a hot day, the hay bales providing a place for a quick nap.

We hold an open house every year to determine which varieties to choose for the following year's catalogue. Samples of all the vegetables, herbs, and fruit that we grow in the trial gardens are harvested, cut into bite-sized pieces, and set up on plates that cover several long tables.

We distribute surveys for comments, and evaluate them to pick the winners.

In 1990, May was especially rainy and cool. We had sixteen cloudy days during the first three weeks, and eight inches of rain. The corn rotted before it could germinate, and by the time we were sure it wasn't going to come up, it was too late to plant more.

So, we got rid of the corn, and replaced it with four dozen varieties of tomato, about thirty kinds of pepper, and another three dozen varieties of eggplant. This was in addition to around one hundred kinds of lettuce and two dozen types each of leek and onion. As soon as the first frost-free date passed (which in these northern climes can be the first week of June), we put in twenty different melons. It is unusual for us to be able to harvest ripe melons, but that year's bumper crop was the highlight of our August tasting event.

Spicy Cheddar Wafers

Makes about 6 dozen thin wafers

Vermont is home to many fine artisan cheese makers who make a wide range of high-quality products. This cracker, which uses the justly famous Vermont Cheddar, may be thin, but it is packed with flavor.

> 1 cup unbleached all-purpose flour
> ¼ cup sesame seeds or poppy seeds
> 1 tablespoon seeded and minced fresh hot chile, such as serrano or jalapeño
> ¾ teaspoon baking powder
> ¾ teaspoon fine sea salt
> ¼ teaspoon freshly ground pepper
> 6 tablespoons (¾ stick) unsalted butter, chilled, cut into 12 pieces
> 2 cups shredded extra-sharp Vermont Cheddar

Pulse the flour, seeds, chile, baking powder, salt, and pepper in a food processor fitted with the metal blade to combine. With the machine running, add the butter, one piece at a time. Add the cheese and pulse until the mixture resembles coarse cornmeal. Sprinkle with 2 tablespoons cold water and pulse just until the mixture starts to form a ball, adding more water if needed.

Gather up the dough and divide into two equal portions. On a lightly floured work surface, form each portion into a 10-inch-long log and wrap each log in waxed paper. Refrigerate until well chilled, at least 2 hours or overnight.

Position the racks in the center and top third of the oven and preheat to 425°F. Cut the logs into ¼-inch-thick rounds, and arrange 1 inch apart on ungreased baking sheets. Bake until the wafers are golden brown (the top rack will probably brown first), about 10 minutes. Cool briefly on the sheets, then transfer to wire cake racks to cool completely. Store the wafers in an airtight container in a cool, dry place for up to 1 week.

HERBED CHEDDAR WAFERS. Add 1 teaspoon dried thyme, oregano, or marjoram to the flour mixture. Omit the chile, if you wish.

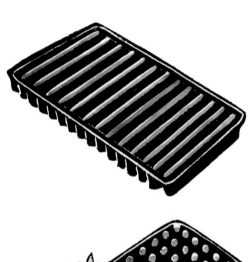

Cheddar, Chile, and Corn Muffins

Makes 12 muffins

A single hot pepper plant will produce a profusion of firecrackerlike chiles. We plant a wide variety, including jalapeño, habanero, serrano, Anaheim, and cayenne, as well as the incendiary, tiny Thai pepper, which is also an attractive indoor ornamental. Coming up with recipes to use them all is easy because we love chiles. These chile-dotted muffins have pockets of melted cheese, and are ideal for serving with chili or the Fiesta Black Bean and Tomato Soup on page 20. You can use any chile you have on hand, adjusting the amount to taste, as each pepper has a different heat level.

1¼ cups unbleached all-purpose flour

1 cup yellow cornmeal

½ cup whole wheat flour

1 teaspoon baking powder

½ teaspoon baking soda

½ teaspoon fine sea salt

1 cup corn kernels, fresh or thawed frozen

1 cup milk

2 large eggs, beaten

5 tablespoons (½ stick plus 1 tablespoon) unsalted butter, melted, plus additional for brushing the muffin tins

½ cup grated sharp Cheddar cheese (4 ounces), preferably Vermont Cheddar

1 jalapeño chile, seeded and cut into very thin ribbons (see Note)

Position a rack in the center of the oven and preheat to 400°F. Brush the insides of 12 muffin tins with melted butter.

Mix the all-purpose flour, cornmeal, whole wheat flour, baking powder, baking soda, and salt in a medium bowl. Make a well in the center, and add the corn, milk, and eggs. Stir the liquids into the dry ingredients just until the batter is barely mixed—it will still be lumpy. Add the melted butter and fold gently just until combined. Take care not to overmix or the muffins will not rise evenly.

Spoon a heaping tablespoon of the batter into each cup. Sprinkle equal amounts of the cheese and the chile over the batter, taking care that the cheese doesn't touch the sides of the cup. Top each with equal amounts of the remaining batter. Smooth the batter in each cup with the back of a spoon to be sure that the batter covers the cheese on the sides of the cup.

Bake until the muffins are golden brown, about 30 minutes. Cool in the pan for 5 minutes, then remove from the cups and serve hot.

NOTE: Chiles contain volatile oils that can be irritating to your skin and mucous membranes. Be careful not to rub your eyes after handling them. If your skin is very sensitive, wear rubber gloves. To slice the chile into ribbons, use a very sharp knife, or even a pair of kitchen scissors.

Summer Berry Muffins

Makes 24 muffins

These cakelike muffins could easily be on the breakfast menu every morning during the height of the summer. As they're made with the berries that grow easily in our garden, I can have a batch mixed and baked in less than an hour. You can make them with all blueberries, if you wish; however, raspberries and chopped strawberries give off quite a bit of juice and could dilute the batter if used in higher proportions. This makes a big batch and while the recipe is easy to divide in half, you'll be happy to have the leftovers in your freezer for another time.

Vegetable oil, for brushing the muffin tins

4 cups unbleached flour

1 tablespoon plus 1 teaspoon baking powder

½ teaspoon ground cinnamon

2 cups granulated sugar

8 tablespoons (1 stick) unsalted butter, at room temperature

4 large eggs, at room temperature

2 teaspoons vanilla extract

1 cup milk

1½ cups blueberries

½ cup raspberries

½ cup hulled and coarsely chopped strawberries

¼ cup raw granulated sugar, or use additional granulated sugar, for topping

Position a rack in the center of the oven and preheat to 375°F. Lightly brush 12 muffin tins with vegetable oil.

Mix the flour, baking powder, and cinnamon to combine. Beat the sugar and butter in a large bowl with an electric mixer on high speed until light and fluffy, about 3 minutes. One at a time, beat in the eggs, then the vanilla. Beginning with the flour, in three additions, use a spoon to stir in alternating portions of the flour and milk, mixing just until smooth. (You can use the mixer on low speed, but do not overmix.) Fold in the berries. Spoon into the muffin tins, filling each tin three-quarters full. Sprinkle the tops with the raw sugar.

Bake until the muffins are golden brown and a toothpick inserted in the center comes out clean, about 35 minutes. Cool in the pan on a wire rack for 5 minutes, then unmold the muffins. Serve warm, or cool to room temperature.

Rhubarb Streusel Coffee Cake

Makes 8 servings

Rhubarb, a reliable perennial, rewards the gardener with ample fruit from early spring until strawberry season, which in our area is the first week of July. Rhubarb cake, with a nice sweet and sour balance between the crumb topping and the fruit, is especially good as a morning treat. To preserve rhubarb for winter use, chop the stalks into 1-inch pieces and freeze in self-sealing bags.

1¼ cups milk

1 tablespoon white distilled or cider vinegar

2¼ cups unbleached all-purpose flour

1 teaspoon baking soda

½ teaspoon fine sea salt

8 tablespoons (1 stick) unsalted butter,
     at room temperature

1¼ cups packed light or dark brown sugar

1 large egg

3 cups rhubarb sliced ½ inch thick

TOPPING

½ cup packed light or dark brown sugar

½ cup old-fashioned rolled oats

1½ teaspoons ground cinnamon

Position a rack in the center of the oven and preheat to 350°F. Lightly butter and flour a 9- × 13-inch baking pan, tapping out the excess flour.

Combine the milk and vinegar and let stand until the milk curdles, about 5 minutes. Mix the flour, baking soda, and salt to combine. Cream the butter and brown sugar together in a medium bowl with an electric mixer on high speed until light and fluffy, about 3 minutes. Beat in the egg. Beginning with the flour, in three additions, use a spoon to stir in alternating portions of the flour and curdled milk, mixing just until smooth. (You can use the mixer on low speed, but do not overmix.) Fold in the rhubarb.

Spread evenly in the pan. Mix the brown sugar, oats, and cinnamon in a small bowl with your fingers until blended. Sprinkle evenly over the batter.

Bake until a toothpick inserted in the center of the cake comes out clean, 35 to 40 minutes. Cool in the pan on a wire rack.

Zucchini-Blueberry Bread

Makes 10 to 12 servings

Zucchini bread is a familiar way to celebrate the annual profusion of summer squash. In my recipe I use butter instead of the vegetable oil you'll find in standard versions, and the added flavor makes a big difference. In most gardens, the blueberries are ripening just as the zucchini is starting to get big, so the two are a natural combination for a tasty quick bread.

3 cups unbleached all-purpose flour

1 teaspoon ground cinnamon

1 teaspoon baking soda

¼ teaspoon baking powder

1 teaspoon fine sea salt

1½ cups sugar

12 tablespoons (1½ sticks) unsalted butter, melted

3 large eggs

1 teaspoon pure vanilla extract

2 cups grated zucchini (about 3 medium zucchini)

1 cup fresh blueberries

Position a rack in the center of the oven and preheat to 350°F. Lightly butter and flour a 9- × 13-inch baking pan, tapping out the excess flour.

Mix the flour, cinnamon, baking soda, baking powder, and salt in a large bowl to combine. Beat the sugar and melted butter in a large bowl with an electric mixer on high speed until combined. Beat in the eggs, one at a time, beating well after each addition. Beat in the vanilla. On low speed, gradually add the flour mixture. Add the zucchini, then fold in the blueberries with a spoon. Spread evenly in the pan.

Bake until a toothpick inserted in the center of the loaf comes out clean, about 1 hour. Cool in the pan on a wire rack for 10 minutes. Remove the cake from the pan and cool.

Old-Fashioned Anadama Bread

Makes 2 loaves

≈

In Anadama bread, cornmeal mush and molasses blend to make a fragrant, moist, dark-brown loaf. Besides being the perfect choice for a tomato and basil sandwich, it makes the best salad croutons. Be careful not to add too much flour when kneading the dough. The molasses and whole wheat flour will give it a tacky surface, and it is easy to compensate with more flour, which would only make the loaf heavy.

½ cup yellow cornmeal

1½ cups boiling water

½ cup unsulfured molasses

3 tablespoons unsalted butter, cut up

2 teaspoons fine sea salt

One ¼-ounce package (2¼ teaspoons)
   active dry yeast

¼ cup warm (105° to 115°) water

4 cups unbleached all-purpose flour, or more
   as needed

2 cups whole wheat flour

Mix the cornmeal with ¾ cup cold water in a medium saucepan. Whisk in the boiling water and bring to a boil over medium heat, whisking often. Add the molasses, butter, and salt, and cook, whisking often, until the cornmeal has thickened to a puddinglike consistency, about 7 minutes. Transfer to a large bowl and cool to lukewarm (no hotter than 115°F).

Sprinkle the yeast over the warm water in a small bowl and let stand until the yeast looks foamy, about 10 minutes. Stir to dissolve the yeast. Stir into the lukewarm cornmeal mush. Mix the all-purpose and whole wheat flours to combine. Gradually stir into the cornmeal mixture to make a stiff, somewhat sticky dough. Turn out onto a lightly floured work surface. Knead, adding more flour as required (but keeping in mind that the dough should remain a bit sticky), until the dough is smooth and elastic, about 10 minutes. If you run out of the flour combination, use all-purpose flour. As long as the dough isn't sticking excessively to the board, you have added enough flour. Gather up the dough into a ball.

Transfer to a large, lightly oiled bowl and turn to coat the dough with oil. Cover with a damp kitchen towel. Let stand in a warm place until double in volume, about 1 hour.

Punch down the dough, cover with the towel, and let rest in the bowl for 10 minutes. Lightly oil two 9- × 5-inch loaf pans. Divide the dough in half. Shape each half into a loaf and place in a pan. Roll the dough in the pan to coat with oil, and turn smooth side up. Cover with the towel and let rest until the dough rises to the top of the pan, about 30 minutes.

Meanwhile, position a rack in the center of the oven and preheat to 400°F. Uncover the pans and bake for 15 minutes. Reduce the oven temperature to 375°F, and bake until the loaves are golden brown and sound hollow when tapped on the bottom (remove a loaf from the pan), about 35 minutes. Let cool in the pans on a wire rack for 10 minutes. Remove from the pans and cool on the rack.

Fragrant Cardamom Braids

Makes 2 braids

≈

Cardamom is as common in India as vanilla is in our country. Its exotic aroma and flavor can be found in spiced main dishes and desserts, but it really shines in baked goods. This dough is soft and exceptionally pliable—just the thing for forming into decorative braids. My preference is for plain braids to serve toasted with soups and stews, but there are many other possibilities. Currants are a wonderful embellishment or the braids may be drizzled with an icing and chopped pecans for a special brunch.

1 cup milk

8 tablespoons (1 stick) unsalted butter, cut up

⅓ cup sugar

2 teaspoons fine sea salt

1½ teaspoons ground cardamom

One ¼-ounce package (2¼ teaspoons)
     active dry yeast

1 cup warm (105° to 115°F) water

1 large egg, well beaten

6 cups unbleached all-purpose flour, as needed

½ cup dried currants (optional)

GLAZE

¼ cup milk or half-and-half

1 large egg

Heat the milk and butter in a medium saucepan over medium heat just until the butter is melted. Pour into a large bowl and stir in the sugar, salt, and cardamom. Let stand until cooled to lukewarm (no warmer than 115°F).

Sprinkle the yeast over the warm water in a small bowl and let stand until the mixture looks foamy, about 10 minutes. Stir to dissolve the yeast. Add to the milk mixture, along with the egg, and mix well. Gradually stir in the flour to make a dough that is too stiff to stir.

Turn out onto a lightly floured work surface. Knead, adding more flour as required until the dough is smooth and elastic, about 10 minutes. Knead in the currants, if using. Gather the dough into a ball. Transfer to a large, lightly oiled bowl and cover with a damp kitchen towel. Let stand in a warm place until doubled in volume, about 1 hour.

Punch down the dough, cover again with the towel, and let rest for 10 minutes. Lightly oil 2 baking sheets. Divide the dough in half. Working with one portion at a time, pat and press the dough into a rectangle about 10 inches long and 5 inches wide. Using a sharp knife, cut the dough vertically, into three thick strips, stopping 2 inches short of the top so the strips are still attached. Braid the strips together. Tuck each end underneath itself. Place each braid on a baking sheet, and cover each with a damp kitchen towel. Let stand in a warm place until doubled in volume, about 45 minutes.

Meanwhile, position the racks in the center and top third of the oven and preheat to 375°F. To make the glaze, beat the milk and egg well in a small bowl. Brush the tops of the braids with some of the glaze.

Bake for 20 minutes. Switch the positions of the braids from top to bottom and front to back. Continue baking until they sound hollow when tapped on the bottom, about 20 minutes. Transfer to wire racks and cool completely.

Herbed Cheese Bread

Makes 1 large round loaf or 2 small loaves

It's a simple thing to bring the scent of the garden into your kitchen—make herb bread. For a more intense herb flavor, allow the bread to rise overnight in the refrigerator (then allow about 2 hours for the dough to warm up and rise at room temperature before baking). Try slices of this bread to make grilled Cheddar cheese and tomato sandwiches.

One ¼-ounce package (2¼ teaspoons)
  active dry yeast
1 teaspoon sugar
1½ cups warm (105° to 115°F) water
4 cups unbleached all-purpose flour, as
  needed
1 cup shredded sharp Vermont
  Cheddar cheese
¼ cup finely chopped fresh herbs,
  such as chives, parsley, rosemary,
  and thyme
3 tablespoons olive oil, plus more for
  brushing the loaves
2 teaspoons salt
½ teaspoon freshly ground pepper
Yellow cornmeal, for the baking sheets

Sprinkle the yeast and sugar over the water in a large bowl. Let stand until the mixture looks foamy, about 10 minutes. Stir to dissolve the yeast. Stir in 1 cup of the flour, the cheese, herbs, oil, salt, and pepper. Gradually stir in enough of the flour to make a stiff dough. Turn out onto a lightly floured work surface. Knead,

adding more flour as required, until the dough is smooth and elastic, about 10 minutes. Gather the dough into a ball.

Lightly oil a large bowl. Place the dough in the bowl and turn to coat with the oil. Cover the bowl with a damp kitchen towel. Let stand in a warm place until the dough has doubled in volume, about 1½ hours.

Sprinkle a large baking sheet with cornmeal. Punch down the dough. Turn out onto a work surface and knead briefly. Divide the dough in half. Form each half into a round loaf. Place the loaves well apart on the baking sheet. Brush the tops of the loaves with olive oil. Cover the loaves with a damp kitchen towel. Let stand in a warm place until doubled in volume, about 45 minutes.

Meanwhile, position a rack in the center of the oven and preheat to 375°F. Uncover the loaves. Bake until the loaves sound hollow when tapped on the bottom, about 35 minutes. Transfer to a wire rack and cool.

Rosemary Focaccia with Onion-Walnut Confit

Makes 4 to 6 servings

On its own, rosemary focaccia can be served for a family meal—kids love to pat out the dough. Other toppings to consider would be caramelized onions, pitted black olives, or even sautéed bitter greens with a sprinkle of fresh thyme. When company comes over, spread it with this savory confit of golden brown onions and chunky walnuts. The confit can also be used as a pasta sauce, tossed with fettuccine and Parmesan cheese.

ONION-WALNUT CONFIT

2 tablespoons unsalted butter

1 tablespoon extra virgin olive oil

3 large onions, thinly sliced into half-moons

4 teaspoons finely chopped fresh rosemary

1 cup dry white wine

⅓ cup walnuts, toasted (see page 12) and coarsely chopped

1 garlic clove, minced

Salt and freshly ground pepper, to taste

ROSEMARY FOCACCIA

One ¼-ounce package (2¼ teaspoons) active dry yeast

¼ teaspoon sugar

¾ cup warm (105° to 115°F) water

¼ cup olive oil, plus more as desired

1 teaspoon fine sea salt

2 cups unbleached all-purpose flour, as needed

1 tablespoon finely chopped fresh rosemary or 1 teaspoon dried rosemary

1 tablespoon freshly grated Parmesan cheese

To make the confit, heat the butter and oil in a large saucepan over medium heat. Add the onions and 1 teaspoon of the rosemary. Cook, stirring often, until the onions are softened, about 5 minutes. Reduce the heat to low. Cook, stirring often (especially toward the end of cooking to avoid sticking), until the onions are very tender and golden brown, about 45 minutes. Stir in the wine, walnuts, and garlic. Bring to a boil over high heat. Reduce the heat to medium and cook until the wine has completely evaporated, about 5 minutes. Stir in the remaining 3 teaspoons of rosemary. Season with the salt and pepper. Cool to room temperature. (The confit can be made up to 1 week ahead, cooled, covered, and refrigerated. Serve at room temperature.)

To make the focaccia, sprinkle the yeast and sugar into the water in a large bowl. Let stand until the mixture looks foamy, about 10 minutes. Stir to dissolve the yeast. Add 2 tablespoons of the oil and the salt. Gradually stir in enough of the flour to make a stiff dough. Turn out onto a lightly floured work surface. Knead, adding flour as required, until the dough is smooth and elastic, about 10 minutes. Gather the dough into a ball.

Lightly oil a large bowl. Place the dough in the bowl and turn to coat with the oil. Cover the bowl with a damp kitchen towel. Let stand in a warm place until the dough doubles in volume, about 1 hour.

Lightly oil a baking sheet. Punch down the dough and turn out onto a floured work surface. Punch and pat the dough to make a 9- × 13-inch rectangle. Transfer to the baking sheet. Cover the dough with a damp kitchen towel and let stand in a warm place until it looks puffy, about 30 minutes.

Meanwhile, position a rack in the center of the oven and preheat to 400°F.

Just before baking, poke indentations with your fingers all over the dough. Drizzle the remaining 2 tablespoons olive oil (or a bit more) on top, then sprinkle with the rosemary and Parmesan. Bake until the focaccia is golden brown on the bottom (lift up a corner to check), about 20 minutes. Cool on the sheet for a few minutes, then spread with the confit and cut into generous squares.

Pesto Swirl Bread

Makes 2 long loaves

Looking for a surefire hit to bring to a potluck? Here it is, a crusty French loaf with a swirl of fresh pesto. To maintain an even shape, use a French loaf mold, available at specialty kitchenware stores, but a free-form loaf will look just fine. See the variation for instructions on how to make equally aromatic rolls.

One ¼-ounce package (2¼ teaspoons) active dry yeast

1 teaspoon sugar

1½ cups warm (105° to 115°F) water

4 tablespoons (½ stick) unsalted butter, melted and cooled to lukewarm

1½ teaspoons fine sea salt

5 cups unbleached all-purpose flour, as needed

1 cup Basil Pesto (page 170)

GLAZE

1 large egg

½ teaspoon fine sea salt

Sprinkle the yeast and sugar over the water in a large bowl. Let stand until the mixture looks foamy, about 10 minutes. Stir to dissolve the yeast. Stir in the melted butter and the salt. Gradually stir in enough of the flour to make a stiff dough. Turn out onto a lightly floured work surface. Knead, adding more flour as required, until the dough is smooth and elastic, about 10 minutes. Gather the dough into a ball.

Lightly oil a large bowl. Place the dough in the bowl and turn to coat with oil. Cover the bowl with a damp kitchen towel. Let stand in a warm place until the dough has doubled in volume, about 1 hour.

Lightly oil two half-cylinder-shaped French bread pans or a large baking sheet. Punch down the dough. Turn out onto a lightly floured work surface and knead briefly. Divide the dough in half. Working with one portion of dough at a time, roll out into a rectangle 12 inches long and 8 inches wide. Spread with ½ cup of the pesto, leaving a ½-inch border on all sides. Starting at the long end, roll up, into a tight cylinder and pinch the seams closed, tucking the ends under the loaf. Place on the baking sheet. Or, if using the bread pans, taper the ends to make a French loaf shape. Cover the loaves with a damp kitchen towel. Let stand in a warm place until doubled in volume, about 45 minutes.

Meanwhile, position a rack in the center of the oven and preheat to 400°F. Beat the egg with the ½ teaspoon of salt to make a glaze. Uncover the loaves and brush lightly with the egg glaze.

Bake until the loaves sound hollow when tapped on the bottom, about 35 minutes. Transfer to a wire rack and cool.

PESTO SWIRL ROLLS. Lightly oil 12-cup muffin tins with olive oil. Spread each portion of dough with pesto, roll up, and pinch the long seam closed. Using a sharp knife, cut the loaves into 1-inch-thick rounds. Place each round in the lightly oiled muffin tin. Cover each muffin pan with a damp kitchen towel. Let stand in a warm place until the rolls look puffy, about 30 minutes. Bake at 400°F until golden brown, about 20 minutes.

Herb Basics

*D*ried herbs should be a staple in every kitchen, but fresh herbs make an incredible difference in flavor and are the mark of a good cook. Planting an herb garden can be as simple as setting up a tub outside the kitchen door, although it's better to devote as much space to them as possible in your kitchen garden.

When a recipe calls for finely chopped herbs, it means that the pieces should be chopped so small that they are no longer identifiable. This can be done in several ways. To cut herbs, it is very important to use a sharp knife, as the pieces should be cleanly cut to avoid bruising, which will discolor the bright green of the leaves. If the herbs are part of a recipe for baked goods, whirl them with the flour in a food processor until finely chopped. My grandmother taught me to strip the herb leaves from their stems, place the leaves in a custard cup, and snip them into small pieces with the tips of sharp scissors. In any case, herbs should be rinsed and dried well before chopping.

For several recipes in this book salad greens or herbs, usually basil, are cut into very thin ribbons (chiffonade). Stack a few wide leaves on top of one other. Starting at a wide end, roll the leaves up into a cylinder. Using a very sharp knife, cut the bundle crosswise into thin slices, then separate the resulting ribbons. It's best to chiffonade an herb right before serving so the cut surfaces don't oxidize (darken).

As a general rule of thumb, if a recipe calls for a fresh herb and you have only the dried, reduce the amount by about two-thirds. In other words, 1 tablespoon finely chopped fresh herbs equals 1 teaspoon dried herbs. To release their essential oils and intensify their flavor, crush dried herbs between your fingers while adding them to the dish.

Pizza Dough

Makes one 12-inch pizza

Making your own pizza at home is fun. You can also make the toppings, so it is one of the most creative ways to bake (see Seasonal Pizza Toppings, pages 192–193). This dough has a fair amount of whole wheat flour, which makes a tasty, nutritious crust. The dough will be more difficult to roll out than the all-white-flour version is. Don't worry. If it retracts excessively during rolling, cover the round with a damp kitchen towel and let it relax for a few minutes. To help keep the dough from sticking to the pizza pan, sesame seeds add another layer of flavor that is irresistible. The best way to keep the crust from getting soggy is to spread a thin layer of cheese on the dough, then bake for 10 minutes. This will firm up the crust before the rest of the ingredients are added.

1¼ cups warm (105° to 115°F) water

One ¼-ounce package (2¼ teaspoons) active dry yeast

1 teaspoon sugar

1 tablespoon olive oil

1½ cups unbleached all-purpose flour, or more as needed

1½ cups whole wheat flour

1 teaspoon fine sea salt

Sesame seeds, for the pan

¼ cup freshly grated Parmesan cheese

Your favorite toppings

Pour ½ cup of the warm water into a small bowl and stir in the yeast and sugar. Let stand until the mixture looks foamy, about 10 minutes. Stir to dissolve the yeast. Pour into a large bowl, and stir in the remaining ¾ cup of warm water and the oil. Mix the flours and the salt. One cup at a time, gradually stir the flours into the liquid until the dough is too stiff to stir. Now knead the dough in the bowl until the dough comes together.

Turn the dough out onto a floured work surface. Knead by hand, adding more flour as necessary, until the dough is smooth and elastic, about 8 minutes. If you run out of flour, use more all-purpose flour. Form the dough into a ball. Place in a large, lightly oiled bowl, and turn the dough to coat with the oil. Cover the bowl with a damp kitchen towel. Let stand in a warm place until doubled in volume, about 1 hour.

Oil a 12-inch heavy-gauge pizza pan and sprinkle the bottom with sesame seeds. Punch down the dough. Roll it out on a lightly floured work surface to make a round of dough about 1 inch wider than the pan. Press into the pan. Fold the edge of the dough over and pinch to create a lip around the circumference. Cover with a damp kitchen towel and let stand in a warm place until the dough looks puffy, about 30 minutes.

Meanwhile, position a rack in the bottom third of the oven and preheat to 425°F. Sprinkle the dough with the Parmesan. Bake until the dough looks set, about 10 minutes.

Remove from the oven and add the toppings. Bake until the crust is golden brown, about 10 minutes. Let stand for a few minutes, then cut into wedges and serve hot.

Fire-Roasted Tomato Sauce

Makes 2½ cups

Once you've tasted the intensity of a fire-roasted tomato sauce, it will become second nature to fire up the grill to prepare the tomatoes. The depth of flavor is perceptible, making this simple sauce the finest for pasta or as a base for pizza. Make up a big batch and store in the refrigerator for a week or the freezer for several months.

4 firm garden variety tomatoes,
    cut crosswise with seeds removed
1 tablespoon olive oil
1 medium onion, chopped
2 garlic cloves, minced
1 medium red pepper,
    roasted (see page 40),
    peeled, seeded, and
    chopped
½ cup chopped fresh basil
2 tablespoons chopped fresh
    thyme
1 bay leaf
Salt and freshly ground
    pepper, to taste

Build a fire in a charcoal grill and let burn until the coals are covered with white ash. Place the tomatoes skin side down on the grill. Cook until the skins are blackened, about 3 minutes. Cool slightly and peel the tomatoes. Finely chop 2 tomatoes with a large knife. Purée the remaining 2 tomatoes in a blender or food processor.

Heat the oil in a large skillet over medium heat. Add the onion and garlic. Cook uncovered, stirring often, until the onion is translucent, about 4 minutes. Add the chopped and puréed tomatoes, red pepper, basil, thyme, and the bay leaf and bring to a simmer. Reduce heat to low and simmer uncovered until reduced to about 2½ cups, about 15 minutes. Season with the salt and pepper. Serve hot.

Seasonal Pizza Toppings

*P*izza dough is my savory blank canvas, and seasonal ingredients are my medium. In spring, my pizzas are often emerald green with sautéed wild greens, fiddlehead ferns, and ramps, decorated with handfuls of pea tendrils. Summer brings together the sizzling colors of roasted red pepper purée spread over paper-thin slices of vine-ripe tomatoes. Cool-weather pizzas might feature the earth colors of caramelized leeks, slivered garlic, and finely sliced grilled radicchio. No matter the season, every pizza brings a rich, sensual delight to the table.

Most of the vegetables for a pizza topping are precooked in some way. Leafy greens should be blanched in boiling water, drained, squeezed of excess moisture, and chopped coarsely, or they can be sautéed in olive oil (add a bit of garlic if you like) until wilted. Other vegetables (zucchini, bell peppers, fennel, leeks, mushrooms) can be roasted, grilled, or sautéed just until barely tender to remove excess moisture. Use the method that makes sense and fits your schedule. Meats should be cooked—pancetta fried until barely crisp, sausage sautéed until it loses its pink color—as they will not cook thoroughly on the pizza.

Not all pizzas have to be laden with cheese, although it can be a fine addition. I don't spread tomato sauce onto every pizza, either. If you use cheese, sprinkle about half of it over the uncooked dough before adding the other toppings, then bake for 10 minutes to "waterproof" the dough against any moisture given off from the toppings and guard against soggy crust.

spring

Spinach, thinly sliced raw radish, and ricotta

Dandelion chicory, and smoked Cheddar

Escarole, cooked pancetta, and Fontina

Smoked salmon, sautéed wild ramps, and sour cream mixed with grated fresh horseradish

Chanterelles, sautéed arugula, and smoked Gouda

summer

Grilled eggplant, sun-dried tomatoes, and pesto

Chopped fresh tomatoes, basil, and fresh mozzarella

Multicolored roasted bell peppers, fresh sausage, and sage

Fennel, yellow peppers, and parsley, topped with cooked, shelled mussels just before serving

Grilled baby artichokes and thyme

fall and winter

Caramelized onions, rosemary, and Gorgonzola

Baked garlic cloves, pancetta, and marjoram

Leeks, pancetta, and goat cheese

Fire-Roasted Tomato Sauce (page 191), coarsely chopped Kalamata olives, and anchovies

Wild mushrooms, leeks, and smoked Cheddar

Broccoli, walnuts, and fresh mozzarella

Roasted and sliced new potatoes and Basil Pesto (page 170)

Tomato-Oregano Bread

Makes 2 round loaves

You can use any of your favorite ripe red tomatoes for this gorgeous bread—plum or beefsteak will both do. Just wait until you use slices for a fresh mozzarella sandwich.

One ¼-ounce package (2¼ teaspoons)
    active dry yeast
1 tablespoon sugar
1½ cups warm (105° to 115°F) water
4 cups unbleached all-purpose flour
2 cups whole wheat flour
1½ cups chopped ripe tomatoes, seeded
2 tablespoons olive oil
2 tablespoons finely chopped fresh parsley
2 tablespoons finely chopped fresh oregano
1 garlic clove, minced
1 tablespoon salt
½ teaspoon freshly ground pepper
Yellow cornmeal, for the baking sheet

Sprinkle the yeast and sugar into the warm water in a large bowl. Let stand until the mixture looks foamy, about 10 minutes. Whisk to dissolve the yeast. Add 1 cup each all-purpose and whole wheat flour and stir well. Cover with a damp kitchen towel and let stand until bubbling, about 30 minutes (this is called a sponge). Mix the remaining 3 cups all-purpose flour and 1 cup whole wheat flour and set aside.

Stir the tomatoes, oil, parsley, oregano, garlic, salt, and pepper into the sponge. Gradually stir in enough of the flour mixture to make a stiff dough. Turn out onto a lightly floured work surface. Knead, adding flour as necessary (don't be surprised if you add quite a bit as the tomatoes give off their juices), until the dough is smooth and elastic, about 10 minutes. Gather up the dough into a ball.

Lightly oil a large bowl. Place the dough in the bowl and turn to coat with the oil. Cover the bowl with a damp kitchen towel and let stand in a warm place until doubled in volume, about 1 hour.

Lightly oil a large baking sheet and dust with the cornmeal. Punch down the dough and divide in half. Form each portion into a round loaf. Place the loaves well apart on the baking sheet. Cover loosely with a damp kitchen towel and let stand in a warm place until doubled in volume, about 30 minutes.

Meanwhile, position a rack in the center of the oven and preheat to 400°F. Using a serrated knife, score the tops with a shallow slash down the center. Uncover and bake until the loaves sound hollow when tapped on the bottom, about 45 minutes. Transfer to a wire cake rack and cool.

Spelt-Squash Rolls

Makes 24 rolls

Spelt, an ancient strain of wheat, has been replaced by modern hybrids. Yet for most wheat-intolerant people, it is easier to digest. That is not the only reason to use spelt—it has a delicious, almost nutty wholesome flavor. It can be found in natural food stores and many supermarkets. Here it is mixed with winter squash purée and a hint of orange to make a very special roll for holiday dinners.

1 cup milk

4 tablespoons (½ stick) unsalted butter or neutral-flavored vegetable oil

1 cup mashed cooked butternut squash, or use any winter squash such as Hubbard, cooking pumpkin, or acorn

¼ cup pure maple syrup or honey

2 teaspoons salt

One ¼-ounce (2¼ teaspoons) active dry yeast

½ teaspoon sugar

¼ cup warm (105° to 115°F) water

2 large eggs, beaten

1 teaspoon grated orange zest

6½ cups spelt flour, as needed

Heat the milk in a medium saucepan over high heat until tiny bubbles appear around the edges. Add the butter and stir until melted. Add the squash, maple syrup, and the salt and mix well. Transfer to a large bowl and let stand until lukewarm (no hotter than 115°F).

Meanwhile, sprinkle the yeast and sugar over the warm water in a small bowl. Let stand until the mixture looks foamy, about 10 minutes, then stir to dissolve the yeast. Stir into the squash mixture. Add the eggs and orange zest. Gradually stir in enough of the flour to make a stiff dough.

Turn out onto a lightly floured work surface. Knead, adding more flour as necessary, until the dough is smooth and elastic, about 10 minutes.

Lightly oil a large bowl. Place the dough in the bowl and turn to coat with the oil. Cover with a damp kitchen towel and let stand in a warm place until doubled in volume, about 1 hour.

Lightly oil 24 muffin tins. Punch down the dough. Turn out onto a floured work surface and knead a few times to expel air bubbles. Cut the dough into 24 equal pieces. Form each piece of dough into a ball and place, smooth side up, in a muffin tin. Cover each pan with a moist kitchen towel and let stand in a warm place until the dough has doubled in volume, about 30 minutes.

Meanwhile, position a rack in the center of the oven and preheat to 375°F. Bake the rolls until golden brown, about 15 minutes. Remove from the tins and serve hot.

VELVET QUEEN. This exquisite sunflower has dark, rich burgundy petals surrounding a charcoal black center. The strong plants are 6 feet tall and well branched, making them great for borders and cutting.

SOLE D'ORO. A fluffy blossom in a rich buttery shade of yellow, this one looks like a furry ball. The center disk is hidden within the bloom by a double ring of petals but still faces and moves with the sun during the day.

ITALIAN WHITE. With a chocolate-colored center ringed by a thin band of creamy white pointed petals, this is a delicate beauty. It is a bushy multiflora plant with an elegantly pointed leaf and given enough space and soil, can reach 6 feet in stature.

PRIMROSE YELLOW. The tallest of the *Helianthus debilis* group, this spectacular sunflower stands 8 feet tall with many branches of yellow blossoms framing a brown center. Easy to grow and wind resistant, it is especially handsome when planted along the face of a barn.

SUNBEAM. This pollen-free hybrid is ideal for bouquets and its uniform 5-foot-high plants bloom early. Sow the seed in warm soil, and in two months, they will be ready to

*M*ost of us are familiar with the classic sunflower, Russian Giant, because it was the mainstay that kids often chose to grow in school gardens. During the past decade, flower breeders have developed more than fifty varieties that go well beyond that tall yellow and black skyscraper. Now you can find sunflowers with petals ranging from dark maroon to lemon yellow and in differing heights that make the plant as easy to grow in a pot as along a fence.

In seed catalogues, the Latin name of the sunflower will give a clue to how the plant will grow. *Helianthus annuus* usually has a single main stalk with one or two large flower heads. *H. debilis* will produce several stalks with many more, smaller flower heads, so this plant may be a better choice for a cutting garden. Many of the newer types are *Helianthus* hybrids, which are bred to be pollen-free to discourage bees—they also stay fresh longer in a vase. Our favorite sunflowers deserve a place in everyone's garden.

harvest for a long-lasting flower arrangement. The center is a cool lime green with contrasting warm yellow petals.

FULL SUN. Another outstanding pollen-free hybrid, this looks like Sunbeam, but is taller and has a dark center disk. It most resembles the classic sunflowers in Van Gogh's famous painting and we found it through the Dutch flower markets. When grown closely spaced, it will reach the perfect height for a cutting flower—meaning that the gardener won't have to do too much bending.

HENRY WILDE. At first glance, this is a standard tall sunflower with a deep chocolate-colored disk and butter yellow petals. But the main stem is host to up to fifteen smaller branches with perfect flowers that match the top bloom; very unusual in the garden, and a great choice for the cut-flower fancier.

AUTUMN BEAUTY MIX. A mix of autumnal earthen shades for cutting or for growing in the fall garden. The 4-inch-wide blossoms are a mix of yellow, bronze, and deep maroon, and will develop into a seed head that birds love. The sturdy 6-foot-tall plants make a nice backdrop to fall crops.

MUSIC BOX MIX. A kid-sized sunflower with a wide color range in well-proportioned flowers on uniform plants that grow only about 3 feet tall. With a mix of fall colors similar to the Autumn Beauty, these are excellent in a container garden or similar small space.

RUSSIAN GIANT. Also known as Grey Stripe, this is the towering sunflower that grows up to 15 feet tall. The huge yellow disks bob in the wind as they follow the sun on its daily round. As a bonus, they yield a bounty of bird seed. Our largest head measured 20 inches across and filled the bird feeder!

VALENTINE. A cut-flower type adaptable for container growing or as a bushy plant for a windbreak around the patio. The flowers, with their small, lemon yellow ray petals surrounding a dark center, grow on 5-foot-tall stems, with plenty of long side branches for lots of blooms.

Desserts

Fruit season in New England is brief, and in southern Vermont, even briefer. Our garden, in Cold Zone Three, allows us to grow only a few basics—raspberries, strawberries, blueberries, and apples. But we grow as many varieties of each one as possible.

Desserts are not everyday fare in our house, but are reserved for guests or special occasions. Many of the desserts in this chapter are those we make with seasonal fruits from our garden. Berries are savored in every way possible, if there are any left after we eat them by the handful while picking off the vine. Rather than buy berries out of season, we freeze the fresh ones in plastic bags, and have learned to adapt our recipes to their frozen state.

Because of the short window of opportunity for cooking with seasonal fruits, I also cook many desserts with vegetables and even grains. One of the classic Yankee desserts, Indian pudding, is made with cornmeal, which is not an ingredient one automatically thinks of when considering dessert, but makes a warm, comforting treat for an autumn evening. It's no secret that carrots, rhubarb, zucchini, and winter squashes such as pumpkin can be turned into wonderful sweets, and a New Englander knows this better than most cooks. The opportunity to savor peaches with lemon verbena may be fleeting, but I can serve my Maple-Carrot Cake at any time of the year.

Blueberry and Cinnamon Basil Custard

Makes 4 servings

If your garden isn't already graced with versatile scented basil, this recipe may be an inspiration to plant some. Cinnamon basil has a subtle spiciness that goes well with delicate fruits, such as the blueberries in this custard. As a substitute, use ½ cup Genovese basil and 1 cinnamon stick.

1 cup packed cinnamon basil leaves, rinsed
   and towel dried
2 cups milk
½ cup heavy cream
¼ vanilla bean, split, or ½ teaspoon pure
   vanilla extract
4 large eggs
¼ cup plus 1 teaspoon sugar
½ pint fresh blueberries
Cinnamon basil flowers, for garnish
   (optional)

Crush the basil leaves with a wooden spoon in a medium saucepan. Add the milk, cream, and vanilla bean and bring just to a simmer over medium heat. Remove from the heat and let stand so that the milk is infused with the basil flavor, about 20 minutes.

Meanwhile, position a rack in the center of the oven and preheat to 350°F.

Whisk the eggs and ¼ cup of the sugar in a medium bowl. Strain the infused milk through a wire sieve to remove the basil and the vanilla bean. Using the tip of a small knife, scrape the seeds of the vanilla bean into the milk. Gradually whisk the milk into the eggs. Strain the custard into a 1-quart measuring cup or pitcher.

Place equal quantities of the berries in four 4-ounce custard cups, and sprinkle each with ¼ teaspoon sugar. Pour equal quantities of the custard into the cups. Place the cups in a large pan, and add enough hot water to come halfway up the sides of the cups.

Bake until a knife tip inserted in the center of the custard comes out clean, about 45 minutes. Remove from the water and let cool to room temperature. Cover each cup with plastic wrap and refrigerate until chilled, at least 2 hours.

To serve, run a knife around the inside of each cup and invert the custard onto a plate. Garnish with the flowers, if using.

Berry Bread Pudding

Makes 4 to 6 servings

Berries are among the most reliable summer fruit crops in our garden, and we grow as many varieties as possible. Rarely found in the markets, green or red gooseberries are well worth planting in a permanent spot in the garden. The Cape gooseberry, which you might find in farmers' markets, is an annual fruit, closely related to the tomatillo. Both gooseberries and tomatillos have a papery husk, and the berries have an intensely sweet-tart flavor that adds distinction to this bread pudding.

4 cups fresh berries, preferably gooseberries or husked Cape gooseberries, or use a combination of gooseberries, blackberries, and raspberries

1¾ cups plus 1 teaspoon sugar

About 9 slices day-old, firm-textured white sandwich bread

4 tablespoons (½ stick) unsalted butter, at room temperature

4 large eggs, beaten

1 cup heavy cream

1 cup milk

1 teaspoon pure vanilla extract

Whipped cream, for serving

Cook the berries and 1 cup of the sugar in a medium saucepan over medium heat, stirring occasionally, until the berries burst and the juices run, about 5 minutes. Reserve ½ cup of the berries, cover, and refrigerate to serve as a sauce with the pudding.

Lightly butter an 8-inch-square baking dish. Removing the crusts, trim 3 slices of bread to fit the bottom of the baking dish. Spread the bread with butter and place buttered side down in the dish. Spread with half of the remaining berries. Repeat with 3 more trimmed slices of buttered bread, and the remaining berries. Top with 3 trimmed bread slices, buttered side down.

Whisk the eggs and ¾ cup of the sugar until the sugar is dissolved, then whisk in the cream, milk, and vanilla. Strain the custard through a wire sieve over the bread. Cover with plastic wrap and refrigerate for 1 hour to allow the bread to soak up the custard.

Position a rack in the center of the oven and preheat to 350°F. Sprinkle the remaining 1 teaspoon sugar over the pudding. Place the dish in a larger pan and pour in enough hot water to come halfway up the sides of the baking dish. Bake until the top is golden brown and feels set when pressed gently in the center, about 1 hour. Serve warm, with the whipped cream and the reserved berry sauce, slightly warmed at room temperature.

Indian Pudding with Gingered Whipped Cream

Makes 6 servings

A slow-cooked cornmeal pudding sweetened with molasses and spices, this dessert is so rib-sticking that we sometimes eat it for dinner. To add a contemporary touch to this very old recipe, serve with ginger-infused whipped cream.

GINGERED WHIPPED CREAM

1 cup heavy cream

1 tablespoon peeled and shredded fresh ginger (use the large holes on a box grater)

2 tablespoons sugar

PUDDING

1 quart milk

½ cup yellow cornmeal

½ cup unsulfured molasses

2 tablespoons unsalted butter

1 teaspoon ground cinnamon

½ teaspoon ground ginger

½ teaspoon fine sea salt

2 large eggs, at room temperature

To prepare the Gingered Whipped Cream, bring the heavy cream just to a boil in a medium saucepan over medium heat. Remove from the heat and add the ginger. Cover and refrigerate until well chilled, at least 4 hours. Strain through a wire sieve into a medium bowl. Add the sugar and whip with a whisk or electric hand mixer until the cream is stiff. (The cream can be prepared up to 4 hours ahead, covered, and refrigerated.)

Position a rack in the center of the oven and preheat to 350°F. Lightly butter a 1½-quart soufflé or round baking dish.

To make the pudding, bring the milk just to a simmer in a medium saucepan over medium heat. Place the cornmeal in the top part of a double boiler and slowly whisk in the hot milk. Cook over boiling water, whisking almost constantly, until the cornmeal is very thick, about 20 minutes. Off the heat, stir in the molasses, butter, cinnamon, ginger, and salt, stirring to melt the butter. In a separate bowl, beat the eggs, then gradually whisk them into the cornmeal mixture. Pour into the soufflé dish.

Position a rack in the center of the oven and preheat to 350°F. Place the soufflé dish in a larger pan and add enough hot water to come halfway up the sides of the dish. Bake until the pudding looks solid and a crack forms on the top, about 1 hour. Remove from the water and cool slightly on a wire cake rack. Serve warm, with the gingered cream.

Apple-Almond Torte

Makes 8 to 12 servings

Flour is used in cakes for structure, but tortes are made from cookie crumbs, bread crumbs, or ground nuts. In this flavorful dessert Italian ladyfinger crumbs, ground almonds, and apples are used to give the moist texture that is the true sign of the finest torte. You can find *savoiardi,* the crisp ladyfingers used in tiramisù, at Italian grocers and many supermarkets. If you like, substitute grated carrots for half of the apples.

2 cups whole natural almonds

1 cup granulated sugar

4 ounces (about 12) dry Italian ladyfingers (*savoiardi*), crumbled

2½ teaspoons baking powder

3 tart apples, such as Granny Smith or Pippin, peeled, cored, and cut into ½-inch cubes (about 2 cups)

1 tablespoon almond-flavored liqueur, such as amaretto, or 1 teaspoon pure almond extract

4 large eggs, separated, at room temperature

Confectioners' sugar, for serving

Position a rack in the center of the oven and preheat to 350°F. Lightly butter a 10-inch springform pan with a removable bottom. Line the bottom of the pan with parchment paper. Dust the sides of the pan with flour, tapping out the excess.

Process the almonds, granulated sugar, and ladyfingers until the almonds are finely ground. Add the baking powder and pulse to blend. Add the apples and liqueur, and pulse to blend. Transfer to a large bowl. One at a time, stir in the egg yolks.

Whip the egg whites in a medium bowl with a whisk or electric mixer on high speed until they form stiff peaks. In five or six additions, gradually fold the whites into the batter. Do not overmix. Spread in the pan.

Bake until a toothpick inserted in the center of the cake comes out clean, about 45 minutes. Cool on a wire cake rack for 10 minutes. Remove the sides of the pan and cool completely. Sift confectioners' sugar over the top and serve.

Melon Mousse and Fresh Strawberry Parfaits

Makes 4 servings

The orange-fleshed Charentais melon, with its smooth skin, intoxicating aroma, and superior flavor, is my first choice for this silky-smooth dessert. If it isn't available, use the very best, ripest cantaloupe you can find. This creamy mousse, reminiscent of a Creamsicle, is a great way to use up overripe melons.

1 ripe Charentais melon (or ½ ripe small cantaloupe)

1 tablespoon honey

2 teaspoons finely chopped fresh mint

Pinch of fine sea salt

½ teaspoon powdered gelatin

¾ cup heavy cream

1 pint fresh strawberries, stemmed and sliced, plus 4 small whole strawberries for garnish

Scoop the flesh from the melon rind, discarding the seeds, and purée in a food processor or blender. You should have 1 cup purée.

Combine the melon purée, honey, mint, and the salt in a medium saucepan, and sprinkle the gelatin on top. Let stand until the gelatin softens, about 5 minutes. Cook over medium-low heat, stirring constantly, until the gelatin dissolves, about 3 minutes. Do not let the purée come to a simmer; adjust the heat as needed. Transfer to a medium bowl. Refrigerate, stirring often, until the purée is cool but not set, about 1 hour.

Whip the cream in a chilled medium bowl with an electric mixer on high speed until it forms stiff peaks. Fold the cream into the purée. Spoon into 4 wine glasses, alternating with layers of the sliced strawberries. Cover each with plastic wrap and refrigerate until chilled and lightly set, at least 2 hours and up to 8. Serve chilled, topping each parfait with a small strawberry.

Charentais: The Best Melon

*T*he melon most commonly found in grocery stores is called a cantaloupe. In fact, it is a muskmelon, a related plant easily recognized by its netted skin and musky odor when ripe. The Charentais melon of France is a true cantaloupe and has long been one of our favorites. It is an old heirloom variety that will ripen even in cool areas. The smooth gray-skinned melon reaches only 2 to 3 pounds when about 5 inches in diameter—just the right size for breakfast or dessert.

Although there are many theories about how to tell when a melon is ripe, the right time is different for each melon. In the garden, a muskmelon is ready when the stem is easily detached from the melon, the background color of the rind changes from green to yellow, the stem end exudes a sweet musky odor, or the blossom end gives slightly when pressed with a finger. True cantaloupe, such as the Charentais, does not slip from the stem, and should be cut, not pulled, from the vine when the melon begins to turn yellow and the bloom end softens, or even cracks. At the market if you find Charentais melon with a crack at one end, smell it to be sure it is fresh and then buy it before someone else does.

Moist Chocolate Zucchini Cake

Makes one 9- × 13-inch cake

Chocolate zucchini cake used to be a big surprise, but as more good recipes appeared, the shock value diminished. This one, made with cocoa powder to reduce the cloying sweetness of lesser versions, is a winner, perfect for dessert or between-meal snacks. If the garden is loaded with yellow squash, you can use that instead of zucchini.

I cup unbleached all-purpose flour

I cup whole wheat flour

½ cup unsweetened cocoa powder

2 teaspoons baking powder

2 teaspoons baking soda

I teaspoon fine sea salt

2 cups sugar

8 tablespoons (I stick) unsalted butter, at room temperature

½ cup olive oil

3 large eggs, at room temperature

⅓ cup sour cream or yogurt

3 cups grated zucchini (about 4 medium zucchini)

Position a rack in the center of the oven and preheat to 350°F. Butter and lightly flour a 9- × 13-inch rectangular pan.

Sift the all-purpose flour, whole wheat flour, cocoa, baking powder, baking soda, and salt together into a medium bowl. Using an electric mixer on high speed, beat the sugar, butter, and oil together in another bowl until well combined. One at a time, add in the eggs, beating well after each addition. Gradually stir in the flour mixture, blending just until smooth. Stir in the sour cream, then the zucchini. Spread evenly in the pan.

Bake until the cake springs back when pressed in the center, about 45 minutes. Cool completely on a wire cake rack. Cut into squares and serve.

Maple-Carrot Cake with Maple Frosting

Makes 8 to 10 servings

When it's time to bake a layer cake for a celebration, this maple-flavored carrot cake can't be beat. We keep a gallon of dark, Grade B maple syrup for cooking and baking, and reserve the milder Grade A syrup to pour onto pancakes and the like. Grade B has a strong maple flavor and is less expensive than Grade A. It is not necessarily inferior—in fact, some people prefer it for all uses.

CAKE

2 cups unbleached all-purpose flour
2 teaspoons baking powder
2 teaspoons baking soda
1/2 teaspoon ground cinnamon
1/4 teaspoon ground ginger
1/8 teaspoon grated nutmeg
I teaspoon fine sea salt
I cup pure maple syrup, preferably Grade B
I cup granulated sugar
1/2 cup vegetable oil
4 large eggs, at room temperature
3 cups shredded carrots (about I pound)
1/2 cup coarsely chopped pecans or walnuts (optional)

FROSTING

I cup confectioners' sugar
One 8-ounce package cream cheese, at room temperature
4 tablespoons (1/2 stick) unsalted butter, at room temperature
2 teaspoons pure vanilla extract
1/4 cup pure maple syrup, preferably Grade B, as needed

Position a rack in the center of the oven and preheat to 350°F. Butter and lightly flour two 9-inch-round cake pans.

To make the cake, sift the flour, baking powder, baking soda, cinnamon, ginger, nutmeg, and salt into a medium bowl. Whisk the maple syrup, sugar, and oil in another medium bowl to combine, then whisk in the eggs, one at a time. Gradually stir in the flour, then add the carrots and the pecans, if using. Spread evenly in the pans.

Bake until the cakes spring back when pressed in the center, about 45 minutes. Cool on a wire rack for 10 minutes. Run a knife around the insides of the pans, and invert the cakes onto the rack. Turn right side up and cool completely.

To make the frosting, pulse the confectioners' sugar, cream cheese, butter, and vanilla in a food processor to blend. With the machine running, gradually enough maple syrup to make a smooth frosting, stopping the machine and scraping down the sides of the bowl as needed.

Place one cake layer, rounded side down, on a serving plate. Spread 1/2 cup of the frosting on the layer. Top with the second layer, rounded side up. Spread the top and then the sides with the remaining frosting.

Apple Crisp with Almond Topping

Makes 6 servings

~

Growing up, we often had desserts, and my favorite was apple crisp. I helped prepare it by putting heaps of peels and cores in one bowl, apple slices in another. It was a rare night that I didn't ask for seconds. My recipe, with a nutty almond topping, is a bit different from Mom's, but it is inspired by one of my dearest food memories. The consistency of the filling will change with the variety of apple, so choose what you prefer. Cortland will hold its shape after cooking; McIntosh will break down into a sauce. Perhaps the best choice is to mix them up.

6 large apples, such as McIntosh or Cortland,
    peeled, cored, and sliced (about 8 cups)
1 teaspoon ground cinnamon
½ teaspoon ground ginger
⅓ cup brandy (optional)
½ teaspoon pure vanilla extract

TOPPING
1 cup unbleached all-purpose flour
½ cup sliced almonds, toasted (see page 12)
    and finely chopped
½ cup granulated sugar
½ cup packed light or dark brown sugar
½ teaspoon fine sea salt
8 tablespoons (1 stick) unsalted butter,
    cut into 8 pieces
½ teaspoon pure almond extract

Whipped cream or vanilla ice cream,
    for serving

Position a rack in the center of the oven and preheat to 325°F. Lightly butter a 10-inch-deep-dish pie pan.

Toss the apples, cinnamon, ginger, brandy, if using, and vanilla. Spread in the dish.

To make the topping, mix the flour, almonds, granulated sugar, brown sugar, and the salt in a medium bowl. Add the butter and almond extract. Using a pastry blender or two knives, cut in the butter until the mixture is crumbly. (You can also pulse the dry ingredients in a food processor, add the butter and extract, and pulse until crumbly.) Crumble the topping over the apples to cover them.

Bake until the topping is golden and crisp, and the apples are tender, about 1 hour. Serve warm with the whipped cream.

Upside-Down Rhubarb Cake

Makes 8 servings

Rhubarb miraculously emerges every spring, its leafy tops providing a welcome shade for pets seeking relief from the heat. The red stalks are so prolific that you are sure to have plenty to freeze to use throughout the year. But with recipes like this and the streusel coffee cake on page 180, you'll have more opportunities to use the stalks beyond the familiar pie.

4 tablespoons (½ stick) unsalted butter

1¼ cups packed light or dark brown sugar

3 cups rhubarb in ½-inch dice

1 cup unbleached all-purpose flour

¾ cup whole wheat flour

1 teaspoon baking powder

¼ teaspoon baking soda

½ teaspoon fine sea salt

¾ cup yogurt

2 large eggs

¼ cup vegetable oil

2 tablespoons finely chopped crystallized ginger

Whipped cream or vanilla ice cream, for serving

Position a rack in the center of the oven and preheat to 350°F.

Melt the butter in a 9- to 10-inch ovenproof skillet, preferably cast iron. Stir in ½ cup of the brown sugar. Bake until the syrup is bubbling, about 5 minutes. Remove from the oven and spread the rhubarb in a single layer in the skillet.

Sift the all-purpose flour, whole wheat flour, baking powder, baking soda, and the salt into a medium bowl. Whisk the remaining ¾ cup brown sugar, yogurt, eggs, oil, and ginger in another medium bowl to combine. Add the flour to the yogurt-egg mixture and whisk until smooth. Pour over the rhubarb and smooth the top.

Bake until the top of the cake springs back when pressed in the center, about 30 minutes. Cool on a wire cake rack for 10 minutes. Run a knife around the inside edge of the skillet. Place a serving platter over the skillet, then invert with the cake to unmold. Serve warm with the whipped cream.

Spiced Baked Apples with Sunflower Seeds and Raisins

Makes 4 servings

Nothing is more comforting than soft, sweet baked apples. Cook a few more than you need, as they are also good for breakfast. Like high-starch baking potatoes, dry-textured cooking apples will hold together better after baking than the soft eating type will, so it is worth learning about the different local varieties.

4 large Cortland apples
½ cup raisins
¼ cup sunflower seeds
Zest of 1 lemon
2 tablespoons fresh lemon juice
1 teaspoon ground cinnamon
¼ teaspoon ground cardamom
1 cup apple cider
2 tablespoons unsalted butter, cut
into small pieces
Vanilla-flavored yogurt, for serving

Position a rack in the center of the oven and preheat to 350°F.

Core the apples with an apple corer. Remove the top third of the peel on each apple with a vegetable peeler. Combine the raisins, sunflower seeds, lemon zest and juice, cinnamon, and cardamom in a small bowl.

Place the apples in a baking dish just large enough to hold them snugly. Fill the apple cen-ters with the raisin mixture. Do not overpack. Pour the cider around the apples and dot the tops with the butter. Cover the dish with a lid or aluminum foil.

Bake, basting occasionally with the juices, until the apples are tender when pierced with the tip of a sharp knife, about 45 minutes. Cool slightly. Serve the apples with the juice in bowls, topped with a spoonful of yogurt.

Peaches and Lemon Verbena in Meringue Cups

Makes 4 servings

The sweet flavor of a ripe, juicy peach is unrivaled, but occasionally even something perfect could use a little embellishment. With peaches macerated with lemon verbena and spooned into crisp meringue cups, this recipe takes a good thing and makes it even better.

MERINGUE CUPS

4 large egg whites, at room temperature

½ teaspoon cream of tartar

1 cup sugar

½ teaspoon pure vanilla extract

½ teaspoon pure almond extract

6 ripe medium peaches, peeled (see Note),
    pitted, and chopped

7 tablespoons sugar

½ cup loosely packed fresh lemon verbena
    leaves, plus 6 leaves for garnish

½ cup heavy cream

To make the meringues, position a rack in the center of the oven and preheat to 250°F. Line a baking sheet with parchment paper.

Beat the egg whites in a medium bowl with an electric mixer on low speed until foamy. Add the cream of tartar and increase the speed to high. Beat just until soft peaks form. One tablespoon at a time, beat in ¾ cup of the sugar to make stiff, shiny peaks. Fold in the remaining ¼ cup sugar and the vanilla and almond extracts.

Using about ½ cup of the meringue for each shell, spoon 4 mounds onto the parchment paper. Using the back of a spoon, make an indentation in the center. Bake until the cups are crisp and lightly golden, about 45 minutes. Cool completely on the baking sheet. Carefully remove the meringue cups from the parchment.

Cook the peaches and 3 tablespoons of the sugar in a medium saucepan over medium heat until the peaches give off their juices, about 3 minutes. Transfer to a medium bowl. Process the remaining ¼ cup sugar with the lemon verbena in a food processor until the verbena is finely ground. Add to the peaches and mix. Cover and refrigerate until chilled, at least 2 hours.

Whip the cream until it forms stiff peaks. Refrigerate until ready to use, but no longer than 4 hours.

To serve, place a meringue cup on a plate. Spoon the peaches into the center, top with the whipped cream, and garnish with the lemon verbena leaves.

NOTE: To peel peaches, bring a large pot of water to a boil over high heat. Add the peaches and cook until the skins loosen, about 30 seconds (longer if the peaches are not quite ripe). Using a slotted spoon, transfer the peaches to a bowl of cold water. The skins should then slip off easily.

Spearmint Granita

Makes 1 quart, 6 to 8 servings

Granita, commonly made with fruit purée, can be served in small quantities to cleanse the palate between courses at a big dinner, or as a light dessert with a cookie or two. Herb granita captures the essence of botanical flavors and is especially refreshing. This light green granita is flecked with tiny bits of mint, but the recipe can be used for any culinary herb to your liking. If you have bergamot, also known as bee balm, growing in your garden, use half mint and half bergamot leaves. Although granita is supposed to be slightly gritty, you can produce a smoother texture by whirling the frozen granita in a food processor (freeze the bowl and blade until well chilled to reduce melting) right before serving.

1 cup gently packed fresh spearmint, plus
    mint sprigs for garnish
1 cup superfine sugar
3 tablespoons fresh lemon juice

Chill a 9- × 13-inch metal baking dish and a large metal serving spoon in the freezer for about 30 minutes.

Meanwhile, chop the mint and sugar in a food processor until the mixture forms a green paste, about 30 seconds. Add the lemon juice and pulse to combine, scraping down the sides of the bowl as needed. Add 3 cups water and pulse until the sugar dissolves.

Strain the mint liquid through a fine wire sieve into the chilled pan, discarding the solids in the sieve. Freeze until the mixture sets around the edges, about 1 hour, depending on your freezer's temperature. Using the metal spoon, mix the frozen edges into the center (leave the spoon in the pan). Freeze, repeating the stirring procedure about every 30 minutes, until the mixture has a slushy consistency, 2 to 3 hours total freezing time. Serve immediately, spooned into chilled glasses, each garnished with a mint sprig.

Lemon-Ricotta Fritters with Lavender-Infused Honey

Makes about 12 fritters, 4 to 6 servings

The batter can be made before dinner, and then it is just a question of deep-frying the fritters. The reward will be crisp, freshly cooked, melt-in-your-mouth morsels with soft lemony centers, just the thing to dip into fragrant lavender honey. In Provence, lavender honey is made by the bees that frequent the wild purple-budded bushes growing near their hives. Be aware that this homemade version, infused with lavender flowers, needs to stand for 24 hours before being used. If you purchase dried lavender flowers, be sure that they are culinary quality. Lavender purchased at hobby shops is often meant for potpourri or other decorative and scenting purposes and may have been sprayed with preservatives and perfume.

LAVENDER HONEY

I cup raw clover honey

24 fresh lavender sprigs with buds, or

    I tablespoon dried lavender flowers

FRITTERS

I pound whole milk ricotta cheese

4 large eggs

²/₃ cup unbleached all-purpose flour

3 tablespoons unsalted butter, melted

2 tablespoons finely chopped fresh lemon

    verbena (optional)

Grated zest of 2 lemons

¼ teaspoon fine sea salt

Vegetable oil, for deep-frying

Fresh lemon verbena or mint leaves, finely

    sliced, for garnish

To make the lavender honey, warm the honey in a small saucepan over low heat. Stir in the lavender. Remove from the heat, cover, and let stand at room temperature for 24 hours.

Warm the honey again over low heat until it is liquid enough to pour freely. Strain through a wire sieve into a clean jar. Cool and cover. Store in the refrigerator for up to 6 months. Serve at room temperature.

To make the fritters, whisk the ricotta and eggs until blended but not quite smooth. Gradually stir in the flour, then fold in the butter, lemon verbena, if using, lemon zest, and salt. Cover the batter with plastic wrap and let stand at room temperature for I hour.

Position a rack in the center of the oven and preheat to 200°F. Line a baking sheet with crumpled paper towels. Pour enough oil into a large saucepan to come halfway up the sides of the pan and heat over high heat until a deep-frying thermometer reads 365°F.

In batches without crowding, drop tablespoons of the batter into the hot oil. Cook, turning once, until the fritters are golden brown, about 3 minutes. Using a wire skimmer or slotted spoon, transfer the fritters to the paper towels and keep warm in the oven while making the remaining fritters.

Serve a few fritters on each plate, drizzle with a generous tablespoon of the lavender honey, and sprinkle with the lemon verbena. Serve hot.

Fresh Peach–Berry Cobbler

Makes 4 to 6 servings

Cobblers are a great way to serve seasonal fruit. During the summer, a combination of berries and peaches celebrates one of the great culinary matches. My biscuit topping has a touch of cardamom to accent the juicy fruit. And I bake the berries first so that the topping stays light and airy.

FILLING

1/2 cup sugar

1 tablespoon cornstarch

1/8 teaspoon ground cinnamon

1/8 teaspoon salt

2 pints fresh blueberries

1 pint fresh raspberries or blackberries

6 ripe peaches, peeled (see Note, page 213), pitted, and sliced into wedges

1 lemon, zest grated and juiced

TOPPING

1 cup unbleached all-purpose white flour

2 tablespoons yellow cornmeal

1/4 cup sugar, plus 2 teaspoons for sprinkling

2 teaspoons baking powder

1/4 teaspoon baking soda

1/4 teaspoon fine sea salt

4 tablespoons (1/2 stick) cold unsalted butter, melted

1/3 cup buttermilk

1/2 teaspoon pure vanilla extract

1/2 teaspoon ground cardamom

1/8 teaspoon ground cinnamon

Vanilla ice cream, for serving

Preheat the oven to 375°F.

Stir the sugar, cornstarch, cinnamon, and salt together in a large bowl. Add the berries and peaches and mix gently until evenly coated. Stir in the lemon zest and juice and transfer to a 13- × 9-inch baking dish. Place on a baking sheet and place in the hot oven and bake for about 25 minutes.

For the topping, whisk the flour, cornmeal, 1/4 cup sugar, baking powder, baking soda, and salt together in a large bowl. Whisk in the melted butter, buttermilk, vanilla, and cardamom in a small bowl. Stir the remaining 2 teaspoons sugar and cinnamon and set aside until the berries come out of the oven. A few minutes before the hot berries emerge from the oven, assemble by adding the wet ingredients to the dry ingredients, stirring gently until just combined.

Remove the hot bubbling berries from the oven; increase the oven temperature to 425°F. Spoon out eight equal pieces of biscuit dough and place evenly on the hot berry filling, spacing them at least 1/2 inch apart. Sprinkle with the cinnamon sugar, bake until the biscuits are golden brown and cooked through and the filling is bubbly, about 15 minutes. Cool slightly before serving with vanilla ice cream.

Chai

Makes 2 to 4 servings

Hot or cold, *chai* is refreshing and invigorating. A staple in India, the tea stimulates the mind and body while the gentle fragrance of the spices creates a calming effect. Iced *chai* will keep in the refrigerator for up to 3 days.

2 cinnamon sticks

4 slices fresh ginger or crystallized ginger

10 cardamom pods, crushed to reveal seeds

1 teaspoon coriander seeds

½ teaspoon whole black peppercorns

½ teaspoon whole cloves

2 teaspoons black tea

¼ cup raw honey, as needed

1 cup milk, warmed if
    serving hot

Bring 4 cups water, the cinnamon, ginger, cardamom, coriander, peppercorns, and cloves to a boil over high heat. Reduce the heat to low, cover with the lid askew, and simmer for 20 minutes to release the flavors. Remove from the heat and stir in the tea. Let steep for 3 to 5 minutes. Strain into a pitcher. Sweeten to taste with the honey. If serving warm, stir in the warm milk. If serving cold, cool to room temperature, stir in the milk, and refrigerate until chilled.

Fragrant Gingerbread with Crystallized Ginger

Makes 12 servings

The aroma of freshly baked gingerbread is sure to bring back memories of an old-fashioned kitchen. This batter is thin, and will seem incorrect, but it will bake up into a moist and spicy cake. Crystallized ginger, available at Asian markets and specialty food stores, gives an additional spicy accent. Serve the cake topped with warm Spiced Dessert Applesauce or cool whipped cream, and don't forget a cup of hot tea.

2 cups unbleached all-purpose flour

2 teaspoons baking soda

I teaspoon ground ginger

I teaspoon ground cinnamon

I teaspoon ground cloves

½ teaspoon fine sea salt

I cup sugar

I cup unsulfured molasses

I cup vegetable oil

3 large eggs, at room temperature

I cup boiling water

½ cup finely chopped crystallized
    ginger

Spiced Dessert Applesauce
    (page 222) or whipped cream,
    for serving

Position a rack in the center of the oven and preheat to 350°F. Lightly butter and flour a 9- × 13-inch baking pan, tapping out the excess flour.

Sift the flour, baking soda, ginger, cinnamon, cloves, and salt into a medium bowl. In another medium bowl, beat the sugar, molasses, oil, and eggs with an electric mixer on high speed until well blended. Stir in the flour mixture. Add the boiling water and mix to make a smooth, thin batter. Pour into the pan.

Bake until the cake springs back when pressed in the center, about 45 minutes. Let cool for 10 minutes, then serve warm.

Prize-Winning Pumpkin Cheesecake

Makes 8 to 12 servings

Pumpkin cheesecakes abound, but this one is outstanding. Considering the praise it receives, it is a very simple recipe, and for several years in a row has won prizes at our local harvest festival.

CRUST

1 cup graham cracker crumbs

6 tablespoons (¾ stick) unsalted butter, melted

1 tablespoon sugar

Two 8-ounce packages cream cheese, at room temperature

1 cup sugar

2 cups cooked and puréed pie pumpkin, such as sugar pumpkin (see Note)

1 teaspoon ground cinnamon

¼ teaspoon ground ginger

¼ teaspoon freshly grated nutmeg

⅛ teaspoon fine sea salt

2 large eggs, at room temperature

2 cups sour cream

1 teaspoon pure vanilla extract

To make the crust, mix the crumbs, melted butter, and sugar in a medium bowl until combined. Press firmly and evenly into the bottom of a 9-inch springform pan. Refrigerate until chilled and firm, about 30 minutes.

Position a rack in the center of the oven and preheat to 350°F.

Beat the cream cheese and ¾ cup of the sugar in a medium bowl with an electric mixer on high speed, scraping down the sides of the bowl as needed, just until smooth. Beat in the pumpkin, cinnamon, ginger, nutmeg, and salt. One at a time, add the eggs, beating after each addition. Spread evenly in the crust.

Bake until the filling seems almost completely set when given a gentle shake (the center will seem a little moist), about 50 minutes.

Remove the cake from the oven and increase the oven temperature to 400°F. Mix the sour cream, remaining ¼ cup of the sugar, and the vanilla in a small bowl. Spread over the top of the cheesecake. Return to the oven and bake until the topping looks set, about 8 minutes.

Transfer the cheesecake to a wire cake rack and cool to room temperature. Cover with plastic wrap and refrigerate until chilled, at least 4 hours. Run a sharp knife around the inside of the pan and remove the sides of the pan. Slice with a hot, wet knife, and serve chilled.

NOTE: For pumpkin pies and other desserts, bake a squash with a firm, not-too-wet flesh, such as a small sugar pumpkin or Red Kuri. One pound of untrimmed winter squash will yield about 1 cup purée.

Cut the pumpkin into quarters. Place with one of the cut sides down in a roasting pan and pour in about ½ inch of water. Bake in a preheated 375°F oven until the flesh is tender, about 1 hour. Cool. Discard the skin and seeds and mash well in a bowl with a fork. The purée should have the same density as canned pumpkin, so drain it in a wire sieve lined with paper towels, if needed.

Pumpkin Crème Caramel

Makes 8 servings

Add pumpkin purée to the classic custard with caramel sauce, and you'll get a dessert with a rich, dark color and autumnal flavor. It's sure to come to mind when you're looking for an upscale dessert for a fall dinner party.

CARAMEL

¾ cup sugar

1 cup half-and-half

1 cup milk

1 vanilla bean, split in half lengthwise

6 large eggs

⅓ cup plus 1 tablespoon sugar

1 tablespoon dark rum

¼ teaspoon ground cinnamon

¼ teaspoon freshly grated nutmeg

⅔ cup cooked and puréed pie pumpkin (see Note, page 219), such as sugar pumpkin

Position a rack in the center of the oven and preheat to 300°F.

To make the caramel, pour ¼ cup water into a medium saucepan and stir in the sugar. Bring to a boil over high heat, stirring just until the sugar dissolves. Cook without stirring, swirling the saucepan by the handle occasionally, until the syrup has turned a dark golden brown, about 5 minutes. If the sugar crystallizes on the insides of the pan, cover tightly for 1 minute, and the collected steam should dissolve the crystals. Or dip a pastry brush in water, and press it against the crystals to wash them back into the syrup.

Immediately pour equal quantities of the hot caramel into eight 4-ounce ramekins or custard cups. Set aside.

Heat the half-and-half, milk, and vanilla in a medium saucepan over medium heat until tiny bubbles form around the edges of the liquid. Remove the vanilla bean and scrape the seeds back into the milk with the tip of a sharp knife. Whisk in the eggs, sugar, rum, cinnamon, and nutmeg until combined, then whisk in the pumpkin. Gradually whisk in the hot milk. Pour equal amounts of the custard into the custard cups.

Place the custard cups in a large roasting pan. Add enough hot water to come halfway up the sides of the cups. Bake until a knife inserted about ½ inch from the center of the custard comes out clean, about 1 hour. Remove the cups from the water and cool completely. Cover each cup with plastic wrap and refrigerate until chilled, at least 2 hours or overnight.

Run a dinner knife around the inside of each cup. Hold a dessert plate over the cup. Invert together and give them a sharp shake to unmold the custard. Serve chilled.

Rum-Pumpkin Pie

Makes 8 servings

Once you've made pumpkin pie with fresh puréed pumpkin, you will never turn back to the canned variety. The color is more vibrant, and the flavor is much richer. This is an exceptional version of an American classic that deserves to be made outside the holiday season.

I recipe Pastry Dough (page 74)

1½ cups cooked and puréed pie pumpkin (see page 219), such as sugar pumpkin

½ cup granulated sugar

½ cup light or dark brown sugar

3 tablespoons dark rum

1 tablespoon unsulfured molasses

1½ teaspoons ground cinnamon

¼ teaspoon ground ginger

⅛ teaspoon ground cloves

2 large eggs

1 cup milk, heated to scalding

Whipped cream, for serving

Position a rack in the center of the oven and preheat to 450°F.

Roll out the pastry on a lightly floured work surface to a 12-inch round about ⅛ inch thick. Fit into a 9-inch pie plate. Fold the overhang under the pastry and flute the edges. Refrigerate the crust while making the filling.

Whisk the pumpkin, granulated sugar, brown sugar, rum, molasses, cinnamon, ginger, and cloves until the brown sugar dissolves. One at a time, beat in the eggs, then the milk. Pour into the crust.

Bake for 10 minutes. Reduce the oven temperature to 325°F and continue baking until a knife inserted in the center comes out clean, about 40 minutes. Transfer to a wire cake rack and cool completely. Serve at room temperature.

Spiced Dessert Applesauce

Makes 4 cups, 8 servings

This is my grandmother's recipe for applesauce, which has more character than most versions. It is an ideal match as a sauce for gingerbread, but it can certainly stand on its own, topped with cool tart yogurt. If you like a spicier sauce, tie the spices and lime slices in a piece of rinsed cheesecloth and cook them with the apples. For a chunky sauce, use Cortland or Golden Delicious apples, McIntosh or Macoun for a smooth sauce, or a combination. Try it as a filling for warm crêpes, sprinkled with confectioners' sugar.

1 cup sugar

½ teaspoon fine sea salt

1½ cinnamon sticks

½ teaspoon freshly grated nutmeg

½ teaspoon finely grated fresh ginger
(use the small holes on a box grater)

6 whole cloves

4 thin slices of lime, rind included

8 medium cooking apples (see suggestions),
peeled, cored, and coarsely chopped (2 pounds)

Bring 1 cup water, the sugar, salt, cinnamon sticks, nutmeg, ginger, cloves, and lime slices to a boil in a small saucepan. Reduce the heat to low and simmer for 5 minutes to release the flavors.

Strain the syrup through a wire sieve into a medium saucepan. Add the apples and cover. Cook over medium-low heat, stirring often, until the apples are barely tender, about 10 minutes. Don't overcook the apples, as they will continue to cook off the heat. Transfer to a large bowl. For a smoother sauce, mash the apples with a fork. Cool and serve warm, or cool completely, cover, and refrigerate until chilled.

Homemade Granola

Makes 20 servings

Homemade granola is the best way to incorporate a wide variety of grains into your diet. It has many other uses beyond the breakfast table—sprinkle some on top of fresh fruit for an afternoon snack or scatter a handful on a bowl of yogurt on the nights when you want a quick dessert. Now that genetically engineered plants are being used for so many commercial cereals, seek out organic ingredients to ensure that your granola is pure. Stored in an airtight container at room temperature, granola will keep for a couple of months, and it makes a nice gift for friends.

I cup raw peanuts, almonds, cashews, or
  skinned hazelnuts

I cup sunflower seeds

I cup hulled pumpkin seeds

I cup wheat germ or millet flakes

I cup raisins or coarsely chopped dried fruit,
  such as dates or apricots

I cup raw clover honey

I cup vegetable oil

5 cups old-fashioned rolled oats

2 cups barley flakes

2 cups wheat flakes

I cup rye flakes

Position the racks in the top third and center of the oven and preheat to 350°F.

Toast the peanuts, sunflower seeds, and pumpkin seeds in a large skillet over medium-high heat, stirring often, until very lightly browned, about 5 minutes. Transfer to a large bowl. Add the wheat germ and raisins and mix well. Set the mixture aside.

Stir the honey and oil in a medium saucepan over medium-low heat just until the honey is fluid. Mix the oats, and the barley, wheat, and rye flakes in a very large bowl. Pour in the honey mixture, and mix well with your hands until the flakes are evenly coated. Spread on two shallow roasting pans.

Bake, stirring often, until the flakes are toasted to a light golden color, 20 to 30 minutes. Do not let the flakes brown, especially around the edges of the pan. Cool completely.

Return the baked mixture to the large bowl and add the nut and seed mixture. Store the granola in an airtight container at room temperature for up to 2 months.

Pear Galette with Almond Cream

Makes 8 servings

A galette is a French fruit tart made from yeasted sweet dough or puff pastry, something like a sweet pizza. This yeast dough is kneaded for just a minute, so don't expect it to rise much. The combination of pears and almonds in this unusual crust makes it a spectacular autumn dessert.

DOUGH

I teaspoon active dry yeast

1/3 cup warm (105° to 115°F) water

I large egg yolk

1 1/4 cups unbleached all-purpose flour,
   plus more for kneading

I tablespoon sugar

Grated zest of 1/2 lemon

1/4 teaspoon salt

4 tablespoons (1/2 stick) unsalted butter,
   chilled, cut into 1/4-inch cubes

1/4 cup maple syrup

Seeds from 1/4 vanilla bean

I tablespoon fresh lemon juice

3 firm, ripe pears, such as Bosc or Comice,
   peeled, cored, and cut lengthwise into
   1/4-inch-thick slices

1/4 cup whole almonds

2 1/2 tablespoons sugar

2 tablespoons unsalted butter, at room
   temperature

I large egg

To make the dough, stir the yeast into the warm water in a small bowl and let stand until the mixture looks foamy, about 10 minutes. Stir to dissolve the yeast. Add the egg yolk and mix. Mix the flour, sugar, zest, and salt in a medium bowl. Using a pastry blender, cut in the butter until the mixture looks like coarse cornmeal. Make a well in the center, add the dissolved yeast mixture, and mix until the dough comes together. Cover the bowl with a damp kitchen towel and let stand for 5 minutes.

Turn out the dough onto a lightly floured surface. Knead, adding just enough flour to keep the dough from sticking to the surface (keep in mind that the dough should feel tacky), until the dough is smooth, about 1 minute. Do not overknead. Place in a buttered medium bowl, turn to coat with butter, and cover with the damp towel. Let stand in a warm place until doubled in volume, about 1 1/4 hours.

Position a rack in the center of the oven and preheat to 375°F. Bring the maple syrup, vanilla seeds, and lemon juice to a simmer in a small saucepan over low heat. Mix with the pear slices in a medium bowl. Steep the pears in the syrup for 15 minutes.

Lightly butter a 9-inch tart pan with a removable bottom. Punch down the dough and press into a disk. Roll out on a lightly floured work surface into a 12-inch round and fit into the tart pan. Fold the edges of the dough inside the pan, and press to give the sides a double thickness.

Process the almonds and sugar in a food processor until the almonds are ground into a flour. Add the butter, pulse to combine, then add the egg and process until smooth. Spread into the dough shell.

Drain the pears, reserving the juices. Fill the dough with layers of overlapping concentric circles of pear slices, filling the center with the smallest slices. Brush the pears with some of the reserved juices.

Bake until the custard is set and the crust is golden brown, about 45 minutes. Cool on a wire cake rack for 20 minutes. Remove the sides of the pan and serve warm, or cool completely.

Preserving the Bounty

When we started our business almost twenty years ago, it mostly revolved around selling our bounty to the weekenders with summer homes in the area. We set up our farm stand like a still life overflowing with a tumbling cascade of just-picked produce. As irresistible as it was, our overstocked shelves inevitably revealed a mountain of leftover fruits and vegetables on Sunday night. Equally inevitably, I learned the art of preserving.

My first specialty was chutney, the unsold but perfectly ripe peaches and plums turned into a piquant relish that would be added to our farm stand inventory by the next weekend. I learned the basics of canning from my neighbor Fay La Prade, who told me, "The first canning session of the year is like learning how to drive on ice. It's a little tricky at first, but once you remember how to do it, it's easy." I always keep this in mind when I set up the canning kettles, jars, scoops, and funnels.

If you aren't already a dedicated canner, it is well worth learning the joys of making your own preserves. My choice of recipe depends on what fruit is most abundant—some of my favorites are combinations of peaches and ginger, and pears with plums or tomatoes. My routine begins when I reach for my faithful preserving kettle and set a brine of vinegar and spices on to simmer. Bags of sugar, ginger knobs, and red-skinned garlic clutter my counter next to clean jars and lids. Soon my pantry shelf is filled with flavorful condiments sure to heighten my winter menus. At other times, I might put up a zesty salsa from a late summer explosion of tomatoes and chiles, or sweet-crisp bread and butter pickles, or even homemade mustard seasoned with the garden's onions, shallots, and garlic.

Beyond canning, there are other ways of preserving the bounty. Freezing is a great way to store many, but not all, fruits and vegetables. I provide an outline of what we have discovered works well on pages 231–232. And, although the flavor of fresh herbs from the garden is exquisite, in most parts of the country, it can be seasonal. Happily, these herbs can be dried to use throughout the year with most of their aroma and taste intact.

The Joy of Preserves

Making your own preserves is very satisfying, but some basic equipment is required for the best results. Once you have the tools, and a garden full of ingredients just waiting to be turned into a tasty condiment, follow the simple step-by-step canning procedures.

■ Canning Equipment. A *heavy-bottomed stainless steel or enameled pot* will cook acidic food such as tomatoes or chutneys without picking up the flavor of the metal—a danger when cooking with aluminum pots. The heavy bottom discourages scorching. For hot-pack processing (which is not always necessary), get a *large canning kettle* with a lid. They are usually made from thin metal so the water will come to a boil quickly. To transfer the jars in and out of the water bath, a *canning rack* and a *jar holder* are practically essential. With a wide-mouthed *canning funnel*, you can transfer the preserves into the jars without a mess. *Canning jars* must be spotlessly clean and without any cracks or nicks. Do not reuse jars from commercially processed foods, such as mayonnaise or jam. The *bands* must have no dents and be rust-free. Because the lids are not reusable (the heat destroys the seal), purchase new *canning lids* every time.

■ Canning Procedures. Heat is an important factor in canning. In all cases, the preserves must be boiling hot when placed in the hot, sterilized jars. It is usually most convenient to sterilize the jars either in a kettle of boiling water or in the dishwasher while the preserves are cooking, but remember that the jars must be piping hot when you add the preserves.

1. Wash the jars in hot soapy water and rinse well. If you use a dishwasher to do the job, you won't have to sterilize the jars in a kettle of hot water, as long as you use the jars while they are piping hot. In this case, keep them stored in the dishwasher until ready to fill.

2. To sterilize the jars, fill a canning kettle or large pot about two-thirds full with water and bring to a boil over high heat. Place the clean jars in a canning rack, and submerge in the boiling water for 10 minutes. If necessary, add more boiling water to cover the jars. Remove the jars from the pot, and use a jar handler or tongs to pour the water from each jar. Invert the jars onto a clean tea towel until ready to fill.

3. To soften the rubber seals, place the lids in a bowl and cover with hot tap water or more boiling water. Do not boil in a saucepan, or the rubber seal will soften too much.

4. Using a canning funnel, spoon the *hot* preserves into the *hot* jars, leaving a ¼-inch gap at the top. With a hot, wet towel, wipe any spills from the lip and sides of each jar. Attach the lids and bands, but do not screw them on tightly. Place the jars on a thick towel or a wooden board (a cool hard surface could make the jars crack) and let cool. When the seals take, you might hear a gentle pop. After a few hours, check the lid to be sure it is flat.

5. If required, process the filled jars in a hot-water bath. Fill a canning pot two-thirds full with water, and bring to a full boil over high heat. Place the jars in a canning rack and lower it into the water. Add enough boiling water to cover the jars by 1 inch. Return to the boil. Time from the point at which the water reboils, and process for the length of time directed in the recipe. Remove from the water, and place the processed jars on a towel or wire cake rack to cool.

We bought our first freezer as soon as the walls were up on our house and it shared the temporary electrical circuit with the carpenters' power tools. That first summer, we tossed everything from our garden in the freezer, from herbs to carrots and squash. Later, eating our frozen inventory, we found that much of it didn't taste as good as we had hoped. We have since learned not only what vegetables are best to freeze, but also how to freeze them so that they remain at their flavorful peak.

There are several reasons for freezing failures. Fluctuating freezer temperatures, which occur when the door is opened, are very detrimental. The ideal freezing temperature is 0°F or lower. Purchase a freezer thermometer to be sure, because uneven temperatures will encourage moisture to form inside the containers and cause dreaded freezer burn. If you are serious about freezing produce, it is worth the money to buy a free-standing deep freezer. The freezing compartment of a kitchen refrigerator is unreliable because the refrigerator door is opened often, affecting the temperature of the entire unit. Each time the door is opened, the temperature in the compartment fluctuates, causing ice crystals to form inside the frozen foods.

Two techniques, quick-freezing and blanching, are used for successfully freezing produce. During freezing, the water in the fruit and vegetables forms sharp ice crystals that can puncture the cell membranes, making the internal structure deflate like a punctured balloon. Quick-freezing the produce makes smaller ice crystals that do less damage. To quick-freeze, spread the fruit or vegetable out on a baking sheet and freeze until solid. Transfer to self-sealing freezer bags, then suck out the air through a straw before closing. If using a container, be sure it is airtight.

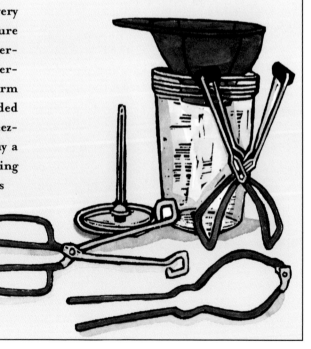

$\mathcal{B}$lanching, briefly cooking the vegetables in boiling water, slows down the enzyme action that can affect the flavor, taste, texture, and vitamin content of frozen foods. It is an essential step for freezing many, but not all, vegetables and fruits.

Unblanched frozen vegetables will rapidly lose quality because freezing, (unlike canning, where high temperatures kill bacteria and stop enzyme production) only slows, but does not stop, the chemical breakdown and the enzyme-changing process. To blanch vegetables, add them to a large pot of boiling water, and cook until they turn a brighter shade of their natural color, usually just a few minutes. Always cool blanched vegetables completely before freezing them.

No matter what method you use, remember that frozen fruits and vegetables do indeed have a shelf life. Always mark the containers or freezer bags with packing dates and, if you haven't used the frozen produce within a year, it may have lost most of its nutritional value as well as culinary merit.

We still freeze vegetables from our garden for eating outside their seasons, but are much more conservative with our time, food, and freezer space than in the past. We now freeze only the crops that we know will freeze particularly well. We are not interested in spending a hot and humid August afternoon swathed in steam from a boiling kettle while we blanch unsuitable vegetables. Here is a list of the herbs, vegetables, and fruits that we try to get in the freezer each summer, and our suggestions for their preparation.

BEANS, GREEN. Blanch in boiling water just until beans turn a brighter shade of green, about 2 minutes. Drain, rinse under cold water, and cool completely. Seal in freezer bags.

BERRIES. Quick-freeze strawberries, blueberries, or raspberries on baking sheets until solid; seal in freezer bags.

CORN. Boil corn on the cob until the kernels are barely tender. Cut the kernels from the cobs. Cool and seal in freezer bags.

GREENS, INCLUDING SPINACH. Rinse well to remove grit. Blanch in boiling water just until wilted. Drain and rinse under cold water. Spin in salad spinner to expel excess moisture. Seal in freezer bags.

HERBS. Chives and parsley are the best choices. Chop and seal airtight in small freezer bags. Do not blanch.

LEEKS. Rinse well, dice into ¼-inch pieces and seal in freezer bags. Do not blanch.

PEACHES. Peel, pit, and cut into wedges. Quick-freeze on baking sheets until solid; seal in freezer bags.

PEAS, SHELL. Remove peas from pods. Blanch in boiling water just until bright green, about 2 minutes. Rinse, cool completely, and seal in freezer bags.

PEPPERS, BELL OR CHILE. Do not blanch. For convenience, remove stems, seeds, and ribs from bell peppers, and chop as desired; seal in freezer bags. Stem whole chiles and freeze without chopping.

TOMATOES. Drop tomatoes in a kettle of boiling water until the peels split, about 1 minute. Cool slightly, slip off the peels, and trim the stem ends. Seal in freezer bags along with sprigs of fresh basil.

WINTER SQUASH. For purée for pies, bake quartered squash (see page 219), purée, cool, and seal in airtight containers or freezer bags. For side dishes or casseroles, boil peeled cubes until tender, cool, and seal in freezer bags.

Plum and Pear Chutney

Makes 4 pints

I am especially fond of this recipe, which combines two glories of the autumn harvest, pears and dark Italian prune plums, in a perfect dance. Use any pear, as long as it is hard and unripe so the fruit retains its shape after cooking. This brilliant red chutney will be ready to serve just in time for the holiday season.

I cup packed light brown sugar

I cup granulated sugar

I cup cider vinegar

I small onion, thinly sliced

¼ cup finely chopped crystallized ginger

I cayenne chile pepper, seeded and minced, or use I teaspoon cayenne pepper

I tablespoon black mustard seeds

I tablespoon pickling (plain or noniodized) salt

2 garlic cloves, minced

2 pounds pitted and halved ripe prune plums

I pound firm Bosc or Bartlett pears, peeled, cored, and cut into ½-inch dice

½ cup raisins

½ cup dried figs, in ½-inch dice

Bring the brown sugar, granulated sugar, and the vinegar to a boil in a large stainless-steel or enameled kettle over high heat, stirring often to dissolve the sugar. Stir in the onion, ginger, cayenne, mustard seeds, salt, and garlic. Reduce the heat to medium and cook at a brisk simmer for 10 minutes.

Add the plums, pears, raisins, and figs. Simmer, stirring occasionally, until the cooking liquid is reduced and the chutney looks glossy, about 45 minutes. Take care not to overcook the fruit, so the chunks are visible.

Fill the jars according to the instructions on page 230. Store in a cool, dark place for at least 3 months to meld the flavors.

Ginger and Peach Chutney

Makes 4 pints

≈

Sweet with the summery flavor of ripe peaches and an undertone of the warm spiciness that only ginger can provide, this chutney will turn simply grilled chicken into a work of art.

2 cups cider vinegar

2 cups packed dark brown sugar

1 medium onion, thinly sliced into
   half-moons

1 cayenne chile pepper or other medium
   hot chile, seeded and minced, or use
   1 teaspoon cayenne pepper

1 tablespoon yellow mustard seeds

1 tablespoon pickling (plain or noniodized)
   salt

4 pounds ripe peaches

1 cup dried cranberries

¼ cup grated fresh ginger (use the large
   holes on a box grater) or finely chopped
   crystallized ginger

Bring the sugar and vinegar to a boil in a large stainless-steel or enameled kettle over high heat, stirring often to dissolve the sugar. Stir in the onion, cayenne, mustard, and salt. Reduce the heat to medium and cook at a brisk simmer for 10 minutes.

Peel and pit the peaches according to the instructions on page 213. Coarsely chop into ¾-inch dice.

Add the peaches, cranberries, and ginger to the pot. Simmer, stirring occasionally, until the cooking liquid is reduced. The chutney should look thick and glossy, about 45 minutes. Take care not to overcook the peaches, so the chunks are visible.

Fill the jars according to the instructions on page 230. Store in a cool, dark place for at least 3 months to meld the flavors.

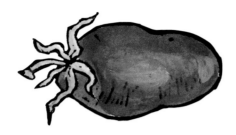

Tomato and Pear Chutney

Makes 4 pints

This lively chutney is especially good with Indian foods and curries. If you have green tomatoes, and you probably will if you grow tomatoes, substitute them, unpeeled, for half of the ripe red ones.

2 cups packed light brown sugar

2 cups cider vinegar

1 medium onion, thinly sliced

¼ cup finely chopped crystallized ginger

1 cayenne chile pepper or other medium hot
    chile, seeded and minced, or 1 teaspoon
    cayenne pepper

1 tablespoon coriander seeds, crushed in a
    mortar or under a heavy saucepan

1 tablespoon pickling (plain or noniodized)
    salt

1 teaspoon ground cinnamon

3 whole star anise

8 ripe tomatoes, peeled (see page 115),
    cored and cut into ½-inch dice
    (about 4 cups)

1 pound firm Bosc or Bartlett pears, peeled,
    cored, and cut into ½-inch dice (about
    4 cups)

Bring the sugar and vinegar to a boil in a large stainless-steel or enameled kettle over high heat, stirring often to dissolve the sugar. Stir in the onion, ginger, cayenne, coriander seeds, salt, cinnamon, and star anise. Reduce the heat to medium and cook at a brisk simmer for 10 minutes.

Add the tomatoes and pears. Simmer, stirring occasionally, until the pears and the cooking liquid look glossy, about 45 minutes. Take care not to overcook the pears—they should retain their shape.

Fill the jars according to the instructions on page 230. Store in a cool, dark place for at least 3 months to meld the flavors.

Carrot and Orange Marmalade

Makes 8 pints

*

This delectable spread is one of the best sellers at our farm stand. The carrots add a whole new flavor dimension to citrus marmalade, and contribute to the light orange color, too. The tart taste is a refreshing wakeup on toast or on crackers at tea.

2 pounds carrots, scrubbed and trimmed

2 oranges

½ cup fresh lemon juice

7 cups sugar

2 teaspoons ground ginger or cinnamon (optional)

One 3-ounce pouch liquid pectin

Cook the carrots in a large saucepan of boiling water until tender, about 15 minutes. Drain, rinse under cold water, and cut into ½-inch dice. Transfer to a bowl.

Scrub the oranges under cold water and dry well. Grate the zest. Cut off the white pith, and chop the pulp into ½-inch dice, discarding any seeds and membranes. Mix with the carrots. Stir in the lemon juice. Measure out 4 cups of the carrot-orange mixture, and transfer to a large stainless-steel or enameled pot. Set aside any leftovers. (Note: The key to make sure jams jell is to keep fruit and sugar proportions accurate.) Stir in the sugar and the ginger, if using.

Bring to a boil over high heat, stirring constantly. When the mixture reaches a rolling boil, boil hard for 1 minute, being sure to stir constantly to prevent scorching. Remove from the heat and immediately stir in the pectin. Skim off the foam on the surface of the marmalade with a metal spoon. Stir for 5 minutes, skimming as needed.

Fill the jars according to the instructions on page 230. Serve when cooled, or store indefinitely in a cool, dark place.

Tomatoes are the single most popular garden vegetable. Even in the extreme climate of Vermont, where just getting a tomato to ripen requires the gardener to go to all kinds of trouble, tomatoes can be found in gardens everywhere.

Like beans and squash, tomato plants are available as bush plants and vine plants. Bush tomatoes are called determinate because their eventual size is largely determined from the beginning. Indeterminate, or vining, tomatoes continue to grow unless the growing point (the very tip of the main stem) is removed or they are killed by frost. In general, determinate varieties fruit earlier, but are less disease resistant than the indeterminate. Either type can be grown sprawling on the ground or trellised.

The unique taste of tomatoes is a delicate balance between sweet and sour. The vegetable sugars that develop at maturity shouldn't be overpowered by the acidity of the juice. Many cooks and gardeners feel that tomatoes without the bite of acidity—this includes many of the golden, yellow, and so-called white varieties—are almost an entirely different vegetable and not the one they're after. Low-acid varieties of tomato have opened up a whole new range of taste treats for those who find the acidity of standard tomatoes too much. Whichever you prefer, keep in mind the difference: Red tomatoes are highest in acidity, and as the color (at maturity) pales toward white, the variety will likely be less acidic, and what sweetness there is will be even more noticeable.

There's no point in harvesting tomatoes until they are perfectly ripe, that is, fully colored and easily depressed by the touch of a finger.

GARDEN PEACH. An heirloom variety, Garden Peach is just 2 or 3 inches in diameter when full size. The fruit is pale yellow with a slight rose blush at the blossom end. The skin is slightly fuzzy like a peach, and the taste is rich without being overly sweet.

PERSIMMON. A winner of our open-house taste tests, this heirloom variety is deep orange, setting it apart from the generic red tomato. The oblate fruit resembles a ripe persimmon with a mild, meaty, and sweet flavor. Served on a platter with red and yellow tomatoes dappled with finely chopped fresh basil, it is a visual treat.

BIG RAINBOW. Named for the ruby red mandala radiating from the blossom end and the streaks of red running through the

flesh. Sliced, it is a thing of beauty and great for sandwiches, or for eating with just a dash of herbed salt. A true heirloom tomato.

BRANDYWINE. Regarded by many tomato connoisseurs as the finest tasting tomato, these large fruits are deeply lobed and slightly purplish red. The vigorous plants have leaves that more closely resemble a potato and they will produce a large, long-season crop.

GREEN ZEBRA. A favorite of the kids' garden, these relatively small fruits have a rich golden green color at maturity, with forest green stripes. Their flavor is tart, and they are best combined with a more classic red or exotic purple tomato.

SUN GOLD. One of the few new hybrids that we adore. These are cherry tomatoes that bear large clusters of flavor-packed, deep golden fruit on very strong, indeterminate vines. Among the first tomatoes to bear in our gardens, they continue to produce fruit all summer.

RED AND YELLOW CURRANT. Tiny, tiny tomatoes that are labor intensive to harvest, but their rich flavor is well worth the effort. Use them as edible garnishes, or snip off an entire bunch and eat them like grapes.

SAN MARZANO. The long fruit of San Marzano are our first choice for making tomato paste or sauce. The fruits mature with a small seed cavity that can be scooped out, leaving all meat. They are also excellent for drying in a low oven for winter sauce and pizza topping.

PRINCIPE BORGHESE. One of our long-time favorites, this cherry tomato is the true Italian drying tomato. The plants bear profusely and hold the fruit on the vine so well that gardeners in arid climates sun-dry whole plants.

BLACK KRIM. Named for its home—the Crimean peninsula of the Black Sea—and its color, which is really a brownish purple that develops as the weather warms. Unusual yet excellent in flavor and quite stunning when served in an overlapping pattern with vine-ripe red tomatoes.

Raspberry and Peach Jam

Makes 4 pints

Raspberries and peaches are old friends, and they are rarely more convivial than in this bright jam. Spread onto toast on the grayest winter morning, it is sure to bring back memories of summer.

2 pounds ripe peaches, peeled (see page 212), pitted, and cut into ½-inch dice

1 pint fresh raspberries

¼ cup fresh lemon juice

6 cups sugar

One 3-ounce pouch liquid pectin

Stir the peaches, raspberries, and lemon juice together in a medium bowl. Measure out 4 cups and transfer to a large stainless-steel or enameled pot. Stir in the sugar. Bring to a boil over high heat, stirring often. When the mixture reaches a rolling boil, boil hard for 1 minute, being sure to stir constantly to prevent scorching. Remove from the heat and immediately stir in the pectin. Skim off the foam on the surface of the jam with a metal spoon. Stir for 5 minutes, skimming as needed, to cool the jam.

Fill the jars according to the instructions on page 230. Serve when cooled, or store indefinitely in a cool, dark place.

Yellow Plum Tomato Marmalade

Makes 4 pints

Yellow plum tomatoes are sweet but low in acid, so without the addition of sugar and lemon juice, they don't can well. The solution is a delectable yellow plum tomato marmalade. This makes an original gift, and the sweet tomato flavor is beyond compare.

2 pounds yellow plum tomatoes, coarsely chopped (about 3½ cups)

6 cups sugar

Zest of 1 large lemon

¼ cup fresh lemon juice

Two 3-ounce pouches liquid pectin

Bring the tomatoes to a boil in a large stainless-steel or enameled pot over medium heat, stirring often to prevent scorching. Cook to evaporate some of the excess liquid, stirring often, until slightly thickened, about 10 minutes. Measure out 3 cups, saving the remaining cooked tomatoes for another use. Return to the pot and stir in the sugar, lemon zest, and juice.

Bring to a boil over high heat, and when the mixture reaches a full rolling boil, one that cannot be stirred down, add the pectin. Continue to stir and once it comes back to a boil, set the timer for 1 minute. Remove from the heat, and skim off any foam on the surface of the marmalade with a metal spoon. Stir for 5 minutes, skimming as needed, to cool the marmalade.

Fill the jars and process for 10 minutes in a boiling water bath, according to the instructions on page 230. Serve when cooled, or store indefinitely in a cool, dark place.

Tarragon Mustard

Makes two 4-ounce jars

Homemade mustard is a snap to make and tastes so fresh. I prefer to grind my own seeds for mustard because it makes it possible to control the texture, depending on how fine the seed is ground. A mortar and pestle are a lot of work but will make the best mustard. If using a food processor, soak the seeds in water for 2 to 3 hours before grinding.

1½ cups yellow mustard seeds, freshly ground
½ cup water or white wine
¼ cup white wine vinegar
½ teaspoon fine sea salt
¼ teaspoon freshly ground pepper
2 teaspoons honey or pure maple syrup
1 tablespoon fresh tarragon, minced

Blend the mustard with the water and vinegar in a small bowl. Add the salt, pepper, honey or maple syrup, and tarragon, and blend well. Pack into jars and refrigerate. This will keep for 3 to 4 weeks.

Hot Pepper Jelly

Makes 3 pints

〜

Sweet and spicy hot pepper jelly is quite versatile—serve it with Cheddar cheese as an hors d'oeuvre or snack, add to a stir-fry for a zesty accent, or use as a condiment for Mexican food such as the Spinach Enchiladas on page 106. You can vary the peppers according to what's in your garden, but keep in mind that some of those peppers are *hot*. While the jelly boils, don't be tempted to take a deep whiff: the fiery fragrance can be alarming. It will eventually mature into a sweet-natured condiment.

> 4 bell peppers (red, yellow, and green in any combination), seeded and coarsely chopped (4 cups)
> About 12 chile peppers, such as jalapeño, serrano, and habanero, seeded and coarsely chopped (1 cup)
> 1½ cups cider vinegar
> 6½ cups sugar
> Two 3-ounce pouches liquid pectin

Pulse the sweet peppers and chiles in a food processor until minced. Measure 3 cups of minced peppers and juice, and transfer to a large stainless-steel or enameled pot.

Stir in the vinegar. Bring to a boil over high heat. Reduce the heat to medium low and cook, stirring occasionally, for 5 minutes. Stir in the sugar and increase the heat to high. Bring to a full rolling boil, stirring often, until the boil is so strong that it can't be stirred down. It may take up to 15 minutes to reach this stage. Add the pectin and stir at the full boil for 1 minute.

Fill the jars according to the instructions on page 230. Serve when cooled, or store indefinitely in a cool, dark place.

Maple Tomato Salsa

Makes 8 cups fresh salsa or 3 pints canned

Vermont cooks love to use the local maple syrup whenever they can. It works well to balance the acidity of tomatoes in this vibrant salsa. This recipe works equally well with fresh or canned tomatoes, and it can be served freshly made or canned for later.

3 pounds ripe tomatoes, peeled, seeded and
    cut into ½-inch dice (5 cups) or use 5 cups
    drained, chopped canned tomatoes

2 medium onions, chopped

2 medium green or red bell peppers, seeds
    and ribs discarded, cut into ½-inch dice

1 jalapeño chile, seeded and minced

1 habanero chile, seeded and minced

2 garlic cloves, minced

¼ cup finely chopped fresh dill

¼ cup finely chopped fresh parsley

3 tablespoons fresh lemon juice

2 tablespoons fresh lime juice

1 teaspoon ground cumin

⅓ cup pure maple syrup, plus more to taste

2 tablespoons soy sauce

Salt, to taste

Mix the tomatoes, onions, peppers, chiles, garlic, dill, parsley, lemon and lime juice, and cumin in a large ceramic or glass bowl. Stir in the maple syrup and soy sauce. Season with the salt. Balance the sweetness with more syrup, if needed.

To serve fresh, cover and refrigerate for at least 2 hours, but preferably overnight, to blend the flavors. Drain off the accumulated juices before serving chilled. (The salsa can be prepared up to 3 days ahead.)

To hot-pack, transfer the salsa to a large stainless-steel or enameled pot and bring to just to a boil over medium heat, stirring occasionally.

Fill the jars and process for 20 minutes in a boiling water bath according to the instructions on page 230. Store in a cool, dark place for at least 1 month to meld the flavors.

Fiery Hot Pepper Sauce

Makes 1 cup

One chile pepper plant will produce mountains of hot peppers. The smallest ones dry easily in the hot summer sun, and the large ones can be frozen whole in a self-sealing plastic bag. For a super-hot pepper sauce to add heat to stir-fries, Mexican specialties, and other dishes, make this easy recipe. For a milder sauce, remove the ribs and seeds before chopping the chiles, but remember that a hot sauce is supposed to be hot!

> 6 jalapeño or habanero chiles, stems removed, coarsely chopped
> 1 teaspoon honey
> ½ teaspoon cider vinegar
> ½ teaspoon fine sea salt

Bring the chopped chiles with their seeds and 1 cup water to a boil in a small saucepan over high heat. Reduce the heat to low and simmer for 5 minutes. Drain in a sieve, reserving the cooking water.

Transfer the chiles to a blender, and add the honey, vinegar, and salt. With the machine running, add enough of the reserved water to make a pourable sauce. Transfer to a small bottle or jar and cover tightly. Store in the refrigerator for up to 6 months.

Spicy Salsa with Tomatillos and Herbs

Makes 8 pints

This is not your typical salsa. The tomatillos provide a tart edge and the basil and parsley give it an herbal character. As it is also good freshly made, I provide a smaller batch as a variation.

> 20 pounds large ripe tomatoes, peeled (see page 115), seeded, and cut into ½-inch dice
> 6 medium onions, chopped
> 12 tomatillos, husked, cored, rinsed, and cut into ½-inch dice
> 1 cup seeded and finely chopped chile peppers, such as jalapeño and serrano (about 24 chiles)
> 4 garlic cloves, minced
> 4 tablespoons pickling (plain or noniodized) salt
> 1 cup cider vinegar
> ¾ cup olive oil
> ½ cup finely chopped fresh basil
> ½ cup finely chopped fresh cilantro
> ½ cup finely chopped fresh parsley

Mix the tomatoes, onions, tomatillos, chiles, and garlic in a large colander. Toss with the salt and let drain in the sink for 2 to 3 hours.

Stir the mixture well so a bit more juice can be expelled, then transfer to a large stainless-steel or enameled pot. Stir in the vinegar, oil, basil, cilantro, and parsley. Cook over medium heat, stirring occasionally, just until the salsa comes to a boil.

Fill the jars and process for 20 minutes in a boiling water bath according to the instructions on page 230. Store in a cool, dark place for at least 1 month to meld the flavors.

FRESH SPICY SALSA. Use 3¼ pounds ripe tomatoes, 1 onion, 2 tomatillos, 2 to 3 tablespoons minced chiles, 1 garlic clove, 1½ teaspoons salt, 3 tablespoons vinegar, 2 tablespoons olive oil, and 2 tablespoons each fresh basil, cilantro, and parsley. Make according to the directions above, cooking in a medium saucepan until boiling. Cool completely. Cover and refrigerate overnight. Serve chilled.

Oven-Dried Tomatoes

Makes 2 pints

Homegrown oven-dried tomatoes are much better than commercial sun-dried tomatoes, which are often too salty, but you must use the right tomato variety. Principe Borghese and San Marzano are beloved by Italian cooks for their thick and meaty flesh that is perfect for cooking into a sauce or tomato paste, and they are great candidates for oven-drying, too. In the arid Sicilian weather, the whole plant is pulled up and hung out in the sun to dry the fruit, and if you live in such a climate, you might want to try the same method. For the rest of us, here's the oven method.

2 quarts ripe plum tomatoes,
    such as Principe Borghese or San Marzano
1 tablespoon fine sea salt, as needed
1 cup packed fresh basil leaves
8 whole garlic cloves, peeled
1 cup olive oil, as needed

Slice the tomatoes in half lengthwise. Using a small spoon or your fingers, poke out the seed pockets. Sprinkle the cut surfaces lightly with salt. Place the tomatoes, cut side down, on kitchen towels and let stand to drain excess juices for 30 minutes.

Position the racks in the center and top third of the oven and preheat to the lowest setting (150°F on most ovens). If you have an efficient commercial-style range, the heat of the pilot light may be sufficient.

Transfer the tomatoes, cut side up, to two lightly oiled baking sheets. Place in the oven and let the tomatoes dry until they have a leather texture, at least 8 hours and up to 16 hours, depending on the heat of the oven. About halfway through baking, when the tomatoes look as if they are beginning to dry out, turn them over. Do not try to rush the baking by increasing the oven temperature, or the tomatoes may burn.

Pack the tomatoes in pint glass jars, alternating the layers with a few basil leaves and the garlic cloves. Pour in enough olive oil to cover the tomatoes completely. Place the lids on the jars. Store the jars in the refrigerator for up to 1 year.

Bread and Butter Pickles

Makes 6 pints

The most difficult thing about making pickles is deciding which recipe to use. Here is my recipe for sweet and crunchy bread and butter pickles. It can be adapted for other garden vegetables, such as baby zucchini or even small round lemon cucumbers. If you have them, place a washed, unsprayed grape leaf or two in each jar before adding the pickles—they contain an enzyme that keeps the pickles crisp.

24 medium unwaxed pickling cucumbers,
    cut into ¼-inch-thick rounds (about
    6 quarts)
6 small yellow onions, thinly sliced
1 cup pickling (plain or noniodized) salt
6 cups cider vinegar
6 cups sugar
½ cup yellow mustard seeds
1 tablespoon celery seeds
1 fresh cayenne chile pepper, seeded
    and minced
Unsprayed fresh grape leaves, washed
    (optional)

Mix the cucumbers, onions, and salt in a large bowl. Add cold water to cover and let stand for 3 hours. Drain in a large colander and rinse well under cold water.

Bring the vinegar, sugar, mustard seeds, celery seeds, and cayenne pepper to a boil in a stainless-steel or enameled pot over high heat. Stir in the cucumber and onions. Cook just until the liquid reaches a simmer, but do not boil, as this will make soft pickles.

Place a grape leaf or two in the bottom of each hot sterilized jar. Fill the jars according to the instructions on page 230. Store in a cool, dark place for at least 3 months to crisp the pickles.

Refrigerator-Pickled Cornichons

Makes about 1 pint

Not all pickles have to be processed in jars and kept for months on the pantry shelf. Here is a reliable way to pickle tiny cornichons in refrigerated brine. The method is especially useful as additional cornichons can be salted and added to the crock as they are harvested (top off with more vinegar as needed). Cornichons (we carry the Vert de Massy variety) are not just immature large cucumbers but a specific variety that grows no longer than 3 inches, with fierce little thorns, so wear gloves while harvesting and washing them. Chopped into a tuna salad or served next to a slice of pâté, they provide a tart bite.

> 3 cups cornichon cucumbers
> 3 tablespoons coarse sea salt
> 5 sprigs fresh tarragon
> 1 teaspoon yellow mustard seeds
> White wine vinegar, as needed

Scrub the cucumbers, rubbing the sharp spines off the skins. Pat the cucumbers dry. Mix the cucumbers and salt in a large ceramic or glass bowl. Let stand at room temperature for 24 hours. Drain in a colander, and pat the cucumbers dry again.

Place the cucumbers, tarragon, and mustard seeds in a covered crock or 1-quart canning jar, leaving at least 2 inches of space at the top. Add enough vinegar to cover the cucumbers by 1 inch. Cover and refrigerate for 4 weeks before using. Pickle as you harvest the cucumbers, and add more salted, drained, and dried cucumbers, with more vinegar and extra spices as needed to compensate for the volume displacement, for the first 2 weeks. After that period, start a new crock.

Organic gardening is the original method used by people to grow food. Hardly a new concept, it is simply a way of recycling—what comes from the earth goes back to the earth. The plots at The Cook's Garden have always been organic, and we actively support the concept of feeding the soil naturally in order to feed ourselves. Chemical farming has dominated during the past fifty years and infiltrated our food supply. As gardeners and consumers, we can promote sustainable farming practices by seeking and supporting organic sources of food. Here, adapted from the Northeast Organic Farmers Association, are ten reasons to buy organic food.

1. TO TASTE BETTER. Organic foods taste better because organic farming starts with the soil. Rejecting chemical fertilization, an organic farmer feeds his soil by planting cover crops, encouraging the growth of micro-organisms, and using natural weed control. These all benefit the soil, which leads to the nourishment of the plant and ultimately us. Studies have shown no difference in the health benefits, but try your own test: Taste organic carrots from your own garden or a local farm against those from a chemically based agribusiness.

2. PROTECT FUTURE GENERATIONS. In children, because they are small and absorb chemicals more readily than adults do, the effects of at least eight cancer-causing pesticides in food are quadrupled. The food choices you make now will affect your child in the future, both in matters of health and in awareness.

3. PREVENT SOIL EROSION. It is estimated that more than 3 billion tons of topsoil are eroded from U.S. cropland each year. Soil is eroding seven times faster than it can be replenished naturally. In conventional farming, soil is regarded merely as a medium for holding plants in a vertical position so they can be chemically fertilized. For organic farmers, soil is the foundation of the food chain.

4. PROTECT WATER QUALITY. Water makes up two-thirds of our body mass and covers three-quarters of the planet. The Environmental Protection Agency estimates that pesticides contaminate the groundwater in thirty-eight states, thus polluting the primary source of drinking water for more than half of the country's population.

5. SAVE ENERGY. In the past three generations, American farms have drastically

changed from the family-based small farm to large-scale food factories dependent on fossil fuels. Modern farming, consuming twelve percent of our total energy supply, uses more petroleum than any other single American industry. Organic farming is still mainly based on labor-intensive practices, such as weeding by hand and using green manure and crop covers rather than synthetic inputs. Organic produce also tends to travel shorter distances from farms to your plate.

6. KEEP CHEMICALS OFF YOUR PLATE. Pesticides are poisons designed to kill living organisms, and they can be harmful to humans. Many pesticides approved for use by the EPA were registered before extensive research had established links between these chemicals and cancer and other diseases. Now the EPA considers that sixty percent of all herbicides, ninety percent of all fungicides, and thirty percent of all insecticides are carcinogenic.

7. PROTECT FARM WORKERS' HEALTH. An estimated one million people are poisoned annually by pesticides. Farmer workers' health is a serious problem in developing nations, where pesticide use can be poorly regulated. Several of the pesticides banned from use in the United States are still manufactured here for export to other countries.

8. HELP SMALL FARMERS. Although many large-scale farms are converting to organic practices, most currently certified organic farms are small, independently owned and operated family farms of less than one hundred acres. It's estimated that the United States has lost more than 650,000 family farms in the last decade.

9. SUPPORT A TRUE ECONOMY. Although organic food is more expensive than conventional groceries, the latter's prices reflect hidden costs borne by taxpayers, including nearly one billion dollars in federal subsidies. Other hidden costs include pesticide regulation and testing, hazardous waste disposal, and clean-up of environmental damage.

10. PROMOTE BIODIVERSITY. Monocropping is the practice of planting large plots of land with the same crop year after year. This tripled farm production between 1950 and 1970, but the lack of natural diversity in plant life has left the soil deficient in natural minerals and nutrients. Planting many crops is the best way to keep the soil healthy.

If you would like more information about The Cook's Garden, please visit www.cooksgarden.com

Planting Healing Herbs

After our kitchen and cutting gardens were well established, we put in a healing herb garden. Many of our culinary herbs were also beneficial to health, but I wanted a garden that was planted exclusively with herbs for making teas, tinctures, and salves as natural remedies for my family.

I started with an 8- × 10-foot rectangle, with a ceramic birdbath in the center, surrounded by a hedge of lavender. The plot was divided into four triangles. One contained gentle herbs that were specifically for children with red clover as a soothing salve, thyme for coughs and sore throats, and various mints for tea. Another contained herbs for the digestive system, primarily chamomile, calendula, and lemon balm. The garden of herbs for the immune system included nasturtium, echinacea, and feverfew—all good during cold and flu season. The fourth section was filled with herbs to benefit the nervous system: large plantings of skullcap, Saint-John's-wort, and hyssop.

My garden flourished, as did my knowledge about how to use these plants medicinally. I continue to make simple tinctures and herbal salves for the family and to give as gifts. I've been fortunate to study herbalism with Pam Montgomery of Danby, Vermont, and Rosemary Gladstar, of Barre, Vermont, my studies increasing my appreciation for the gifts our green friends, herbs, bring into our lives.

Letter from the Garden

The American organic movement is still growing, but European consumers have been more vocal about the degree of community responsibility demanded from multinational food and agricultural companies. Still, when agribusiness lobbyists tried to change the pending United States Food and Drug Administration's organic food regulations to allow more genetically modified organisms (GMOs) under the definition of organic, more than 275,000 Americans sent protests. The regulations, which had been altered against the wishes of the National Organic Standards Board, were withdrawn. Let's not only hope but also work to be sure that the people who started this movement—the organic growers and their customers—are not cut out of the process in the future.

By some estimates, GMOs are already used in half of the food products (especially processed foods) in our supermarkets. Much of the American corn and soybean crop is planted with genetically engineered seed, and these two crops are the raw materials for countless processed foods.

Plants are not toys or machines. They are evolving organisms, recombining their genes in each generation, now and forever. Once we set in motion the process of gene modification, we have no control over the result. There is no way to recall a new and harmful plant form if it appears, and no way to clean up the genetic problem that caused it. I, for one, don't consider the risk to be worth the promised benefits.

Who's Who at The Cook's Garden

Ellen Ogden is the cook at The Cook's Garden and develops the recipes for each new seed catalogue. Herbs and flowers are her passion; she leaves the more challenging vegetable crops to the real gardener in the family.

Shepherd Ogden is the gardener at The Cook's Garden catalogue trial gardens in the summer months. During the rest of the year he writes the catalogue copy and descriptions for the new seed varieties, and designs and maintains the website and the planting guides that come with each seed order.

Molly Ogden learned to pack seeds from the day she could hold a spoon, and once she started walking she was put in charge of the children's garden. When the trial gardens were at the farm, her garden tours always included a romp to the chicken house to view her flock of exotic chickens.

Sam Ogden prefers to mow the lawn on the riding tractor and drive the farm truck rather than weed the garden. Yet he's made some pocket money over the years, growing seedlings of some special dark hollyhocks from seeds he brought back from Holland.

Index